Alaska *MORE BEAR* Tales

Alaska *MORE* *BEAR* Tales

Larry Kaniut

Alaska Northwest Books®
Anchorage • Portland

I lovingly dedicate this book to my parents.
—L. K.

Library of Congress Cataloging-in-Publication Data
Kaniut, Larry.
    More Alaska bear tales.
    Includes index.
  1. Bear hunting—Alaska. I. Title
SK295.K24   1989   799.2'774446'09798   89-6187
ISBN 0-88240-372-9

First published by Sammamish Press, 1989

Editorial development and book design and production by
Laing Communications, Inc., Bellevue, Washington

Cover design by Elizabeth Watson
Front cover photograph by Mark Newman/AlaskaStock Images
Back cover photograph by Bill Ivy, Toronto

Alaska Northwest Books®
An imprint of Graphic Arts Center Publishing Company
P.O. Box 10306
Portland, Oregon 97296-0306
503-226-2402 / www.gacpc.com

Printed in the United States of America

Look for the original *Alaska Bear Tales*
at gacpc.com or kaniut.com.

Contents

Introduction

T he spectacular nature of bear attacks and the resulting publicity can give the impression that Alaska is filled with bears just waiting to maul visitors. Not so. The chance of a bear attacking a reasonably prudent backpacker is slight. Bears are naturally shy, and most flee at the sight of man, especially in areas where they are hunted.—Jim Rearden, "Killer Bears of Alaska," Outdoor Life March 1981

Unfortunately, sensationalistic accounts of man-bear encounters are often the public's main source of information on bruins. Not only are these accounts exaggerated, but they instill unnecessary fears about the wilderness-outdoor experience.

More than a decade ago, when I was completing work on Alaska Bear Tales, I was contacted by a senior editor of a national magazine. He asked me if I could confirm a specific bear mauling which had taken place in Alaska. His magazine had received a story about a spectacular hand-to-hand fight between a man and a grizzly.

The editor proceeded to summarize the story. A

man had been fishing on the Klutina River near Copper Center when he encountered a grizzly. The 850-pound beast attacked him, and after several minutes of "hand-to-hand" combat, the man allegedly killed the bear with his bare hands.

It doesn't take much common sense to question the author's credibility. Next time you see an eighty-five-pound Doberman pinscher, ask yourself if you could kill it with your bare hands. Then multiply its weight by ten.

After reading *Alaska Bear Tales*, some people criticized me for giving the impression that there is a bear behind every tree waiting to attack someone. Certainly that was not my intent. My goal then—and now with the sequel—was to present exciting, factual accounts that informed the public about the nature of bears.

You seldom have to worry about seeing bears, because they usually don't want you to see them. In all likelihood bears will not bother you, but you need to be alert. Don't take bears for granted.

John Sarvis, former manager of Izembek National Wildlife Range, probably said it best: ". . . bears are not deliberately out to harm people. In nearly every adverse encounter between bears and people, humans have precipitated or aggravated the situation. It is true that bears are normally and naturally afraid of people and will avoid humans unless conditioned otherwise. If bears actually wanted to harm or eat people they could have and would have had a 'field day' already. The surprising thing is how few adverse encounters do occur considering the numbers of people going into bear habitat each year."

A major factor contributing to the public's fear of the outdoors is lack of accurate information about bears. Inexperienced people have unwarranted fears that either keep them from enjoying the outdoors or lead them into trouble.

Many outdoorsmen feel that it is safer in the woods than in town. Do we quit driving on the freeways because there's traffic or because we might run into another car? Why should we quit going into the woods for fear that we might see a bear? In the past twenty-two years of living and outbacking in Alaska, I have never been charged or mauled by a bear. I have seen my share of bears, but I have never had a problem with one, other than the two brown bear cubs in our yard one June!

Many of my most treasured moments have taken place outdoors, a fact that has had enormous impact on my life.

One of my first outdoor memories involves a family camping-fishing trip in the Washington Cascades. My stepfather, Charley Jenkins of Lewiston, Idaho, was carrying a mountain of rolled blankets on one shoulder when a startled whitetail fawn scooted between his legs and down the trail.

In grade school, I proudly trudged home one day with a BB gun in one hand and chickadees in the other. My mother's stern advice was "clean them, because we don't shoot what we don't eat." That was the last of my killing for sport.

On another occasion, I spotted a porcupine beside the road near Quartz Creek in Alaska and stopped for a little family nature study. As the porcupine slothed its way up a tree, our then-pre-school-aged children watched in amazement. One daughter, Jill, pointed and exclaimed, "Look at the pine cone!"

I was born in Deer Park, Washington, and raised on my grandparents' coastal dairy farm. Growing up in the Pacific Northwest and later living in Alaska molded my love affair with the outdoors and gave me a determination to preserve the wilderness experience and the environment where that experience exists.

I have long been intrigued by the triumph of the human spirit. I have an insatiable interest in survival stories, because they show how man has battled the odds in the outdoors.

In this book, I have tried to present facts in a way that will be valuable and inoffensive. I have tried to describe bears accurately and have tried to avoid over-emphasizing the bears' destructive actions.

Good taste and a sense of balance are essential in reporting bear-man encounters. I didn't want *Alaska Bear Tales* to be another *Jaws*, so I eliminated much blood and gore. Nevertheless, it still contains a great deal of graphic material. Some of this is necessary, because bear attacks should be closely studied. Our best weapon in dealing with bears is to arm ourselves with knowledge.

I've spent ten years researching and writing two collections of *Alaska Bear Tales*. My goals have been to entertain, but even more so to educate. Certainly, I hope these stories provide exciting reading. But more important, they should serve as a reminder of how powerful bears are and how vulnerable we can be when armed with little more than our curiosity and an ignorance of the wild.

> Larry Kaniut
> Anchorage, Alaska

1

The Hunt

They spent almost an hour creeping up on the bear in the dark. Slaughter said he was trembling so hard from fear that he began to worry lest he wouldn't be able to shoot straight when the time came. . . .

Slaughter mustered his nerve. There was nothing to do but shoot, now! It wouldn't do to get panicky and run. Then the bear would probably kill them both. He pointed the gun, but it took all the strength of will he possessed to keep from breaking down.—Katherine Bayou, *Alaska Sportsman*, January 1946

The first shot . . . is all important. . . . Four times out of five it will be in brush at distances from ten to fifty feet with all the odds favoring the bear.—Virgil Buford, *North to Danger*

. . . behind me came a blood-curdling roar!
I whirled about to face the mad monster.
I thrust my gun forward against that hairy chest. To this day I can see the stream of fire from my rifle entering the massive body only inches away.

The huge body shuddered and reeled as if some giant invisible hand had lain hold of it and swung it around. Down it went in a heap, where it lay kicking and thrashing. . . . One last shudder, and the giant body was still. The quiet of the forest closed in like a curtain at the end of a tragic drama.—Otis H. Speer, *The Alaska Sportsman*, December 1943

Sgt. Rock

One big-game outfitter who shared some of his stories with me was Larry Rivers. One of Larry's guides, Garth Larsen, had this amusing story to tell about his outing with an enthusiastic ex-marine.

I knew I was in trouble when at daylight (3:45 A.M. in May) my six-foot, three-inch, 160-pound, ex-Marine client sprang up in his bed and bugled, "Gee, it's great to be alive and in the corps!"

"Oh, God," I thought as rain spattered our tent and I tried to return to my dream . . . sailing in the Bahamas, cold Heineken in hand with mermaids splashing around my boat. . . .

"Hey, big guide? Which mountain are we gonna assault today?" he questioned.

"Ugh. Hey, man, you don't holler at the guide, and this isn't a safari, so back off! Besides, you don't walk around while bear hunting, you sit and look," I managed to mumble with some emphasis.

This tack usually cools out most over-zealous hunters, but not "Sgt. Rock." He takes it as a challenge and launches into a dissertation on how he ran the drill sergeant into the ground on a thirty-mile march. All the while he cooks us one cup of tea and one package of instant oats and puts his small lunch in the vest pocket of his ten-pound, wool mackinaw raingear and sleeping bag combo.

"What the heck, this guy wants to kill something," I thought to myself.

I was pawing this over in my mind and working on my third cup of coffee when Rock passed the opening of the tent on his third lap up and down our mile of beach. Outside the tent, as I stuffed a thermos, scope and my six-pound lunch in my pack, I noticed the undue assortment of glass balls, rope and five-gallon cans, already scavenged from the beach and piled around the tent. Rock was nervous. The rain hissed as it hit his combat boots, hot from his six miles of beach combing.

We wandered our way up the valley to a good vantage point on a low ridge. Here we gazed at the grassy bear trails, the blue ocean on either side of the peninsula, the peaks dusted with snow and listened to the squawk of gulls and sea birds.

A beautiful spring day in the Aleutians, and I think Rock sensed the uniqueness of this beautiful spot. After eight and a half minutes of glassing, Rock was ready to roll.

"Hey, what's behind that hill? Is that the ocean over there? What's on top of that mountain?" he questioned.

Afflicted with a touch of spring fever myself and having a difficult time doing what the Big Guns taught me, i.e. sit, look and don't walk around and stink up the place, we threw caution to the wind, took the bit in our teeth and "boogied" on down the trail.

In the first five days (to hell with the weather) we walked from the Bering to the Pacific twice and investigated the old village of Morzhovoi where we watched a friend of mine repairing his gear for the coming red salmon season on the Ikatan Peninsula. We saw False

Pass from five different peaks, walked no less than ten miles a day and commonly did five-thousand-foot verticals in a day and left the valley smokin' with our tracks.

When our outfitter, Larry ("Skychief") Rivers dropped in to check on us later that week, I was ready to cut my hair, enlist in the Marines and go down to Nicaragua or wherever the action was. Rock was infectious. Instead, I got scowled at, lectured to and flown out of our playground to the base of a big peak where we immediately proceeded to bemoan the fact that we had no axes, ropes, or crampons—not to mention skis! (Rock lived at the base of Mount St. Helens in Washington, and before it blew he would climb it three times a week. Now he just runs, eats health food, does yoga, drives his Mercedes fast and sells plywood to anyone who'll buy it).

We cooked indoors for two days while we played war games with our dome tent during a steady, fifty-knot windstorm that hosted gusts of up to seventy knots. We trenched our tent, buried blazo, ate too much and got tired of each other's lies and idiosyncrasies. Rock was babbling about companies and assaults in his sleep and waking me each day with, "Gee, it's great to be alive and in the corps." And me, moaning about various women who took the money and ran.

We were ready for some mindless fun and hunting to appease our broken lives, when at last the weather abated. That day we saw a bear at the head of one fork of the valley—just our style, off came the raingear and on with the charge. Crazed with our previous inactivity, we did a twenty-miler in ten hours (with a thirty-five-hundred-foot vertical thrown in) to check out a three-year-old, six-and-a-half-foot bear.

The next day we did a repeat performance on the

other side of the valley in under ten hours. It was like training for the Iditarod, living on jerky and seal meat.

The following day my sense of duty caught up with me. Guilt-ridden with fears of stinking up another valley and invoking the wrath of my employer, we hid behind a rock, out of the wind with a good view of the entire valley. Peering through our "sportviews," we tried to make bears out of various tussocks and rocks until our eyes twitched and watered. We then began eating pudding and tuna out of boredom. Knowing this was far too mellow, we fell asleep in the afternoon sun and were tormented by nightmares of being overweight in an old folks' home in Pensacola.

Back at Camp Foxtail that same evening, as the alpenglow lit the upper icefalls of our peak, we stood discussing whether or not we should burn all the camp gear and food, save the pilot bread and Hefty garbage bags and sleep up on top. Or, as ol' Ray McNutt would say (as he searched the black spruce bogs for his horses), "Get lean in the belly and hungry in the eye." When suddenly, what do we see but ol' Billy Bear kickin' the snow from his hole some one thousand feet up the south flank of our mountain. Throwing our gear together and on the assault by 7:30 p.m., we began to realize this day of inactivity was all part of a master plan to save us for a "Night Mission."

Two hours later we are positioned on the same lateral plain as the bear and two hundred yards away. Mr. Bear is nowhere to be seen, and we soon are discussing what the enemy will do if fired upon near his encampment. I contend he will run for cover and seek security in his den. "Mr. Commando" views bears with the discerning eye of the urban guerilla and contends that when those little pig eyes see us, he'll come directly at us!

Desperately, I tried to convince Rock of his insanity, telling him not to shoot until I could judge the bear and until he was at least fifty to seventy-five yards from his den. But all this time Rock is setting up on his rest, peering through the semi-fogged, two-power Weaver scope on his J.C. Penney 7mm magnum loaded with "Herter's delux" ammo. Soon, who appears, but Mr. Bear groggily wandering about his hole, sniffing the air for signs of spring, fish or a new love. I'm eyeballing through the spotting scope telling Rock that he's not rubbed and looks to be about nine-foot-plus, when all of a sudden, crack . . . *wwwzzz* . . . *thwack*. . . . Rock lets off a round!

Mr. Bear swaps ends and is gone before Rock can work his bolt. I'm speechless for a hundredth of a second, then I give him my rendition of a drill instructor's welcoming and storm off toward ground zero. One hundred and fifty yards from the bear's den I jack in a shell and tell "Trigger Happy" to do the same. We then advanced on the enemy, feeling all the excitement I wanted for a hundred dollars a day. As we approach ground zero, the law of Karma dictates.

I place Rock on the low side of the hole. We holler and jive around, and I fire a couple of rounds into the hole trying to entice an eight-hundred-pound bear to take us on. Fortunately, he didn't take us up on it, and I regained my senses, realizing that two thousand feet up a thirty-degree snow field, pumped up on adrenalin was no place to be at eleven P.M.

I said with the calm assurance of the seasoned big-game guide, "We'll let him sleep on it and come back tomorrow." Sgt. Rock had been very quiet since the enemy had not charged.

The walk back to Camp Foxtail was a quiet one followed by a quiet dinner and an introspective and short night. The next morning we began our assault with a ten-foot alder as a prodding tool and Marlin Grasser's favorite weapon, a short-handled spade.

Back at the scene of the crime, all was quiet as we pondered our next move. Just then we see the Cub land at camp. Skychief dismounted, stretched and walked to camp.

I relished the next few minutes as I watched him ponder the note written with a bullet on a paper plate: "Gone to dig a bear out of his hole on south flank of mountain." I'm sure he thought he had a couple of live ones and was thinking about his insurance premiums and trying to remember names of the next of kin. Back to the Super Cub, Skychief went looking for us. But as everyone knows, you can never find anything from the air when you want to, Murphy's Law #100.

Shining my flashlight down the hole did not illuminate the situation, so next we decided we would poke the alder down through the snow, into the entrance. We would slowly move the alder into the hole until we hit the den or the bear itself. But first we had to dig a fifteen-foot-long trench above the entrance so we could reach the hole with our ten-foot probe.

Slowly, we moved our probe down into the entrance. Just out of sight, Rock hit something soft. Bingo. We punched it a couple of more times and, sure enough, it was soft and didn't move.

Figuring it must be the dead bear, I donned my raingear and Ruger. 357 pistol and assumed the fetal position for entry into the war zone. About halfway down the hole, I realized it would probably break my ear drums to shoot the .357 in there, and about that time I lost my footing and . . . *zipppp.*

My Ruger and I went streaking down the hole and came to an abrupt stop against a dead brown bear.

Oddly enough, I had no sensation of fear—my days of downhill racing, my belief that God protects the innocent and my acceptance of Murphy's Law #101, "If you're gonna be dumb, you gotta be tough" had led me to the interior of this large den in search of bear, and he was home.

With the interest of an amateur naturalist, I was intrigued by my surroundings. The den wasn't a small, dingy hole, but rather a cathedral-like snow dome. There was enough room for ten big bears. I hollered for Rock, and soon we both stood staring at the power of the 7mm magnum and wondering why we were so fortunate.

Skinning a bear in his own home is a bit unnerving, and owing to the cool temperature and a bit of claustrophobia, we moved right along. Somehow, I didn't feel like I belonged in there. I took a break to take a look around and crawled up the entrance, which was a tunnel about three and a half feet in diameter, fifteen feet long and at about a thirty-degree angle, pushing loose snow ahead of me as I went along.

Unknown to me on a far ridge about four miles away, another guide and client were watching as snow came from the hole. Ol' Don perks up and says to his hunter, "We got a bear now, Duane." About that time I popped out.

A bear in raingear? Don's ego was irrevocably damaged. (His relations with his client were already strained due to his food preparation, such as breakfasts of dry oatmeal cereal with a package of dry whipping cream, instant coffee sandwiches for lunch and maybe cold Spam or some other mystery meat for dinner. Like Don tells his clients, "I'm here to hunt, not cook.")

Meanwhile, I'm back down the hole skinning away,

and on my next trip to the surface what do I see but a three-year-old bear chuggin' up the slope eight hundred yards below! This gave me, as well as Don and his client, some tense moments.

I practiced some disco moves and talked in tongues convincing Junior to change his route. He finally moved off to a position about six hundred feet above, where he sat down and observed the strange sight. Rock and I then decided to post a sentry around the war zone, so he stood guard while I finished removing Mr. Bear's jacket. We worked our way up the hole for the last time, dragging his hide. I stuffed what I could of the hide in my pack and headed for camp.

By this time Rock had regained his old stature and was visibly puffed up from his one-shot kill. He double-timed it to camp to prove his superiority. As he marched past, all I could do was watch while I stumbled along, burdened with ninety pounds of bear hide on my back.

The remaining two miles from the base of the mountain to Camp Foxtail were a series of rotten snow gullies and rocky ridges. My weight plus the weight of the bear hide caused me to break right through our old tracks. I became lodged to my armpits in the snow and rocks, anchored by my "hideous burden," as Poe would say.

For twenty minutes I pondered my situation and wondered what Rock was up to, when finally he appeared on the ridge above me like some demigod. At last he had me where he wanted me. I admitted they didn't make men like him anymore, and he glowed as he helped dislodge me.

It had been a wonderful hunt, and after fifteen days Rock had his nine-foot, six-inch brownie, and I had the oosik (veteran Alaskans know this to be a walrus penis—traditionally "made" in Alaska of 100% ivory), a plane ticket on Reeve and a date with a chiropractor in Anchorage.

All fun and humor aside, Sgt. Rock is in fact Doug Stinson, a hard-hunting, hard-working timber cruiser from Oregon.

Who Says There Are No More Big Bears?

Some say there are no more big bears, but one of Larry Rivers' clients disagrees. Bill Katen, a custom-builder from New York, tells about how he proved that there are still plenty of trophy-bears to go around.

My guide and I worked our way up the mountainside to our lookout point in a low overcast sky with a light drizzle coming down. The wind had dropped off to a light breeze, a welcome relief from the powerful gusts that had been pounding us the last two days. We had seen three bears since the beginning of my trip, but I wasn't looking for just *any* bear. This trip was my second into this area, and I knew what I wanted.

Billy moved ahead, picking his trail carefully. We wanted to come out on a grassy hillside overlooking the valley floor, then move across to a small rock outcrop that gave us a protected view of all sections of the valley.

I was just emerging from the alders into the high, wet grass when Bill stopped in the trail ahead of me and quickly motioned for me to ready my rifle. Not fifty yards away, a bear sat in the alders with his head up. He must have heard us because the next thing I knew he had swung around to look. In a split second he was on his feet and coming straight for us.

As he ran, his flesh rippled with the motion of stored fat, and he broke through the alders as easily as if they were grass. I grabbed my rifle, threw off the safety and was ready to fire, when he stopped. Now, just yards away, he stood shaking his head and snorting. Still I held my fire, hoping I wouldn't have to shoot. I remember thinking of how long I had waited to make this second hunt and how I didn't want to end it by shooting an animal out of necessity.

Then, just as suddenly as he had charged, the bear turned and ran like hell. We watched him run until he left the valley. Billy had estimated him to be eight or nine feet in size.

Hunting this area started with a phone call in December 1978. I had been to Alaska on several previous occasions, hunting with the famous bush pilot and guide Don Sheldon in the Talkeetna area. Unfortunately, Don had passed away in 1975, and his air-taxi license had been sold. I called his wife Roberta to ask her if she could recommend any other outfitters now that Don was gone. She suggested calling Larry Rivers, who I telephoned immediately. I booked a hunt on the Alaska Peninsula for the following October.

I arrived in camp in October 1979. After a quick lunch and change of clothes, we packed the Super Cub and departed for spike camp and my long-awaited bear hunt. About thirty minutes out, Larry pointed out a camp pitched at the edge of a partially dried-up lake. As we set up to land, he pointed out the landmarks I would need to know. My guide was waiting for me as Larry touched the tires to the sand and taxied to a stop.

"Bill, I would like you to meet Billy," Larry said as I climbed out. "He'll be your guide on the hunt."

Billy was twenty-six years old, about five foot, seven inches and a solid 155 pounds. He had grown up in Boston but had lived the last several years around Alaska, mainly in the small tents and cabins he used on his trapline.

"Come on, let's get this gear into the tent, so Larry can get back into the air," Billy said. We soon had my gear unloaded, and as Larry and Billy discussed the last-minute details, I had a chance to look around.

We were on a small, shallow lake located on the floor of a large valley. The lake was perhaps one hundred yards across and two feet deep. Climbing up on the bank, I could see several miles up the valley to a point where the bank turned sharply to the right and disappeared. Later, I would learn that this was a pass through the mountains to the Pacific Ocean. Looking down the valley a mile or two, I could see where the land came to an end, on a bluff overlooking a large bay. Beyond that were flat lowlands that ran for several miles and ended at the Bering Sea.

The valley floor was almost flat, made up of high rows of dark green niggerheads and sections of grassy muskeg. Numerous small lakes dotted the landscape and drained into one large stream that emptied into the Pacific. The only brush and alder was located on the western wall about two miles away.

The day was overcast and the breeze from the north carried with it the fresh, clean smell of ocean, beach, grass and rain. I was excited and pleased to be in such a beautiful location.

"Bill," Larry called, bringing my attention back to camp, "Billy seems to have everything under control. We're expecting some bad weather to roll in, so I'll be back in three days to check on you. Good luck."

"Bad weather" was an understatement! The first day out the wind and rain were fierce, but we still managed to take an excellent bull caribou at a range of about two hundred yards. The second morning we saw another twenty or thirty caribou and two wolves far out on the valley floor. At about eleven A.M. I spotted a bear feeding up the valley, and my heart began to pound.

I had come for a big bear, and now I was looking at one of obviously large size. The conditions were right, and soon we reached a spot within thirty yards of him. The bear was feeding on the bottom of a small creek. If I stood up, I could see the top of his back, but couldn't get a shot. It would have been foolish to move closer, so we waited for him to move up on the bank.

The next twenty minutes seemed like hours as we sat and waited. At last, our impatience got the best of us, and we stood up to look. He was gone! After a quick and careful search, we spotted him in the thick brush about 150 yards away. But no sooner had we located him, he seemed to vanish into the grass. We were never able to find him again.

The third day the wind and rain battered our camp with even more force than the previous days. Still, the weather didn't dampen our spirits, and we hiked out and took a white wolf a few miles from camp. On the trip back to the tent, we leaned into a wind so strong that when it quit momentarily, we would fall to the ground. Several hours later we arrived at camp, exhausted.

The fourth morning we dried our gear, ate a good breakfast and headed back into the field. We had only been on the hill a few minutes when Billy leaned over and pointed to a large, brown shape moving at the edge of the alders about a mile and a half away. He reached across my pack and picked up the spotting scope to have a better look. I continued to watch through my binoculars, awaiting his decision.

"Looks to me like the best bear we've seen," he whispered at last. "Probably go well over nine and a half feet." That was what I was waiting to hear.

While Billy watched the bear, trying to decide what he was up to, I was busy putting my gear back into my pack. It would be a difficult stalk; we would need to use every low area and creekbed for cover.

Four hours later we were still several hundred yards from where the bear was feeding along the base of the mountain at the west side of the valley. It was mid-afternoon, and we expected him to lay down at any time, allowing us the chance to move in for a shot. Because the wind was blowing steadily at about fifteen knots in our favor, we were not concerned about the bear scenting us, and the rush of the cool ocean breezes was drowning out our sounds. Still, I could hear a nagging noise in the distance.

Suddenly, it occurred to me that this was the day Larry had said he would return to check on the camp; the sound I was hearing was the drone of his Super Cub! I scanned the sky and saw the small aircraft headed up the valley. My thoughts were yanked back to the ground as Billy tugged on my sleeve and pointed to the bear, now standing on his hind legs and looking in the direction of the aircraft.

From the corner of my eye I could see Larry turning away, his engine cut to an idle. Apparently, he had seen the bear also and was trying to leave as quickly and quietly as possible. Now, the big bear had dropped to the ground and started walking purposefully back up the mountain toward the alders.

It would be a long shot for my .375 H & H, but I knew that it was now or never. I would have to take the best shot possible and hoped that my hours of practice would make up the difference. Billy was right beside me as I threw myself on the ground, lined up on the bear's shoulder and fired.

"You hit him!" Billy exclaimed. "Bust him again!"

I quickly followed with two more shots that I was sure had connected, just before the bear disappeared into the grass. When the bear appeared again, he was moving at a steady pace up the face of the mountain. We could see blood on his leg, and he walked with a limp but didn't slow down for a minute. By now, he was approaching the top of the mountain, and we were moving after him as fast as we could go. But he was gone. Billy and I spent the remainder of the day looking for his trail, but tracking was impossible on the rocky mountainside.

I was unbelievably disappointed. The bear's tracks indicated the bruin was well over ten feet in size. Needless to say, our camp was not a very happy one that night.

Larry arrived the next morning and after hearing our story decided to move us to another valley. He would continue to try to locate the bear by air.

A short time later we landed on the beach with the surf breaking a few feet away. We set up camp behind the first dune and set about anchoring down our supplies. For two days we hunted this area, seeing only smaller sows and cubs. And unfortunately, the winds were picking up again, making it especially difficult to hunt.

The third evening at the new camp, Larry flew over at high tide and dropped a note. The weather pattern that year had been unusually bad, and another strong system was moving in. He wanted to move us out of the area. We would have to walk about a mile and a half to a flat behind the sand dunes where he could pick us up with two planes.

We worked our way across country through the alders. Soon, we reached the stream that separated us from the airplanes. It had turned into a raging river, which we tried to cross two times without success.

Larry was standing on the opposite bank, but

couldn't hear our shouts over the high winds. We motioned that we couldn't cross and indicated that he would need to pick us up on our side. The only problem was that we were standing on a sand strip only ten feet wide and less than one hundred feet long with tall grass on one side and river on three.

Larry headed back to his plane and in a few minutes was flying overhead very low. The Cub made four passses over our spot to check the turbulence. On his last pass, Larry opened the door and yelled, "When I touch down, grab the wings!"

Landing like a helicopter, the plane touched down, and we grabbed the struts. The winds were so strong that it seemed as if the plane would lift off the ground with the engine at an idle. Larry opened the door, and I hurled myself into the Cub. We took off quickly, directly from the position where the plane had stopped. After dropping me off behind a large sand dune where the other plane was parked, Larry returned for Billy.

Although I had more thrills than I ever asked for, I returned to New York with an unfilled tag, comforting myself by booking another hunt for the fall of 1981.

A short time later I heard from Larry. He told me that he had spotted my bear from his plane, but the animal had moved again during the night before he could do anything about it. Johnnie Lowe of Houston, Texas, came into camp on the following hunt and took an eleven-foot, five-inch brown bear. While skinning the animal, they found a fresh bullet cut on the brisket and a single .375 H & H bullet lodged in its right foot. When officially measured, the skull went twenty-nine inches and is listed in Boone and Crockett under number 87.

I was disappointed but not beat.

When I arrived at Larry's camp for my next hunt, I

was pleased to find that Billy would again serve as my guide. And this time I came prepared for the worst with plastic bags for my gear, waterproofed supplies and even extra-long aluminum stakes to anchor my tent. The weather was better this year, and I had a full sixteen days to look for the bear of my choice.

On the first day of our hunt we saw nothing except for a small bear heading in our direction, looking over its shoulder very nervously. No wonder! A short time later a very large bear appeared, following in the small bruin's tracks.

As quickly as we could, we moved to the valley on a course plotted to intercept him at the river. He got there ahead of us, and we moved into position just in time to see him emerge on our side, dripping wet. He was moving steadily, looking for salmon and feeding on the vegetation along the stream. Upon reaching the bank, he turned and started away from us at a rate that would be hard to follow. I estimated the range to be two hundred yards, within the capability of the .338 Winchester I was carrying that year.

I laid my rifle across my jacket for a rest and told Billy that I would fire the next time the bear came out of the creek. In a moment he stepped up on the gravel bank. I fired for his shoulder. There was a sharp s*plat* as the bullet hit his wet hide, and he let out a huge roar. Instantly, the bear started to run for the mountain we had just left. I hit him two more times before he reached the slope, and there he turned and headed straight for us.

"This is my last shot!" I yelled to Billy as I took aim. The bullet hit him square in the chest and spun him around in his tracks, but he never went down. Instead he headed back to the mountain and took refuge in an alder patch.

With heart pounding and Billy standing cover, I quickly reloaded. Billy led the way around the patch in an attempt to catch some sight of the wounded bear. All was silent except for occasional movement of brush somewhere below. After about fifteen minutes and no sight of him, we decided to throw a stone or two, hoping for some response. The first rock thudded into the soft earth, and the bear stood up less than twenty yards away.

"Bust him," Billy whispered. I placed the crosshairs on his neck and dropped him in his tracks. The shot rolled him down the hill and he came to rest in the swamp.

I thought for sure that shot had killed him, but as we moved down the hill, we could still hear him moving around.

Carefully, we inched into the swamp. Only a small knoll separated us from the bear. We moved closer to a distance of fifty yards, where we could see him sitting and watching. When he caught sight of us, he took off at a run.

Twice more I knocked him down before he rolled back to the swamp, yet he was still not dead. I had to fire one last shot into his neck to finish him off.

It was the biggest bear I had ever seen. Needless to say, Billy and I danced around the swamp for quite some time congratulating ourselves. It took everything we had to skin that bear, and we had to spend a second day fleshing it before it was light enough to pack out to the beach.

I took another fine caribou on that hunt, but the real thrill came when we squared the hide. It measured eleven feet, three inches, just two inches less than the bear I didn't get two years before. It was one of the greatest experiences I have ever had in hunting.

Damn Lucky

Ron Maddox was raised in Arkansas. He now lives in Alaska and hunts every chance he gets. In 1975—the last year they issued brown bear tags from Kodiak— Ron was sixteenth in line and got four permits, allowing him and his hunting partners to hunt in Pinnell and Talifson's area on Red Lake.

Ten years later Ron happened upon a large brown bear across Cook Inlet from Anchorage, and wanted to get this mystery bear in the worst way. As Al Dawson wrote about his chase for a record whitetail deer, "The first time I saw the deer I made myself a promise. I'd hunt him until I hung that strange and magnificent rack on my wall, no matter how long it took, unless another hunter killed him first. I didn't guess then that I was taking on a five-year assignment and the most fascinating outdoor quest of my life." —New Record Whitetail: A Five-Year Stalk, "A Treasury of Outdoor Life, William E. Rae, 1975.

As his story shows, Ron Maddox had the same deep convictions about capturing his brown/grizzly.

After the noise from the five shots had echoed into silence, he was gone. I was stunned.

"Damn," I thought. "After all that, I had my chance, and I blew it."

My mind was racing, trying to sort out all the events of the prior seconds and determine what to do next. I knew the first two shots had scored; however, the last two were questionable. As I crossed the open muskeg field, watching the brush for movement, I hoped I would find the bear lying dead in the brush.

I found the spot where the bear had fallen with the first shot, but no blood trail existed. As I moved closer to the area where he disappeared, my questions were answered. A long, low, guttural growl broke the silence; the bear was definitely alive and very upset.

This all started in the fall of '85 when Ed Deerwent, pilot for Rust's Flying Service in Anchorage and a good friend, asked me to take his son Robert along moose hunting since he couldn't take the time himself. I needed a hunting partner and quickly agreed. We picked an area southeast of Beluga Lake, which was close, inexpensive, had a tent camp and good fishing to boot. To be quite honest, I wanted a few days of rest and fishing more than a moose anyway.

When we flew in, Ed cautioned us about a large brown bear in the area that reportedly had given quite a scare to unsuspecting moose hunters. I had a bear tag, as usual, and welcomed the opportunity for a good brown bear, but I really didn't expect to see one of any size in an area with that much traffic and brush.

It was a good hunt. I took a forty-nine-inch bull moose, and Robert got a good black bear—both on the east side of the lake. But most importantly, to the west I found the mystery brown bear's tracks for the first time. The track was over eight inches wide; he had to be a nine-footer. I didn't catch a glimpse of the bear that year, but I never forgot about him either.

In the past I've hunted bears in the spring—either Kodiak Island for brown bears or Prince William Sound for black bears. Trying to hunt a brown bear in country like this was not exactly easy, with all the brush and lack of open space. I figured my chances of success to be pretty slim and was not quick to plan a return trip. But I did not forget about him. I guess his notoriety helped some, too, as I heard other stories about the bear that liked to steal moose.

The next year came along. A couple of friends and

I decided to hunt moose in the fall. A trip across the Alaska Range for three is pretty expensive, and we had this big bear to consider. We decided to head for the area of my hunt the previous fall. One of the other hunters in our party was fairly experienced, and he picked up on the bear immediately, so I was anxious to claim my hunting area right away.

I said bluntly, "This is where I hunt. You boys have a good time." Serious competition was suddenly too close for comfort.

That year, 1986, I saw my bear for the first time. It was our second day out. I was moving very slowly along the edge of a muskeg field in the early morning fog. All of a sudden, he appeared. But as he moved through the fog and underbrush, it was too difficult to get a clear view from 150 yards away. I didn't dare risk a shot under those circumstances. Soon, my mystery bear disappeared completely. Although I never caught a good glimpse of his actual size, I was sure he was the same bear when I examined his tracks.

From that point on, the hunt deteriorated. Because all the little lakes west of Anchorage are pretty popular, we expected to share our area with others. But this year the population problem was worse than we ever imagined. On our second day, a float plane landed near our campsite and dropped off a camper with a mountain of gear. The plane returned again and again with more and more gear and more and more passengers.

It was a fly-in party. They had everything—motorboats, chainsaws, music and beer coolers, to name a few. One cannot imagine the racket being made by full-grown adults. For some unknown reason, the women were screaming out in the boats. The men were cutting wood with chainsaws. They cleared the entire area of all game, including the bear. As we left the lake, we dubbed the hunt the "Texas Chainsaw Massacre Hunt of 1986."

The last week of brown bear season that year, I decided to try my luck at catching up with the mystery bear again. The husband of a co-worker, Leonard Anderson, agreed to come along. I had just bought a new open-sight carbine, a .338 magnum-caliber Sako Mannlicher, ideal for hunting in thicketed areas, and I felt confident and ready to go. Arriving at the lake, I immediately went looking for sign of the bear down a seismic trail behind our campsite. I found his track, but it was old, maybe two weeks.

The next morning we got an early start. Leonard, who was interested in hunting moose, had no desire to meet my bear, so we went our separate ways. I took off for a muskeg field to the south toward some of the salmon spawning areas. I didn't find the bear, but my spirits boosted as I came across plenty of fresh sign. Then I found his track.

Later that day I decided to try a new approach into the area the bear seemed to dominate. I planned to go northwest into a series of long muskeg fields that might lead me into the salmon spawning stream where he fished. I had never hiked this way before, and I enjoyed seeing some new country.

Soon, I came to a thin stand of spruce trees growing on a mossy knoll. Although the rain was falling lightly, this small rise was dry beneath the trees, so I decided to sit down and watch. The area was perfectly silent, except for the occasional cawing of ravens in the distance.

I had been sitting on the knoll about thirty minutes when I spotted the bear walking down a densely covered ridge, heading south for an open field. He was moving in an extremely deliberate fashion, obviously intent on getting somewhere. I calculated the bear was about 250 yards away, and for a brief second I wished I had my old, scoped Weatherby .340, now sitting in the gun cabinet at home. Despite the distance, I still had confidence in my new open-sight carbine. Although it would be a long shot, the bear was out in the open field by now and there would be time to fire more than once, if needed.

The bear was like something I'd never seen before. He looked as large as a Cadillac as he moved through the grass. There was no doubt in my mind that I had found my bear.

But he was moving away quickly. I had to make a decison. My sitting position was right. I was comfortable. The conditions were ideal, except the increasing distance was becoming a little questionable. Despite this worry, I touched off the first shot. The bear vanished. Then suddenly, I could see his feet waving in the air and faintly hear him squalling from the hit. Then before I knew it the bear was up again, heading in the opposite direction. I was ready for him. I shoved a shell into the barrel and touched it off. Down he went again.

Two for two; now I was feeling pretty cocky.

But the bear jumped up again and headed south. I felt the first waves of anxiety rise over me. I couldn't let him get away. Frantically, I brought the gun up, jacked another shell in, and immediately my pinkie finger touched the trigger by mistake. The shot went wild, firing straight up. If a plane had been flying over, I would have shot it down.

Now the bear seemed to get his bearings, as if he had pin-pointed my location and deliberately headed in the opposite direction. I shot again with no effect. I got another shell and drew a bead, but just as I squeezed it off, the bear disappeared. I had no idea whether my last two shots had hit or not.

Now, I tried to gain some composure. I needed to calm down. I couldn't believe it had all happened so fast. A sick feeling gnawed at my stomach. After all these months of chasing the bear, I could have blown my chances.

The nagging questions bombarded me. Should I have shot? In my anxiety I made my way toward the spot I'd last seen the bear. That's when I heard a low growl.

But I couldn't locate his position in the brush. I looked to the south again and spotted a large dark spot in the grass.

"God, I hope that's him," I thought as I moved nearer. The closer I got, the more I was convinced he was dead. But when I reached the spot, I discovered the dark mound was the remains of a dead moose the bear had covered up. I waited and watched, then picked up the moose leg, hoping to provoke the bear to charge so I could get another chance. A lot of time had gone into trying to take this animal. Now I had shot him, and I wanted to finish what I had started.

Suddenly, the simple realization came over me that I was in a very dangerous situation. Here I was, perhaps within yards of a wounded bear, standing in his territory, next to his kill. My only consolation was the wide, open areas to the north and south of me. I'd have some warning if the bear charged. But I only had two bullets left, and it was getting dark. Would I be able to stop him if he charged? In a last desperate hope, I moved towards the edge of the field in an effort to see into the heavy cover. It was useless; the grass was over my head, five and a half, maybe six feet tall.

"This is stupid nonsense," I thought, as I moved

back to the moose. Now it was becoming so dark that I might not be able to see the bear if he recrossed the clearing, trying to double-back and meet me in the trail. All the stories that I had ever read about maulings raced through my mind.

I hightailed it back across the field and met Leonard, who had heard all five shots and had come to see what had happened. I told him the story and made it clear we should get back to camp. The trail was overgrown and brushy, making us easy prey for the bear. As we walked, Leonard suggested we spend the night in another camp across the lake, which sounded like a great idea. The move would eliminate the scent trail.

We picked up our sleeping bags, food for supper and breakfast and headed for the other camp. As we got settled, I worried about the bear. How could I have possibly lost him? Now, he would probably die of his wounds and never be found.

The next morning we motored back across the lake. It had rained steadily during the night, and any blood trails would have probably been washed away. Any hopes I had of finding the bear were disappearing rapidly. We reached the spot where I had been sitting the day before, and saw the spent cartridges still laying there. I pointed to the area where the bear had been.

Leonard immediately said, "That's three hundred yards."

"Well, I thought it was about 250," I said.

"I play golf," he responded. "And that's a good three hundred yards."

What could I say? I had done it. I felt foolish to have taken the shot at that distance.

We went across the field and found where the first shot had hit. Leonard found spots of blood, but that was the last trace we found. Surprisingly, we were able to find tracks where the bear had moved into the brush and headed up to the ridge. The prints were staggered, not uniform.

The bear apparently headed back to the north toward some trees and deadfalls, but there was no sign of him among the fallen timber. As I made a systematic search up and down the ridge, Leonard covered me from the field. He was carrying a .30/06. Knowing the size of the bear, I was a little worried about relying on a gun that small. After hunting fifteen years in Alaska, this was the first time I had ever looked for a wounded brown bear in the brush. I assure you, it is not fun work.

I had completely given up hopes of finding the bear and was walking back toward Leonard, feeling completely disappointed, when I noticed some grass out of place toward the south. The dry weeds were lying at an angle. Even though it wasn't obvious that anything was amiss, I decided I needed to investigate. I started working down the hill, following the barely disturbed grass, which angled in different directions. Suddenly, I smelled a distinctly different odor, and I called to Leonard, who was still covering me, that he should be ready for anything. The further I walked, the stronger the smell became.

I lost sight of Leonard.

"Ron," I heard him call.

"What is it?"

"Down here," he said

"Do you see the bear?" I asked, slightly annoyed because he wouldn't explain.

"Yes."

My first reaction was to leap for joy. I forgot all the danger. I was so happy that the bear was there, I didn't give a damn whether he was alive or dead. We had found the bear and I was in seventh heaven. At least the bear was found.

Then I thought, "Oh, my God," as I realized that I should be considering the situation more carefully.

"Stay still," I hissed and started toward the direction of his voice.

Leonard had trained his gun on the bear. I told him to touch off a shot or two in front of the bear. I didn't want another hole in him if it wasn't necessary.

Leonard shot. There was no movement. I walked closer slowly, then sighed with relief. It was over.

It appeared that the bear had followed me into the brush when I had found his moose buried in the muskeg field. He had died twenty-five feet into the brush and about 150 yards south of where he had disappeared the night before. His carcass was still warm, so I guessed that he had died in the early morning hours.

The bear squared nine feet, seven inches. Upon inspection, we found that all four of my shots had hit the bear. His skull measured 26 1/8 inches, and he made the Safari International book. I believe the first bullet was the killing shot, although at that distance the shot was too inadequate to do a good job. We measured repeatedly and found that I had fired the first shot from three hundred yards away and the last two shots from about 330 yards—too far to be shooting bears near brush.

Through this ordeal, I gained a new respect for brown bears and learned some lessons I won't soon forget. In my opinion, I took a chance and got lucky, damn lucky.

Bear on Ice

Matt Caldwell is an Illinois veterinarian who special-izes in treating livestock. He is also an avid hunter whose trophies include Alaska record-book animals, as well as turkey and whitetail from the Continental states. This particular hunt took place on the Alaska Peninsula. Matt's story reflects his values and demonstrates that there is more to a hunt than a trophy and more to life in general than killing an animal.

I've wanted to hunt in Alaska for as long as I can remember. Like a lot of people, I grew up reading Jack O'Connor's stories and always dreamed of experiencing that kind of adventure firsthand. After writing to many guides and outfitters, I picked for my first hunt AAA Alaskan Outfitters, run by Brent Jones and Roger Morris. Both Brent and Roger have trophy hunted exten-sively and participate personally in guiding.

On my first trip, I realized Alaska is quite different from anyplace I had ever seen and I would need to come back several times to really appreciate it. Many people who hunt in Alaska are wealthy, high-pressure types who are used to getting what they want when they want it. But Alaska runs on a slightly different schedule. Weather delays lasting days and even weeks at a time are common and accepted in Alaska. A good supply of paperbacks and patience is the best remedy for a socked-in hunting expedition. Side trips, such as beach-combing, fishing, prospecting and sightseeing can add immeasurably to the total enjoyment. Some of my favorite times were spent in camp, just talking to the guides and other hunters.

I learned a lot about how Alaska runs on my first trip, and I was anxious to return. Immediately, I made

plans to come back and try for a bigger bear. Personally, I'm not such a hard-core hunter that I would only
shoot a ten-foot bear or none at all. I just enjoy hunting,
and it sometimes adds to the challenge to set goals;
however, the success or failure of my trips definitely
does not depend on the size of the bear.

On my second trip, I flew into camp without incident and the accommodations were first rate, as usual.
Brent and Roger, both ex-Air Force men, run their
camps expertly and efficiently. My guide was Dick
Koskovitch from Homer, Alaska. I had taken a seventy-
pound halibut out of Homer with Dick the summer
before and spent time with him on my previous hunt
with AAA. Dick, a custom goldsmith by profession, is a
first-rate guide, keeps a very positive attitude and is
always up for adventure. I had no doubts that we would
have a good hunt.

Our pilot, Tony Lee, flew us by Super Cub to a
remote spot on a gravel bar and deposited us with all
the necessary equipment for a week or so. We were at
the head of the bay with mountains surrounding us.
Glaciers dotted the mountains, and we could see ice
blocks the size of houses fall away from the glaciers.
Some days it sounded like rolling thunder overhead for
hours.

The bears were just coming out of their dens, and
we could see their tracks everywhere. Using our binoculars, we could literally follow the tracks right to the
bear making them. We saw sows and cubs playing in
the snow, running up the hill and wrestling and sliding
down for several hundred yards.

One day we decided to hike over to a valley, the
bottom of which we couldn't see from our camp. We
hiked several hours back up to a glacier-filled bowl and
set up to glass. At one point, Dick noticed four to six

bear tracks way up in the mountain goat area. Looking harder, sure enough, there was a bear sleeping peacefully. From his spot, he had a gorgeous view, and what he couldn't see while sleeping, he could smell. We decided our only option was to approach in the dark. Dick had brought white coveralls along in his pack for sheep hunting, so we put them on and started across the avalanche field in the dark.

Because the snow was very crunchy, it took four hours to carefully and slowly walk the 893 steps in unison to a spot closer to the bear. Luckily, in the cold of the night, the snow was fairly stable, and the glacier directly above us was quiet. I was wondering just what might happen when I opened up with my pre-'64 model 70, .375 H & H.

We stopped on some bare rocks poking through the snow and decided to wait for light before seeing if we could get any closer to the bear. The coldest four hours of my life began. We had taken off from our camp on the spur of the moment, very late in the day, without eating supper or bringing along sleeping bags; we hadn't quite anticipated that this would be an all-night ordeal. Fortunately, we had brought along small, foam pads to sit on while glassing, and these were life-savers for keeping us directly off the rock and snow.

Despite my discomfort, I enjoyed the beautiful view. The stars were out in full, and there were herring boats in the bay below us with their lights on. If I've ever seen a more beautiful sight, sitting there surrounded by mountains, I don't know where it was.

We dozed fitfully until the first signs of daylight appeared. Then we realized we still needed to be closer for a shot. To keep from falling through the snow, we crab-walked in close unison, moving close together, to keep our profile to a minimum and to be as quiet as possible. We must have been quite a sight, but the maneuvering served its purpose as we came within three hundred yards of the bear; that distance was about as close as we could get.

Although I was reasonably comfortable with my rifle and my ability to shoot it, three hundred yards is a long way for a bear shot. And the animal had a good chance of falling out of sight down an avalanche chute in one or two jumps. I asked Dick to feel free to sling a little lead in the bear's direction if it looked like he was outrunning my Nosler offering.

In the very first volley the bear went down for keeps. He was a beautiful animal with a coat as gorgeous as they come. We took many good pictures and skinned him quickly. Although we didn't set off any avalanches, one had definitely occurred the day before, and more were sure to follow as it warmed up.

On our way out, we realized we had spent most of the night about ten feet from the bear's den. Had we only known, we could have crawled in and been considerably warmer than out on the ice in the wind. The den was big enough for both of us to crawl in and take pictures.

Even without much sleep, we were anxious to get back to base camp. It had been ten days since our last shower. Rather than wait for the plane to fly over and check on us in a day or two, we headed right for camp about fifteen miles away along the beach. Home-cooked food and hot showers were waiting for us.

I flew out the next day to head down to Soldotna for some King salmon fishing. I caught a thirty-five-pound King, which made a perfect end to a great trip.

. . . So there you have it—a typical Alaskan adventure—out running around at night on a glacier, chasing a bear where a mountain goat should be, using sheep-hunting techniques. . . . That's what I love about Alaska.

The Bears of Arctic Valley

Where bears and humans share the same territory, there is certain to be some conflict. In populated areas, bears can become habituated—they become used to the presence of humans, learn that human's garbage is decent bear food and eventually lose their fear of humans. But the woods are still "the bear's territory." When human encroachment into unpopulated regions adversely affects bear behavior, the humans are the ones who had best be careful.

Areas that are heavily hunted for moose and deer are often also known for the aggressive bear that live there. Kodiak Island is one such place. Some believe that the bears are coming to the sound of deer hunters' rifles—the rifle shots that open the hunting season are like the sound of a dinner bell. The bears are being conditioned and are equating rifle reports with food.

Ship Creek and Arctic Valley, just a few miles northeast of Anchorage, is a popular skiing area. I have heard a number of bear stories about Arctic Valley and Ship Creek—most involving brown-grizzly bears that steal hunters' moose. Of the half dozen hunters I've talked with who have hunted the Ship Creek drainage, all have had problems with bears. Dave Nord and Tom Weismann have successfully hunted the area for a few years, but Dave tells how at least one bear has learned to let the hunters do all the hard work.

Tom and I packed in high on the left side, side-hilling around from the Arctic Valley Ski parking lot on a Friday night. We went about three ridges back and hunted there. We set up camp and then we got up in the morning and hunted the high area because we'd shot a moose there the year before. We hunted the whole area.

About mid-morning we spotted a couple of cows down in a swampy area.

We'd seen a moose walk into a clump of trees but couldn't tell whether it was a bull or a cow. Tom climbed up a little way, circled around and got himself situated. I was dropped down and kinda came in and followed the way the moose had gone.

We'd prearranged a meeting spot where we thought we could find each other.

It was brushy, way taller than my head. I was goin' down and sneakin' 'til I got to this open area and stood around, looked around for quite a while then kinda looked back up the hill, and there was Tom right behind me. I wondered, "What's he doin'? He's s'pose to be goin' the other way."

Tom had followed their plan: "It was a little more woody and open with some grassy areas where I was going. I came to one area, and I looked over there and I saw a brown patch; I knew it had to be an animal. It was about sixty yards away. It was so rounded I knew it couldn't be a moose. And sure enough, I could see it was a bear diggin' around in the earth doing something. Apparently he was intent on what he was doing enough, so I was able to quickly and quietly pussyfoot out of there. Somewhere after that when I was putting distance between myself and the bear, Dave saw me."

We had never hunted down along that creek before and were scouting along, checking it out as a possibility for coming in the lower end and hunting. We'd gotten there about ten o'clock and were looking for a place to rest where we could look at the hillside.

We were walking around when suddenly we heard a *crash, crash, crash*. And a cow moose came runnin' out. Right behind her came a bull! Then there's another bull! The cow moose sensed our presence and stopped. Three moose—our two bulls handed to us!

It was Tom's turn to shoot, so he lined up and *blam*. The moose took two, three steps sideways, but we lost sight of it because it went behind a tree.

We found the downed bull and Tom finished it off. Then we spotted the other one. I shot it, so we had two of 'em down. And as Tom said at the time, "Now we're in trouble."

They were both small bulls about the same size. We gutted and quartered them, left a testicle for proof of sex and carried the quarters across the swamp a hundred yards and hung 'em in some pine trees out of the rain about six foot off the ground which was as high as we could lift 'em. Then we hiked back up to our camp on the hill to get our gear.

We saw a beautiful black bear, the best one we've ever seen; but we passed it up because we already had the two moose down. We packed up our camp and then came back down again.

Then we cut off all the meat from the backbone, ribs and trim meat. We put it in our packs and walked out late Sunday afternoon."

Looking back Tom realized the error of our plan: "We were naive. We always thought the bears would go toward the gut pile, that's why we moved the moose quarters."

We set the tent up on the trail as a landmark and a possible deterrent. That was the last weekend of the hunting season, so we returned to Anchorage and our school-teaching chores for the week. Saturday we recruited Doug Morris and got three horses and returned to where we'd strung up those moose quarters.

We took the horses in as far as we could and left Doug with them while Tom and I grabbed our backpacks and our rifles and hiked up to the moose meat.

At the time, Tom felt a little spooky because of the bear that we'd seen. So we built up our courage by singing, whistling and making noise. We walked in there, and there wasn't a quarter hanging.

We were aghast. They were gone! I couldn't believe it. All eight quarters were gone!

We were just standin' there lookin' around. I thought, "Boy, Doug is gonna be mad at us now. Here we drag him all the way out here and no moose meat."

Tom took his cue from me, but when he heard the safety of my gun go off, *click*, he knew we were in trouble. This wasn't a good situation to be in, and we were both a bit nervous.

I always look around and try to stay pretty alert in the woods. I can usually spot what's out of place—like baby moose hooves in bear crap. Looking down as I stood there in that clearing where our moose quarters should have been hanging, I saw a hoof. I grabbed the hoof and lifted up on it and out came a front quarter. Then I kicked around and picked up another one. We found seven quarters buried there.

Actually we had been standing right on top of 'em. The bear had laid the quarters on the ground just like drumsticks, the big end to the little end. There were four on the bottom, laid in there just as neat as could be . . . big end, little end. I don't know if it was flukey the way it happened, but that's the way we found them.

We were pretty relieved to find the meat and happy that it was in good shape. The quarters were covered and cool—with a layer of moss three or four inches thick over the meat we'd already bagged in the game bags. It was real natural. The bear hadn't urinated or defecated on the meat like we'd heard they did.

Next came the task of getting the moose to the horses. I stood with my rifle while Tom tied a quarter on his pack; then he stood with his rifle while I tied a quarter on mine.

We got the rest of the meat out of there the same way—two quarter, at a time, one of us standing guard with the rifle. We let the bear have the one quarter he'd already taken, and we didn't go crashin' around the brush tryin' to find it. However, he'd eaten the testicle off every one of those quarters. So there we were, a week after moose season packin' out seven quarters of moose without evidence of sex.

The Stick and the String

North American bowhunting is a sport with growing numbers of participants and vast amounts of paraphernalia, but bowhunting today is a world apart from its beginnings.

Bowhunting as a sport is rooted in the Native Americans' principal method of hunting. The natives excelled at improvising with their hunting weaponry. Their bows and arrows were crude by today's standards, but they got the job done.

The bows of the American Plains Indians were short and heavy, making an effective weapon for hunting on horseback. These weapons were powerful enough to drop a wild bison. The arrows were stout and short, tipped with stone rather than iron points. Glue boiled from buffalo hooves or sections of hide was used for attaching the guiding feathers.

Weapons developed by the Eskimos were designed

for an environment vastly different from where the Plains Indians lived. Eskimos used a combination of archery tackle and spears to hunt bears.

These black-haired, brown-eyed, dark-skinned, small, squat people of the Arctic shores combined their creative intelligence and humor to survive the cruelest of environments. They used their ancient weapons and followed polar bears with their dog teams. Once their prey was located, the hunters released their dogs and attacked the bears as a team.

The usual method of fighting the bear was to shoot it with as many arrows as possible, allowing the dogs to distract it while the hunters kept up a constant barrage of arrows. If need be, the native, usually armed with a spear, used the spear as a back up or provoked the bear into attacking him, at which time he jammed the butt of the spear into the snow and let the bear impale himself.

Today's bowhunting equipment is almost as dissimilar to its Native American roots as the Plains Indians' bow was to the Eskimos' spear. The first white Americans used bow-and-arrow materials that linked the centuries and cultures. Our early bow weapons were made using some of the same techniques we use today but were far inferior to modern high-tech archery tackle. Today the archer's equipment includes aluminum arrow shafts with rubberized plastic vanes. And somewhere in this evolution of archery falls the names of the men whose involvement in hunting led to changes in our outlook on the sport. At least five names will always be found in the history of modern bowhunting: Fred Bear, Howard Hill, Dr. Saxton Pope, Arthur Young and Ishi.

Few bowhunters in America today know the story of how early in this century a Native American named

Ishi impacted their sport. In 1912 Ishi emerged from the foothills of Mount Lassen in southern California after witnessing, three and a half years earlier, the death of his mother, the only other member of his tribe. Ishi was discovered cowering in a slaughterhouse corral, clad only in an old, covered-wagon canvas. He was taken from there to the Oroville jail by a sheriff. Amid the clamor of the discovery of this creature, Ishi was released into the custody of two Berkeley anthro-pologists, Alfred Kroeber and Thomas Waterman. These men took Ishi to the Berkeley Museum of Anthropology and began working with him to record his heritage.

At Berkeley Dr. Saxton Pope developed a relation-ship with the Native American. One day while Dr. Pope was watching Ishi work on a bow, Pope fell in love with archery, and their friendship blossomed. In time this man taught the college professor all he could about his bow and arrow heritage. From this beginning Dr. Saxton Pope became the founding father of American bowhunting.

Who would have guessed in 1914 that the friend-ship and activity of two men from vastly different worlds would so impact hunting in America? One was a college-educated doctor while the other was an untutored Native American. It became common to see this cultured man practicing the ancient art of archery with the man from the mountains.

Dr. Pope learned of the bow and arrow's construc-tion from Ishi. The bow or *man-nee* was fashioned from juniper over a fire, and deer sinew was used as backing and deer tendon for the bow string. Arrows or *sa wa* were thirty-two-inch shafts, bound and cured for a month or so. These were later cut at twenty-six inches with a six-inch foreshaft of mahogany added. Hawk or eagle feathers comprised the vanes (owl feathers meant bad luck). The arrow was then painted with pigments from natural sources.

In time Dr. Pope became the world's leading authority on archery, and he is credited with having been the first white man to kill a grizzly with a bow and arrow.

Sixty-five years ago the very idea of taking a grizzly with a bow and arrow was not only foolhardy but also suicidal. The danger merely added to the challenge of Dr. Pope's dream. In 1919 he volunteered services and the services of his friend Arthur Young. After receiving permission to obtain a family group of grizzlies for the California Academy of Sciences in Golden Gate Park, San Francisco, Dr. Pope secured as his guide Ned Frost of Cody, the most experienced grizzly hunter in Wyoming.

Dr. Pope and Arthur Young spared nothing in their preparations—studying the anatomy of bears, using the strongest bows and arrows they could handle, adding to the length of their arrows, using tempered rather than soft steel, constructing spears with torch potential and choosing to hunt from blinds over bait.

Art Young used two bows—one with a draw weight of eighty-five pounds and his favorite stand-by bow named Old Grizzly with a draw weight of seventy-five pounds. Art discovered it was nearly impossible for him to use his eighty-five-pound bow because the cold decreased his strength while adding to that of the bow. Dr. Pope took his two bows, Old Horrible and Bear Slayer. Their arrows were three-eighths-inch birch shafts tipped with tempered, dagger-like steel. A Mr. Compton completed the threesome of hunters who had agreed to have no rifle-shot animals unless all other means of stopping the bears failed.

In preparation for the hunt, Ned Frost instructed

the archers that 1) bears attack when least expected; 2)
a good bear dog is hard to come by—once in a lifetime;
3) bears seldom go up against a man; and 4) bear dogs
are not the answer for hunting a grizzly, only for
locating him.

A party of five stalked the first bear. The pelage of
the brute was not good, and he was a scrawny, male
adolescent. But it was a griz and a good test of the men's
ability. The bear approached within fifty yards of the
waiting men before becoming aware of them. The bear
looked up, Pope and Young drew and fired almost as
one. Pope's arrow grazed the bear's shoulder as Young's
missed. The bear escaped, and to the hunters' joy it
seemed no worse for the encounter.

The second encounter was more nerve-tingling.
Frost, Young and Pope were to sneak up on four bears
they had spotted the night before. The age-old questions flagged their prey-searching minds . . . will we
spook them? How close can we get? Will we hit them?
What will they do?

When they reached the snowfield-bedded bears,
Pope selected the farthest, and both he and Young shot.
With crescendoing roars the brutes fled. Pope's bear
attacked its mother only to have her bite him back. At
that point the three cubs attacked the mother.

As the she-bear reared and roared, Pope and Young
released arrows—one missing and two striking her in
the chest and below her foreleg. With blood running
from her mouth and nostrils in frothy streams, she rose
above her brood, cuffing and roaring. Just as Pope
pulled a fourth arrow from his quiver the red-eyed
brute saw the men and charged!

She was on the men in two bounds but was blown
backward by a blast from Frost's rifle. She fell fifty
yards down the steep snow bank before she righted

herself for another charge, just as two arrows buried themselves in her heaving sides before she died. The cubs vanished. The wounded cub was later found dead. It weighed 135 pounds. At the conclusion of this skirmish Ned Frost, sufficiently impressed by the archers' ability and their weapons' efficiency, admitted to Pope and Young that they had made believers out of him.

Bears were hard to find, and when bears were found, none suited the hunters. Over a month passed and with the passing of time the hunting party diminished in number. In time only Pope and Young were left to try for the bears. Prior to the stalk of their third quarry they inspected their equipment, straightening and sharpening arrows, waxing new bow strings and drying feathers on their arrows.

Their victim was a large male which they proposed to hunt from the safety of a large rock beneath which a trail passed. They had long since concluded that no man could safely evade a charging grizzly's attack by going up a tree if the bear was within fifty yards. On the night of their biggest hunt five bears shuffled towards them in the darkness—a female, three cubs and a monster boar.

The hunters fired at one at the cubs, sending the bear family into pandemonium. Pope drew and released an arrow at the sow, staggering her. Young fired three arrows from sixty-five yards at the monster boar in the shadows of the forest; Pope fired one arrow from what he considered the "point blank" range of seventy-five yards. Within a minute and a half silence reigned.

The sow lay dead; the boar and cubs were gone. At daybreak the men discovered one cub and were elated to note that one of Young's arrows was missing. Late the next evening after having searched all day, the two archers found their prey, one arrow having felled this near-thousand-pound animal. The bear's skull measured eighteen and a half inches in length, and it bore a hide weighing nearly 150 pounds.

So mortal man could slay *ursus* with a stick and a string! What an exciting beginning to a great sport.

Record Bow-and-Arrow Bear

In 1985, Fred Bear's quarter-century-old world record for killing the largest brown bear with a bow and arrow was broken by Dr. Jack Frost, an orthopedic surgeon in Anchorage. Jack has a number of impressive archery kills to his credit; one of his highest honors was to be the first man to take the grand slam on North American sheep—the Dall, Desert, Rocky Mountain and Stone. When I spoke with Jack about his achievements and requested his brown bear story, he cordially invited me to his home where I spent an enjoyable evening hearing about his legendary Unimak Island hunt.

One of my goals had always been to kill a brown bear with a bow and arrow. One of the major drawbacks to hunting with a bow is the fact that once you hit a bear with an arrow, you often have to trail it into brushy areas or patches of alder to take the final shot. For this reason, I had been putting in for permits at Unimak Island—a lightly-hunted island (roughly sixty miles long and ten miles wide) with open beaches and salmon streams, where bears wandered in great numbers.

In the spring of '85 I was fortunate enough to draw a permit for Unimak. Now, my only remaining task was to find a back-up gunner—a good shot, but one who was not too quick to pull the trigger. I invited Tony Oney, a dentist in Anchorage and a certified guide.

Back in the days when polar bears were legal to shoot, Tony led many successful hunts. Besides being a good shot himself, Tony is not easily excitable; he's fun to be around, and he was willing to make the trip and act as my back-up in tight situations. This trip, Tony wouldn't be a guide but would be coming along as a friend.

For safety's sake, Tony and I decided to each fly our own plane to Unimak. The island is a long flight from Anchorage, requiring a ten-hour ride to Cold Bay and then another hour to Unimak. By taking two planes, we could carry extra gas and have enough space to bring along supplies for a very comfortable camp. And most important, if we had trouble with one plane, we would have a back-up vehicle.

When we reached Cold Bay, the weather was overcast and windy, but the next morning dawned warm, sunny and calm—so we took off. Our plan was to fly the entire circumference of Unimak, looking for dead walrus or whales on the beach, where bears would be likely to congregate. We had flown no more than ten miles when we spotted a dead whale on the west side of the island, surrounded by bear tracks. The whale was buried by quite a bit of sand, and the bears had scooped more sand on top of it, so that from the air, the carcass almost appeared to be a large mound of dirt. The whale was laying beside a steep bluff measuring thirty to forty feet high flanked by sand dunes; this looked to be an ideal spot.

We flew the rest of the way around the island, seeing a total of twenty-eight bears. We never found another dead creature, and it became obvious that the whale's beach was going to be a smart place to hunt. We headed back and landed on the beach about two miles from the carcass, taxiing our planes onto the grass to get above the high tide line.

In the morning we hiked up to look at the whale carcass and had almost reached the bluffs that we would use for cover when we ran into a sow and two cubs about one hundred yards back from the beach. Because the wind was blowing from the island out to the sea, we had to be careful about staying downwind from the animals. We tiptoed past them and eased out to the front of the bluff to check the location of the whale. We peeked over the edge of the ridge and saw a big bear lying on top of the whale, spread-eagle as if he was trying to hide that thirty-foot-long carcass from the mass of seagulls flying overhead. We couldn't have asked for a better setup. This bear was a perfect target.

We backed away from the edge and started to move to a spot directly opposite the bear and whale. As we were repositioning, we saw another big bear heading toward us along the top of the bluff. Now, I really began to appreciate having Tony along. The sow and two cubs were still about one hundred yards behind us, one big bear was coming straight for us and another was down on the beach no more than fifty yards away. By the time we reached our new spot, the whale bear was standing on top of the carcass. I could see something white hanging from his mouth, which I thought was a scrap of food at first glance. But looking more closely with my binoculars, I realized one of his lower canines was jutting out a right angle. Now, the other large bear had dropped down off the bluff to the beach and was approaching the whale. Old Snaggletooth bristled all over and rushed out to meet the intruder.

"He's leaving. You better shoot," Tony whispered.

If I had been left to my own devices, I probably would have just waited until one of the bears walked directly beneath me within a fifteen-yard range. But our target was still within what I considered to be an effective bow-and-arrow range, and actually an archer might be better off shooting an animal that's a little farther away, out of the immediate attack zone.

I fired and hit the bear in the back of the shoulder. He immediately spun around and ran down the beach to our left. The other bear was probably thinking, "I've won the whale. That was easy enough." He just walked right up to the whale and sat on top of it.

My bear ran about four hundred yards down the beach, then turned and moved through a little cut in the bluffs and out on the tundra. Tony and I had a difficult time keeping up with the bear as he headed for the tundra. But by the time he reached the flat and open area, the bear was just walking and bleeding enough so that, through the binoculars, we could see blood running down his side.

I couldn't see blood around the bear's mouth and nose, which meant the arrow had hit too high in his spine. Still, the bear was badly hurt and acted extremely agitated, lying down and then rising up several times very quickly. The bear made eight to ten different beds before he settled in one spot. We circled and moved directly downwind from him. Since there were no brush or rocks to hide behind, we started walking towards him cautiously. I led and Tony remained five feet behind me. Each time the bear would lift his head, Tony and I would stop and watch. Finally, we reached a small rise about twenty-five to thirty yards from the bear, which was now lying curled up like a big dog with his back to us. I wanted to move within twenty yards of the target, because I had a large amount of practice shooting at that range, and I wanted to be sure my next arrow was placed perfectly.

As I reached the right spot and put an arrow in the string, the bear looked over his shoulder at us. Although the winds were blowing away from the bear and he couldn't smell us, I'm sure he registered that something was there. We stuck out like sore thumbs on that bare tundra. But the bear looked like he had no desire to charge. As soon as he turned his head, I drew and shot him along the back. The instant the arrow hit, I knew the shot was good.

I remember thinking, "I hope Tony doesn't shoot it because I think that arrow is a good one." On the other hand, the possibility of the bear charging was rushing through my mind, and I was thinking, "God, I hope he doesn't miss."

The bear whirled around unbelievably fast, then stood up on all fours, looking about ten times bigger than he had appeared lying on the ground. He laid his ears back, bared his fangs and his hair stood straight on end. As I waited to hear the muzzle blast over my shoulder, I realized the bear wasn't going to charge after all. Instead, his ears pointed up, his hair flattened and his mouth dropped open. The next thing I knew, he had lain down and rolled over.

That last arrow had hit the bear right in the heart. Because of the position the bear was lying in, I hadn't intentionally been aiming for this spot, but the arrow punctured one lung and hit the heart anyway. Since the animal was already weakened from his first wound, he expired quickly and calmy without needing a bullet to finish the job. When we finished skinning the bear, it was obvious that he was every bit as big as we had thought. The hide squared nine foot, four inches. I wanted to see if I could carry the hide the two hundred yards down to the beach without a packframe, so I just draped it over my shoulders and Tony helped me stand up. Later, after the hide was fleshed, it weighed 105 pounds.

That night we flew out to Cold Bay where we had the skull measured. The results were icing on the cake. If the skull came over twenty-eight inches, it would make Boone and Crockett. It measured 28 7/16 inches, not only making Boone and Crockett but breaking the previous bow-and-arrow world record set by Fred Bear back in 1960.

If there was one world record I wish I hadn't broken, it was be Fred Bear's. From a personal standpoint, the best part of this whole situation was the fact that Fred Bear called me up and congratulated me. A year and a half before Fred died, he also attended the Pope and Young banquet where I was presented with the award for the new world record. I got to spend a lot of time with him there, swapping bear stories. That's an experience I'll never forget.

The Controversy Over Bear Baiting

Bear baiting—intentionally attracting a bear to a shooting site—has long been a subject of controversy. As with many other bear-man situations, bear baiting and its ramifications are complex. Mention bear baiting among Alaskans—particularly those living in rural areas with bear populations where hunters actively bait for bears—and you resurrect a monster.

Baiting bears in Alaska has long been allowed. However, during the construction of the Trans-Alaska Pipeline in the 1970s there were so many problems arising from pipeline workers feeding bears that on July 1, 1977, the Alaska Department of Fish and Game imposed a statewide ban on bear baiting. The ban made it illegal to feed bears, wolves, foxes and wolverines.

The proponents of archery hunting, namely the

Alaska Bowhunters Association, lobbied for the right to bait bears, and in 1982, the Alaska Department of Fish and Game rescinded their earlier ban on bear baiting.

The 1982 ADFG decision resurrected age-old arguments about public safety, proper game management, practicality and sportsmanship. Both residents and hunters disagree on the most acceptable solutions; there are residents and hunters who oppose bear baiting, and there are residents and hunters who favor bear baiting. The controversy and the arguments continue.

Many who oppose baiting argue that it attracts bears into their living space, endangering them and their families. During the summer of 1987 the residents in the area of Hope, Alaska, ninety road-miles but only a few air-miles south of Anchorage, cited several incidents which gave credence to the argument for public safety.

A lifelong resident of Hope, Sue Anderson's thirteen-year-old son John was false-charged several times by a brown bear while riding his bicycle on Resurrection Road. The boy was finally able to escape by climbing onto a shed roof. Anderson told Debbie McKinney of the *Anchorage Daily News*, "I'm really afraid for our children. They play in the woods. The thing is, they're (baiting) so close to our homes."

A two-and-a-half- to three-year-old brown, probably the same one that charged young John Anderson was later killed while attempting to enter the home of Bud Wood.

Girdwood residents have also expressed concern over bear baiting. Two locals, John Heiser and Cynthia Toohey, owners of Crow Creek Mine, circulated petitions and brought the issue up in town meetings. They followed that action with a request to the Board of Game to close their valley to baiting. They were granted their wish on July 1, 1987.

Anyone with any common sense or knowledge of bear nature and behavior would think twice before *luring* bears into populated areas. It is incomprehensible that someone would want to bag a bear badly enough to bait the animal in a manner that would jeopardize a community. Anyone guilty of such behavior should be prosecuted.

People who lure bears into populated areas for hunting blatantly disregard the dangerous problem of the habituated bear. In the last several years more attention has been paid to the significance of human-bear encounters, especially those encounters that relate to the disposal of garbage. Man's presence in bear country brings about a tenuous relationship of co-existence. The man-habituated bear is a real danger, maybe more dangerous than a wild bear because man views a habituated bear with less respect than he would a wild bear, and a habituated bear has little fear of man. Bear baiting is a deliberate attempt to attract bears and endangers the possibility for coexistence.

Stephen Herrero compiled *Bear Attacks* after extensively studying bear behavior within the proximity of humans. He believes that bears can become dangerously food-conditioned and begin to associate food with people. The presence of food-conditioned bears is proportionally related to injuries and attacks to humans. Ironically, the ADFG's policy that sanctions bear baiting seems to deliberately undermine the state's attempt to eliminate the problem of the garbage bears.

John Heiser, a Girdwood resident who has done research with Charles Jonkel for his grizzly study, believes that "If a bear eats food handled by humans, it's going to associate humans with food." (*Anchorage Daily News*, Tuesday, August 11, 1987)

Not only does the bear baiter have to contend with the issue of public safety, but fellow hunters, fishermen and non-sportsmen all criticize the practice as unsportsmanlike.

Shooting a baited bear has been compared to shooting fish in a barrel—it doesn't even come close to being sportsmanlike, and it violates the idea of the fair chase. Former Alaska Bowman Association (founding) member Jay Massey, who also sits on the ADFG board, feels that "It seems sort of incongruous. If you profess to do something dangerous, why climb in a tree to do it?" (*Anchorage Daily News*, Tuesday, August 11, 1987)

Proponents of bear baiting cite a number of reasons for hunting from a bait stand—1) selectivity; 2) killing shot more likely; 3) little chance of error; 4) more humane; 5) safety. The hunter who wants to shoot a large black bear has the opportunity to be selective from a stand, considering that many bears will come to the bait over several days. This hunter will earn his trophy, because he will spend hours preparing the area and bringing bait. If his site is properly set up, he will have a good chance for a killing shot with less chance of error which will be more humane to the animal than a poorly-placed shot from a uncertain distance. And the platform hunter is safe from a ground attack.

Staking Out Bruin

The rapid growth in bowhunting targets the sportsperson with myriad products and activities. Ralph Ertz is an avid bowhunter with a wealth of experience. A Montana state champion archer, he holds the Pope and Young record for being the only man to have taken all

*five species of North American deer with bow and arrow.
He has bagged a number of the North American big-
game species including several Alaskan animals.*

*Ralph has been working with Wade Nolan to pro-
duce a bear hunting video. And since he successfully
shot in 1975, what is now Alaska's number-nine brown
bear, I asked him to express his thoughts on that hunt.*

It was a nice fall day in October, clear as a bell; it
had froze up during the night. We were hunting over an
old moose kill, and we'd thrown some dead salmon
from the nearby stream around the moose. We'd been
there a week, and I'd sat in the tree stand overnight
three or four nights. The night before I shot the bear it
was blowin' and raining. I had a little light tarp that I
put over me to keep the water from runnin' down the
chair and gettin' my sleeping bag wet. I nailed the tarp
to the tree and draped it over the chair. I was nice and
warm and everything was great.

The bear I was waiting for would only come in the
last half hour of daylight. He'd been feeding off the bait
for a long time, but I'd only been in the tree two or three
nights. When he came in the night before, he'd come in
too late to shoot. The night before was the first time I'd
had the tarp because it had started raining, and I
needed it to keep dry. I put the tarp up before the bear
came in. He'd come in, listen and leave. After it got dark,
he could hear the tarp flapping in the wind.

Then the bear came in, and I was only twenty yards
from a grizzly. He was down there grubbin' around
underneath my tree. The only thing between us was
air, and I was up in a tree fourteen or fifteen feet. It's
just like exposing yourself to death—he bein' that close
and all.

He came in three or four times during the night.

Every time he came in I could hear him come because of the dog-panting sound he made. He would walk around makin' a grunting sound—makin' noise to tell everything and everybody he was there . . . he's the biggest, meanest and toughest.

No tenseness or anything like that. I'd slept some earlier and I was warm except for my face. I felt a certain satisfaction at being there listenin' to the bear down below. I was gettin' ready to kill him—gettin' ready to attack him. Basically that's what I was doin'—I'd been gettin' ready to attack this bear after watchin' him two or three days. He'd been clickin' his teeth at me. And I was gettin' ready to kill him. At moments like that I begin to ask the questions . . . "What in the world am I tryin' to do here? Am I going to be able to do this? Will this thing really work?"

Bear Baiting Journal

The following journal documents most of a summer of baiting black bears in Alaska. Wade Nolan kept the journal while producing a video tape on bear hunting and loaned it to me for inclusion in this book. Wade wanted to make a video that was both informative and entertaining and chose as his project hunting black bears from a tree stand.

The baiting began May 12. Wade baited three areas with a variety of materials: donuts, anise rags, beef suet, burnt sugar and honey and jelly. By mid-June the bear activity at his bait sites was heavy. The names of his bait sites have been changed.

June 10

Tundra Lake—Surprised a black bear on the bait. He left after lots of noise. Added suet. Barrel one third empty of donuts. Hanging suet not hit. Grabbers not bit.

June 12

Tundra Lake—Afternoon. Made lots of noise walking in. Spread molasses on a grabber and put it in barrel. Climbed into south tree—got set up. In fifteen minutes the medium bear I'd named Swing came into sight behind north tree and circled downstream. In the next hour he circled the bait twice. I saw him occasionally in three or four spots as he moved. He then approached the bait barrel from upstream and under the hanging burlap. He was very cautious and only stayed in the open for five minutes and retreated into the brush. He came back two more times; once he looked directly at me when my shutter clicked but showed no sign of recognition; I was motionless. He ate about five mouth loads of suet then left the way he came.

Tundra Lake—Evening. Fred Kaltenbach and I went into the Tundra Lake bait at 8:30. We took suet in a box to replenish the bait supply. We got situated in the tree stands at nine and got quiet and still. We had laid the empty suet box a few yards up the trail. I was in the north stand—the hot seat, and Fred was in the photography stand. We had only sat for eleven minutes when I spotted a bear I believed to be Swing, circling to the right behind Fred's stand. The bear moved slowly and kept on the edge of our line of vision. That bear never did come in that night.

The next bit of action occurred at approximately eleven. Two bears came into the bait from down the creek. One medium-sized bear and one smaller, jumpy bear weighing approximately 200 and 125 pounds, respectively. The larger bear walked to the bait and ate some suet and then progressed to the cardboard box which it swatted and bit. It then returned to the bait. The smaller bear moved over to the box, grabbed it in his mouth and noisily charged off into the woods with it.

The larger bear then continued to feed, carrying some suet over to a spot directly under my stand and plopped down about ten feet under me and ate it. I could only see a tiny bit of his back over the corner of my platform. Then for no apparent reason both bears broke for cover, passing under me on the way. Next Brownie showed up approaching from behind and below Fred's stand. His legs seemed especially long and his brown was revealed from rubbing. He fed for thirty minutes before finally leaving. When he departed, so did we.

July 12

Grinny and I got into the treestands at six P.M. He was in the low stand; I was in the first photo stand. Our standard swing bear came in just seven minutes from down the creek. He circled half way around and walked under Bob's tree, looked up at Bob and continued to the bait. We photographed him. Bob even shot a flash at him. He stopped and looked intently at Bob when the flash went off but didn't run. A little later another bear came in—a runt. He was so edgy that he jumped when a squirrel chattered.

The third bear to come in was a medium-large. He walked over to Grinny's tree, stood up and put his claws on the tree. At this point his claws were just eight feet from Bob's feet. He looked up; Bob looked down. We kept the guns handy.

Then he dropped and walked across the clearing

over toward my tree. I got a shot of him in front of the tree. Then he walked under me. My tree was a Sitka spruce and the lower half was not trimmed, and I couldn't see under me. A hundred and eighty degrees to the front was obscured. I lost sight of the bear.

The next time I saw him, he was behind me to my right, standing up. I wiggled around and tried to get a picture. Too many branches were in the way. I glanced over to Bob who was watching intently, and when I looked back, the bear was gone.

I got situated back in my seat and started to search the perimeter of the brush near my tree for a glimpse of him. Then I felt the tree quiver!

I twisted around to my left and looked down toward the ground on the back side of my tree and found the bear. Eight feet below me and he was climbing. There were so many branches on the tree that he had to snake around them in order to move.

I glanced at Bob. He was holding the pistol with both hands at arm's length aiming just under me. The bear stopped. I took note of the location and position of my shotgun and leaned over with my camera. What an opportunity for a picture! I shot two even though the light was real low.

I chose a branch two feet above his head and decided that I would begin talking to him where he was and harvest him when he reached the branch I'd chosen above his head. I leaned over and said, "Ahh, bear, please get out of my tree!" At that he leaned way out and focused his beady, dark eyes on me and began to retreat down toward the ground.

After he hit the ground he walked out into the clearing into my view and stopped. He looked back over his shoulder and up at me. Thinking quickly, I decided to confirm my place in the pecking order and gave him a series of *ooo, ooo, ooo*s. It's the same sound I've heard bears making to one another when they're saying, "I'm a bigger and badder bear than you are!" He ambled off into the brush.

Later I told Bob that I was glad he had been holding that gun on the bear when he was just under me. Bob replied that due to all the branches on my tree at that level he couldn't see the bear but knew he was just under me. The whole episode had been played through with no guns on the bear at all! The next day I took a saw and fixed the visibility problem.

September 2

Tundra Lake—Afternoon. Ralph Ertz and I went into the Tundra Lake stand. I had baited it with caribou trim and salmon heads three days before. The barrel was tipped and had only five pounds of bait left in it. Bones were spread all over the woods.

Ralph got into his stand (the low one) and took six practice shots at a salmon head next to the barrel. First three shots were three inches high; the next three shots were dead center. He had brought a few blunts to blunt a bear if a candidate came in.

Within ten minutes a bear came stalking and sniffing along from behind Ralph. He checked out the barrel, got a fish and wandered off. He did look at Ralph a few times and acted edgy.

Once he left we had a dry spell for nearly two hours. Then in came a medium-sized bear I couldn't identify. We were signaling back and forth as to whether or not to blunt this bear when two tiny cubs tumbled out of the brush and walked up to mom. They were only twenty-pounders and full of action. They grabbed a salmon and had a tug of war right under Ralph.

Once I clicked the shutter and mom huffed. The two

cubs ran for a tree next to Ralph and shot up it like a pair of squirrels. They got eye-level with Ralph and clung there for a few minutes before climbing down.

After twenty minutes of feeding the sow was at the barrel, feeding among the cubby when a floppy-eared bear silently stalked in from the alders and stood at the edge of the clearing. Nearly two minutes lapsed before the sow saw the intruder. She woofed, and the three of them ran for the big tree next to Ralph, and all three climbed it.

It was unusual that she didn't hear the intruder approach. These bears usually know well in advance of an approaching bruin.

The sow came back, and we decided to blunt her so I could practice photographing a flying arrow. Ralph drew on her when the cubs were a safe distance away and nailed her at half draw. She woofed, spun and ran for a tree. The cubs and she climbed.

As it got later, I saw two larger bears stalking around the perimeter. One might have been Swing, but the other, a full-coated, medium-large blackie, came around the corner and walked the edge of the clearing. He was the sixth and largest bear of the night. He was sniffing, cautious and slow. He passed under Ralph and grabbed a fish laying on the edge of the woods and vanished down a trail.

September 3

I took a load of bait and dropped it in the woods near the trail. It was overcast and wet. A light drizzle fell, making the woods silent. I carried my .41 and a full pack of stinky meat. I began talking to the broken log as I always do when alone.

As I neared the bait station, I really chattered it up. I saw the overturned barrel and what I thought was a flash of black from a magpie. I kept talking and when I was twenty-five yards from the can, the bear stood up and took three big jumps up the bear trail past the low stand.

It was a big bear, probably the full-coated bear we saw last night. Then he stopped, turned and woofed, stamped his front feet and took two leaps toward me woofing all the while.

The sound of his warnings filled the damp air. I leveled my gun and pulled back the hammer. This was tense! He was actually defending the bait, and as far as he was concerned, I was not his benefactor but a thief.

I kept talking, and he shook his head and in two leaps reached the big hemlock. He woofed at every move. He scaled the three-foot-diameter hemlock in three giant leaps. I could see his spread paws clutching either side as he climbed. He stood on a big lateral branch and continued to warn me with a constant huffing and head-shaking. The bear was about thirty yards away from me and twenty from the barrel.

I stepped closer to the barrel and he became even more agitated. I wanted to dump that seventy-five pounds off my back but finally decided that it just might precipitate an attack. Still holding the gun on him, I backed off and when out of sight turned and hightailed it up the trail, looking behind me often.

The previous months of watching the bears' antics and being relatively close to them in our stands had made me lose some of the healthy fear I should hold toward these bears. Any bear I'm feeding could reach my tree stand in under five seconds. These are carnivores, scratching out a living. They are powerful and unpredictable.

Later this afternoon Ralph came down, and we took in a half barrel of meat scraps. No bears at the bait station. We set the barrel up so that a feeding bear would be in position for a lethal arrow. Tomorrow we hunt.

September 4

Ralph and Chico came down at 7:30 A.M. Chico was running a telephoto for me. We sat from nine to one P.M. and saw our standard bear all around the clearing, but he was edgy and wouldn't come out to the barrel with three of us sitting there. We saw Swing again at five and then at half past six; with good light Swing got up his confidence and headed for the barrel.

The plan was to come to full draw as he got into position, let down, draw again and shoot. I wanted a full draw in our bear photo. Well, after the first full draw our bear wandered off to the edge of the clearing and never came back. So much for being able to second-guess a bear.

A half hour later another bear entered the clearing and stopped short. His eyes caught Ralph, swung over to Chico and then up to me. He slowly backed up to the alders and disappeared. So much for three people at a bait stand.

September 5

Ralph and I took three boxes of moose trim into Shane Landing this afternoon. I expected the barrel to be empty but it was half full. It had been seven days since Kaltenbach, Chico and I had filled it. Ralph thinks a grizzly is working that bait, due to the condition of the area. It really looks like it was rototilled. We trimmed a few limbs off of the trees to allow a nicer photo of a harvest.

Then we came back for an evening at Tundra Lake. Ralph had his bow ready and we sat until eight P.M. but not one bear showed up. This really seemed unusual. We should have had loads of bears.

September 6

This morning we decided to try a new tactic. We mixed up a scent concoction and put it in a spray bottle. It contained oil of anise, white wine, vanilla and cover-up. We carried it in and sprayed it everywhere— on our legs and boots, every place we walked, on and in the barrel, all over our trees, etc. We hoped to keep that bear so preoccupied with smelling that he would forget about us even being there.

The barrel was empty. The six-foot log that lay in front of the barrel all summer looked like someone worked on it with a chainsaw. An eight-foot section had been chewed and clawed away. Brush, dirt and grass had been scraped up and piled over what was left of the bait. Ralph said it looked like grizzly work.

We sat from twelve 'til two and from four 'til nine, and it wasn't until eight o'clock that our first black came in. It was our standard bear, but he came in from behind me. Very unusual for this bear who camps out on the other side of the clearing.

He came slow, smelling all the potion we'd sprayed. He stopped under my tree and put his paws up on it and sniffed. Then he moved toward the barrel.

Ralph closed his eyes when the bear faced him so as not to alarm the bear with his intensity. I held the camera up to my eye and watched the scene through the viewfinder.

He stopped at the barrel for a second and picked up a scrap and moved over toward the demolished cubby. This bear wasn't timid today. We had this guy's number.

He began walking toward the barrel with deliberation. Once he traveled the next ten feet and turned for a mouthful of bait, we would only need five seconds. Ralph was at one-third draw. The bear was lining up—all was silent. My heart was pounding; my finger tensing on the motor-driven shutter release.

Without warning a huffing grizzly charged out of the edge of the clearing and at the black bear. He covered half the distance before the black even moved, but then Swing moved into high gear and took off. The grizzly had silently stalked to within ten yards of Ralph's tree before making the charge. I nearly jumped out of my tree stand.

He then stomped around the clearing huffing at each step. The brownie was wide-chested, cocoa brown on the back and had dark legs. His disposition was just poor. He was irritated. He was just out in front of me when I snapped his picture. At the sound of my motor drive many black bears have spooked and headed for the woods, but this bear's head raised. His eyes met mine and he woofed, jumped at me and stomped both front feet. I was real glad to be in my tree right then.

He huffed around some more and then entered the woods behind Ralph, circled around and came out ten yards in front of Ralph. The griz looked at Ralph and stomped and woofed. This bear was mad at us for even being there. Ralph was trying to nock a blunt in order to sting this bear's behind when he moved further into the woods.

Ralph said that this griz was saying, "Alright you knuckleheads, I'm in charge. Everybody out of here! I'm the boss."

Well, after he left, we took his advice and left, talking plenty on the way out. The bait was also gone, and Ralph thought the bear would lose interest once the food was gone.

September 7

The griz came in every night for the next four nights and always with the same disposition. The black bears were gone for the next two weeks.

September 29

Kaltenbach and I set up a new bait station two and a half miles farther up Tundra Lake. It is high on the west mountainside where hemlocks give way to alders. We built a big cubby out of logs and deposited three hundred pounds of suet.

October 6

I walked in to check the new bait on Tundra Lake Mountain. I took my shotgun along. The one problem with this station was that the station was not visible until you were twenty-five yards away, due to a crest of a hill on the trail.

As I crested the hill—I had been hollering—I stopped and stared with amazement. The neat cubby and the entire area had been excavated and there was a pile of dirt over the bait four feet high. It looked like a backhoe had scraped up enough dirt and brush to fill a dump truck and then covered up a Volkswagen with it. The bait was under the mound of dirt. The mound looked compacted as if the grizzly had been lying on it.

I began to walk over closer when I heard a big branch snap and heard the grizzly woofing just out of my range of vision in the alders. I was backpedaling from that moment on, gun held ready, glancing over my shoulder. I'd seen a griz attack the black bear on Tundra Lake and realized just how rapidly it can happen. I was glad to cross the creek and head down the mountain.

The Monster of High Lake

A registered guide from Homer, Cecil Jones, permit-
ted me to use some of his hunting stories. The following
one was written by Dennis Frings, one of his clients.

Cecil Jones patiently scanned the meadows that lay far below us. Suddenly, he dropped down to a sitting position behind his spotting scope, squinting at what seemed to be nothing but Alaskan landscape. "Brown bear," he said, "and he's a big one." He looked up at me and grinned, "Going to be a heck of a stalk though. Better not get your hopes up."

I sighed. We'd had extreme bad weather for the previous eight days, and so far had not seen a single bear. Cecil reacted to my excitement by growing even calmer. Looking over at his brother Troy, he asked, "What do you think?" The bear, over a mile away, was contentedly eating mountain ash berries along the edge of High Lake.

Troy leaned against the rocks, frowning. "Look at the wind on the lake. It's blowing from every direction, and those alders are goin' to make it rough to get close to him."

Cecil shrugged. "Let's just wait here a while." He lay peacefully behind the spotting scope, his head resting in his hand. As for me, I could barely restrain myself from jumping up and running straight down the mountain. I wanted that bear badly and he looked to be the only chance I was going to get.

It had all started when I casually looked through the classified ads in *Safari Magazine* one day. It was summertime, 1986, and I had not yet booked any hunts for the fall. I had hunted in Africa the previous three years and had a fourth hunt booked in Ethiopia in January 1987. That left a lot of good autumn hunting months free, and besides, I had always wanted to try my luck at a brown bear. I spotted Cecil Jones' ad and wrote him, describing my interests. He replied that on the Kenai Peninsula the only decent time to hunt the big bears was during the last ten days of the season, in late October.

By that time, the cold weather freezes much of the runoff from the glaciers, making the streams that feed them clear, and the salmon swimming in them are visible to hungry bears. Cecil had one problem, however, with scheduling my hunt; he was fully booked with goat hunters during that part of the season. He asked me to wait a couple of weeks and he would try to rearrange some of the other hunts. I waited only a few days before he called back and told me we were going bear hunting.

October 6 found me climbing off an Alaskan Airlines Twin Otter in Homer, and looking at five grinning faces. Since I was the only one getting off the plane, I kind of figured they were grinning at me. "Cecil Jones?" I asked. Cecil stepped forward, introducing himself, his lovely wife Ina and three hunters who were about to board the same plane for the return trip to California. The smiles on their faces told me how successful their trip had been—three mountain goats and three black bears with several days left at the end to feel good about it all. Now that was the kind of luck I liked to see. I was ready to get started.

Several hours later, I clambered into Cecil's Super Cub and soon we were bumping along to a stop on a narrow landing strip along the banks of the Sheep River, a short distance from our base camp. Cecil and Troy would both accompany me on this hunt. I was awed by the beauty of the landscape. Fast flowing water splashed in an enormous river valley rimmed by the majestic peaks of the Kenai Mountains. The blue ice of mighty glaciers glinted in the sunlight. Even more exciting, we had already spotted brown bear tracks that were no more than a day old.

For the first two days we hunted from base camp, spending much time on mountain overlooks and carefully glassing the valley below. We saw a variety of game—eagles, ravens, goats, black bear—but no brownies.

On the third day, after a conference, we decided to head for a more distant camp. The brothers felt that the hunting would be better further upriver. The move entailed riding horseback over the mountains through one of their high camps and then descending to another river, the Fox. The trip started out with only a few rain clouds, but by the time we had ridden into camp nearly ten hours later, rain was falling in great, horizontal sheets. The wind was so strong that we had to lean far forward into the powerful gusts just to stay in the saddle. We didn't know it then, but the massive floods of October 1986 in Alaska were beginning. During the next two days and nights, the rain fell continually in a torrential downpour. The wind pounded the canvas, while we huddled inside, grateful for the warmth of a wood stove.

By the sixth day the clouds finally broke early in the morning. We hurriedly saddled the horses, happy for a respite, no matter how brief. The river, surrounding our camp on three sides, was rising to alarming levels. That fact made hunting the river bottom impossible. We decided to move to higher ground.

We reached our high camp in the middle of the afternoon, and by then the rain had started all over, pounding down with incredible intensity. It was back to the tent and the wood stove for another twenty-four hours. By now my visions of a brown bear were floating away.

On the morning of the seventh day, we again discussed our situation. There was little chance for a brown bear now that the river valleys were flooded. With the high waters, it was also impossible to hunt bear from the thick spruce stands surrounding the rivers. That left the high country—not very choice hunting ground with its lack of cover and few berries this late in the season. Cecil shook his head. Unfortunately, the dying chances of getting a brown bear weren't our only worry. Down in the constantly swelling flood plain, a Piper Super Cub was tied down.

We decided to head higher into the mountains to set up our spotting scope so we could at least determine if our plane was still intact. If we spotted a black bear on the way, well, I'd fill my bear tag that way. Shooting a black bear wasn't to my liking, but the hunt was only a day and a half from being over.

The spotting scope revealed that the plane was indeed intact, but that its landing gear, as well as the landing strip, were underwater. Both Cecil and Troy breathed a sigh of relief. At least the plane hadn't floated away . . . yet. Troy suggested that since there was little else we could do, we should ride over to the other side of the mountain and do some glassing. Maybe we might locate a bear.

An hour later we spotted that bear by High Lake. Interestingly enough, not five minutes after seeing the brownie, we spotted a black bear feeding directly off to our right. Troy grinned. "If we'd seen that bear first," he said, pointing to the black, "you might never have had a chance at the other."

The brothers continued to patiently observe, discussing strategy. My stomach was churning. "Hey fellows," I wanted to say, "we're not going to get any more chances. Let's go."

Cecil at one point turned around as if reading my thoughts. "If that bear decides to move outta here and we're halfway down the mountain, you'll never see him again. Let's just wait and see what he does. It's still early in the day."

We waited and waited. Soon the bear disappeared into a dense thicket of alders, not to emerge for what seemed like hours but was really only twenty minutes. Suddenly, we spotted him in the lake, swimming along complacently with his head under water; only his hump was visible. He put on quite a show. In and out he went. I thought he might be fishing, but Cecil said there were no fish in that lake. Maybe he just liked swimming. Finally, he climbed up on the bank and lay down not ten feet from the water.

After a few minutes Troy looked back at me. "You ready?" he asked. I nodded.

"Get rid of everything you don't need and anything that'll make noise," he said. "We're only gonna get one chance."

"I'll bring up the horses behind you two," Cecil added. "Just make sure that bear don't get away!"

Troy nodded, "Let's go." He led off with a quick jog. Down the mountain we went moving from alder thicket to alder thicket. At one point in my haste to keep up, my feet flew out from under me, and I landed with a crash. Troy never even looked back. He wanted that bear as much as I did.

Finally, after getting down the mountain, we had to climb up a short, steep slope covered with a thick grove of cottonwood trees. Just before we reached the top, Troy stopped.

"Get your breath," he said, his voice tense.

He produced a roll of electrical tape from his pocket and proceeded to wrap the cuff of each leg of my pants tightly to each boot. "Follow my footsteps and stay close. Don't make any more noise than you can possibly help," he said.

Thirty seconds later we popped over the top of the last rise. The lake was there, the alders were there, but no bear. Troy dropped to one knee, and I followed. He said nothing while he carefully scanned each branch of each bush. Suddenly the bear appeared, moving slowly through the alders toward a little finger of land projecting out into the lake. A few moments later the bear moved into a small clearing and lay down again.

"How far?" I asked.

"Three, maybe 350 yards," he replied into my ear. "Pretty long shot."

"I think I can do it though," I whispered. "There's a good rest here." I had a lot of confidence in my handmade, left-handed .338, meticulously prepared by my close friend, Leonard Muse. It had done its job well on many other hunts.

"No, he's too far," Troy replied, his voice so quiet he merely breathed the words into my ear. "Let's go straight down this alder patch toward him and see if we can get in closer."

We crouched on all fours to keep our profiles from sight. Alders slapped my face, but I carefully, methodically concentrated on putting one foot very slowly in front of the other. After what seemed an eternity, we reached the bottom of the hill. Unfortunately, we were also in a dense thicket. There was no way for a shot in this stuff unless we liked our bear eyeball-to-eyeball. I didn't have *that* much confidence in my .338.

A small ridge, maybe fifty feet high, lay between us

and where we had last seen the bear. Without a word, Troy started to move parallel to that ridge, his direction away from the lake. I followed.

We walked quietly, but quickly. We both knew the bear was very near. After moving about two hundred yards, Troy turned toward the top of the ridge. I realized that he was attempting a flanking maneuver. If the bear stayed lying in the same spot, this would put us above and behind him.

But what if he hadn't? My stomach churned. The wind was blowing first from one direction and then another. There seemed no way that the bear could avoid smelling us. I felt that queasiness of knowing too many things could go wrong.

On top of the ridge we turned again, this time back toward the lake. Troy looked back at me only once. His level gaze left no doubt that the bear was close. We stepped forward now by inches. No noise was tolerable. Inch by inch, we crawled, careful to lift each branch, sidestep each stone. Suddenly Troy stiffened, and in the next instant frantically waved me forward.

I plunged ahead. The bear, fifty feet below us near the edge of the brush, was about to run.

"Shoot!" he whispered. I threw my rifle up and fired. The bear let out a bellow and roared into a thicket of alders. Both Troy and I fired again, but by then the bear was concealed.

"You hit him," Troy yelled. "Reload, reload, he's coming around this knoll below us." We could hear the bear roaring and thrashing through the alders, still no more than fifty feet away. We both fired again, but the cover was too thick.

I desperately wanted that bear, but I felt he was getting away. We both ran frantically to the opposite side of the knoll where we knew he would emerge.

Troy was a bit lower on the hill than I was. Suddenly he fired. "Shoot him!" he yelled. "He's coming out of those alders!"

I waited, and then instantly the bear appeared, moving quickly toward a stand of spruce. I shouldered the rifle, located the cross hairs on his back and pulled the trigger. The bear stopped, hesitated only a moment, and then rolled over backward end-over-end to the bottom of a little draw.

In spite of the fact that he had run in a long circle around the ridge we were on, he was still only twenty feet from the water. His body was now all but concealed by the brush.

"Good shot," Troy yelled.

We proceeded slowly forward, careful to make sure he was dead. There wasn't a quiver.

I let out a whoop. This bear was one very big bruin. Even a greenhorn, eastern hunter like me could tell that. Troy's grin was nearly as big as the bear. It turned out that we both hit him in the last ten seconds. Troy's shot had slowed him down, and my final shot had finished him. Pure relief flooded through me. I had read enough trailing-the-wounded-bear stories to make me reluctant to try that alternative.

"You got yourself one big bear," Troy exclaimed. "He's ten feet, if I'm an inch. And look at those teeth. You must have knocked them out with one of your shots."

The bear's two lower canine teeth were hanging by strips of skin from the corners of his mouth. On closer inspection we saw that they had been knocked out years before; the broken part of the teeth were worn smooth. Apparently, this ol' boy had gotten into a fight with another brownie, or perhaps his teeth had been kicked out by a moose's hoof. Either way, the pain he suffered must have been incredible. One eye socket had been damaged, and coupled with the broken teeth, the injury gave the old veteran a monstrous appearance.

Many hours later, after skinning the bear and making the long night-ride back to camp, we found out just how big that bear was. He measured ten feet, ten inches square, the biggest bear Cecil and Troy had taken in their many years of guiding.

There was more to come on this hunt—pouring rain, swimming horses through raging floodwaters and a flight out that barely got the plane aloft from what was left of a crumbling gravel bar. But it all seemed anti-climactic after felling that bear. The government biologist in Homer later confirmed that he was twenty-seven-and-a-half years old, one of the oldest bears ever taken from the Kenai Peninsula.

It was an extraordinary hunt with two very fine professionals. I'll carry fond memories of the hunt for Old Snaggletooth for the rest of my days.

Two Close for Comfort

Randy Bridwell is a hunter's hunter. Employed at Spenard Builders in Anchorage, he spends as much time as possible outdoors, pursuing his favorite hobby —hunting. Randy has collected a number of big game animals, including caribou, moose goat, Dall sheep, musk ox and bear.

He had a close call with not one, but two world-class brown bears in the spring of 1988.

Alaska's 1988 brown bear season opened in 1987 for my hunting partner, Ron King, and me. We had dreamed about big bears for an entire year, and we eagerly waited for the hunting season to open on the Alaska Peninsula. Brown bear season there is only open to hunters every other year.

In the months approaching our May hunt, we began our planning with great anticipation. We jogged as often as possible to prepare for the long hikes over rough terrain, and we also made detailed travel arrangements. We would fly from Anchorage International Airport to King Salmon, then board a Cessna 180, which would land us on the beach of the bay we had chosen to hunt. Since we had decided to hunt the Pacific side of the Peninsula, we were almost certain that another hunting party would choose the same area. With this in mind, we studied maps and decided that during the first week we would hunt five miles up the main river valley from our drop-off point.

Ron and I had both lived in Anchorage since 1982 and had been on numerous hunting trips. But with the preliminary arrangements made well ahead of time, the remaining weeks before our trip seemed to pass very slowly. Finally, we were down to buying our groceries and what little gear we still needed. The decision to hike five miles up the river valley narrowed the choices of food we could take along. Instead of steak and pork chops, we had to settle for Top Ramen and Cup-O-Soup as the main courses. Breakfast would consist of granola bars, oatmeal and trail mix.

Arriving at the bay on a Saturday at five in the evening, we began unpacking the base camp immediately. We pitched the tent, emptied our backpacks and began to repack a spike camp to carry the five miles up the valley. We decided to take a small Moss two-man tent, a backpacker's stove, five day's worth of Top Ramen and Cup-O-Soup, sleeping bags, a few extra articles of clothing and, of course, our guns. At six A.M.

on Sunday we were up and on our way. The weather was fair as we made our way up the valley, which was crisscrossed with rivers meandering down to the ocean. Although forced to cross several deep streams, we decided not to wear hip boots because of their weight and lack of ankle support; we opted for rain pants, tying them securely at the ankles, over our water-proofed, leather boots.

When we had walked about two and a half miles, we decided to set up the tent and wander around the surrounding valley to make sure we hadn't overlooked any good bear country. We set out for a small knob to do some glassing. Ron and I hadn't moved more than twenty feet from the tent when we spotted an enormous set of brown bear tracks in the mud. We were surprised, expecting the bears to still be high in the mountains instead of roaming the river bottoms with us.

After reaching the knob, we glassed the snow-covered hillsides, looking for the large trails the bears leave in the snow when coming out of hibernation. We spotted caribou, fox and ptarmigan all around us and a couple of bear trails leading down from the snowy peaks.

Since it was still early in the day, we left our spike camp and continued up to the head of the valley to survey the area we had originally chosen to hunt. When we rounded the last bend, we were awed by the sight of the bowl at the head of the valley and the surrounding snow-covered mountains. We returned to the spike camp that night and decided to move up to the bowl the following day.

The next day we chose a camp site that allowed us to glass 360 degrees around our spot. We had already discovered several sets of large tracks in the snow and still had two days to glass and relax until the season opened. But suddenly the weather changed. The clouds dropped in, completely hiding the mountains and making glassing impossible. A pelting rain began to fall, driven sideways by the powerful wind gusting up the river valley. Since we were socked in with no visibility, we holed up in our small tent for the next twenty-four hours, missing the chance to hunt opening day—May 10.

Finally, the weather began to let up around noon on the eleventh, so we crawled out of the tent and decided to take a short walk to stretch our legs. Since Ron had his gun and we were walking a short distance, I didn't carry my rifle. As usual, the short walk turned into a long one. The further we went, the better it looked. We ended up three quarters of a mile from the tent.

The four small streams we crossed had all shown extremely good signs of bears. The trails along the streams had swaths of grass growing in the middle with well-worn paths on each side where the bears' feet landed as they walked; bones and various other salmon parts had been dropped all over the trails.

From the knob we began glassing, looking for any strange objects. The wind finally calmed down, and when it did, the bugs began to swarm around our faces, making it difficult to concentrate on spotting. As I scanned the area, I noticed an object that appeared to be a rock; but its location seemed peculiar, so I kept my binoculars focused on the rock for some time.

Suddenly, to my surprise, the rock began to move. Four legs pointed up in the air. This was no rock, but a brown bear lying in the snow on his back. And then, out of the corner of my eye, I saw another movement. About two hundred yards up the mountain was another brown bear.

The first bear was a blonde with dark legs, the second, chocolate in color. Sighting these two beasts within seconds of each other made the hair on my neck stand straight up. We set up the spotting scope and agreed I should hoof it back to camp to get my backpack and gun. I ran the mile and a half to the tent and back.

After returning to the spot where Ron was keeping an eye on the bears, we saw the blonde bear get up from where it was lying and begin to move toward the chocolate bear. As the blonde bear closed the gap to forty yards, the other bear rose out of his bed and headed toward the blonde. When they met, the bears began to fight, biting and swatting at each other. Both stood on their hind legs. As they clashed, a loud roar echoed across the valley. It was one of the most awesome sounds in nature that I have ever heard. The bears tumbled through the snow, thrashing at one another, finally coming up face-to-face. There was a thirty-second stand-off, and then the bears both turned away and headed back for their beds. The entire battle lasted three minutes.

We packed up the spotting scope and began making our way to the base of the mountain where the bears were lying. After crossing several streams, we shed our rain gear and backpacks, then inched our way along a two-foot wide bear trail worn down to the dirt. On our left the snow was three feet deep, and on our right an eighty-foot cliff dropped off into the valley below.

We hadn't hiked more than 150 feet up the mountain when Ron realized that he had left his extra ammunition in his raincoat. Rather than take a chance on going back to get the ammo, and since we were both shooting .300 Winchester magnums, I gave Ron two of my extra shells. That gave us each a grand total of six bullets. I told Ron to put one shell in each pocket so they wouldn't rattle on each other—a move that later proved nearly fatal.

As we inched our way up the hogback, my heart pounded like a drum. A light breeze was blowing in our faces from the bears to us. The cover along the ridge was very sparse, so much of the stalk was on our hands and knees. We worked to within 120 yards of the blonde bear—the one I had chosen to shoot. Both bears, lying about two hundred yards apart, were sleeping in the thawing spring snow.

Although I didn't want to take the head-on shot, it was all I had. The bear suddenly raised his head to look around, and I aimed at the front of his chest and squeezed the trigger. At the same instant, the bear dropped his head. The 180-grain Nosler bullet hit him two inches above the right eye, penetrating the skull into the brain. To my amazement, the bear didn't even flinch before falling, but dropped directly to the ground. I couldn't believe I had killed him so quickly.

I looked back at Ron to ask what the chocolate bear had done. We had both expected it to jump up and run away at the sound of my shot. Surprisingly, the bear was still sleeping soundly. Perhaps all the avalanches in the area had desensitized him to loud sounds.

We decided to creep over to my bear to get a better angle for Ron's shot. I had the hardest time not letting out a yell after my bear was down, but now we had the chance of a lifetime—we could get two big brownies together.

We crawled toward my bear. I had told Ron it would make a great story to shoot his bear while resting his gun on my animal, but he found a better rest and clearer shot about ten feet away. I lay across my bear and couldn't believe what was happening.

The big, chocolate bear was lying in a depression he

had dug out of the snow. Ron looked through his scope, and quickly decided the angle of the shot was bad because of the bear's position. I told Ron that if he hit the bear anywhere, it would stand up and give him a good second shot. So Ron aimed and pulled the trigger, and, as we expected, the bear stood up. We learned at that moment that a non-fatal shot only gets a brown bear's adrenaline pumping, making him damn near unstoppable.

Ron unleashed a second shot, which only seemed to aggravate the bear. The animal was convinced that the pain he was feeling had somehow been inflicted by the blonde bear. In an unbelievable display of speed and strength, he charged directly toward my bear. Ron fired two more shots, emptying his gun. I looked over and asked Ron if he would mind if I started shooting, too. His reply was, "Hell, no. Go ahead!"

Just as I pulled my gun up to let off a shot, the bear disappeared into a small gully. Ron reloaded with the one shell from his right pocket, not having time to reach into his other pocket for his last shell. I used the break in the action to move out of the direct line of the bear's charge. I made three leaps along the edge of the cliff, covering twenty feet. Ron didn't realize, as I ran past him, that I had stopped just a few feet away. "Don't run!" he shouted. "Stay here and shoot."

Just then, the bear reappeared only twenty-five yards away, charging at full speed. Ron took his fifth shot, emptying his gun. The bullet hit the bear solidly behind the front shoulder, but he didn't even flinch. Ron turned back toward me with panic in his eyes. His last bullet was in his pocket, not in his gun. I pulled up my rifle and fired just as the animal was getting ready to maul my bear.

The bullet struck the enraged bear in the chest,

throwing him onto his back against my bear.

As the bullet hit, Ron was frantically trying to reload his gun, thinking the bear was barreling down on top of him.

"Where is the bear?" he yelled.

"It's dead," I said.

Only after the bear stopped moving could we breathe a sigh of relief. Ron and I sat down, trying to collect our thoughts. Soon, we walked up and admired the bears. I raced down the mountain to get my backpack and camera. We each posed by our bears and took many pictures, and although we didn't need photographs to remember our adventure, we still weren't finished with this hunt. It was time to begin the task of skinning our trophies.

Because of the position and the weight of these bears, it was impossible to roll the huge carcasses around. We couldn't even roll them downhill, because they'd fallen only five feet from the edge of an eighty-foot cliff, to roll them anywhere was to risk losing them over the cliff.

We began skinning Ron's bear first. By 11:30 P.M. we still hadn't finished but quit for the night and hiked back to the spike camp just before dark. The next day we were up early and back on the mountain, working to finish the job. Six hours later we'd skinned them both. The next step was getting the hides off the mountain. The snow was deep and rotten, so we couldn't carry the hides on our backs. We dragged them across the snow all the way down the mountain. At the bottom we tied one of the hides onto a backpack frame. But it took two of us just to lift the one frame! The 150 pounds of weight on the pack forced us to make two trips down the mountain with our hides. On the trip up to camp for the second hide I looked up the mountain and couldn't believe it—another large chocolate-colored bear had moved in on the carcasses we'd left at the kill site.

This was one hunting trip we'd never forget! Aside from our great luck, it took us five hours to cover the four and a half miles from the spike camp to base camp—for each bear. Then we had to make a trip back to the spike camp for our gear. When our bodies recover we'll be ready for our next bear hunt!

Alaska's Bear Cubs

This is guide Ben Forbes' story of a hunter from New York and his bear.

The whole story is kind of crazy. I had an inquiry from a gentleman from New York City. He wanted to go on a bear hunt in the spring, so I sent him the usual information about hiring a guide and when hunts were scheduled. And he was full of further questions.

When was the earliest we could hunt? When did the season open? How many hunters would I take out and at what price? What was the success ratio on my trips? And a lot more details. And besides the questions, he also added some things he wanted on the trip.

He said, "I don't want to see anybody. I want to get out alone. I don't want to go into any of the Indian villages. I don't want to go to any canneries. I don't want to see anybody. In fact if you weren't necessary, I wouldn't even take you along."

So, I made arrangements for him and suggested he come on the fifth of May and hunt until the fifteenth for a ten-day bear hunt. He wrote back said no, he wanted to start hunting on April 27. He said, "I want to be out there before the woods are full of hunters."

Well, he didn't know Alaska or bear hunting, because nobody goes out in April. I couldn't convince him that his date was a little too early, so he came, and he started hunting on April 27. I met him at the airport, and as soon as he got off the plane, he started asking questions, "How many bear are there in this country?"

And I told him, "I don't know, I've never counted, but Fish and Game says there're five thousand bears."

"Nope, there aren't that many." And he asked, "How big are they?"

This time I gave him some very factual figures I knew from personal experience, but he said, "Nope, they don't grow that big."

Now, this guy really had me puzzled. "Well, what's your reasoning?" I asked.

"I've seen lots of bear in zoos and there isn't one of them that big."

I tried to explain that in the wild bears live a different life; they have the capacity to grow much larger with more food and more activity. He said, "Aw, that's a crock of you-know-what. They have all the food in the world in the zoos, and they receive the best care in the world there, so zoo bears should be the biggest bears in the world."

And any question of his that I answered, he always contradicted my answer—I was wrong.

It wasn't long before I wasn't giving him any arguments about anything. He'd ask me a question, and I'd answer it and just let it go. He had his mind made up and there wasn't anything I could tell him that was going to change it.

And now, because we were hunting the last week of April, we had a heck of a time finding any bear. We'd been out about three days, hadn't seen bear one and just a very few tracks. So I decided to take him in to a favorite bay of mine, where I knew of a rather unique situation. The bay at the head end is almost square, and a river comes in each corner. A bear trail goes down one river, crosses the beach and up the other river, and the bears travel the trail going in both directions.

Now, a bear trail that's used a great deal shows a very interesting and incredible detail. The bears all step in the same footprints, and after a few years of use, these footprints are worn down into the ground, maybe as deep as six or seven inches. And in places where they've walked over hard ground, the impressions are actually visible. And this bay was an ideal one for seeing this kind of trail, because the trail went up and down the river and was quite deeply marked with paw prints way down into the ground. Where they crossed the beach, the bears walked across rocks, and they had walked on these rocks enough to leave good, slight depressions in the rock.

We went ashore, and I walked up on these rocks and could see where the bear tracks were.

So I said, "There's been a bear along here," which was an understatement, because there'd been thousands of them along there to make a trail that heavily marked.

And he says, "Where? I don't see any tracks?.

I said, "Look, see the depressions here in the rock." And he looked at those tracks, and I could see he was completely startled. He stamped his heel on the ground, and of course, he didn't even leave a mark. He looked at those tracks again, and he didn't know what to make of it. All I said was, "Well, let's see where he went."

I followed the trail to the left, knowing what I would find. The trail went along the beach, turned and went up the bank, between two trees. And these trees were what we call bear rubbing trees. They're . . . well, I suppose they serve as a post office or something like that for the bear, because the bears go up and rub their sides against the trees. They stand up and bite them or scratch them up as high as they can reach, and they scratch a little bit in the spring. I guess they want to rub their fur to get some of the matted hair off.

Well, when we went up to this tree, we were lucky. There had been a bear by the night before or maybe even that morning, and he'd stopped and stood up and rubbed his back against one tree. And in his wiggling, his hind feet had left footprints that looked like violin cases. So I pointed the tracks out to my hunter, and he looked at them.

Then I said, "Take a look at the bark here." And there was hair in the bark . . . four feet off the ground, five feet, six feet, seven feet, eight, nine feet high there was hair in the bark on that tree. Not much, just little tufts of it. And I pointed that out to him.

Now these trees were about three feet apart, and the trail went between them.

So I stepped back, took a look at the trail between the trees and said, "You know, it looks like that was a tight fit."

And my poor hunter, he looked at those tracks, he looked at that hair on the tree nine feet high, and then he said, "Let's go back to the boat."

So I said, "Okay."

Back down at the skiff, we started to row out to the boat, and he was sitting on the seat, looking at his rifle—he had a .375 rifle that must have cost him close to five hundred dollars. He said, "Is this thing big enough to kill a bear?"

Well, I wasn't going to give just any answer, so I said, "Oh, it'll kill him all right, if you hit him in the right place."

Well, I got him back to the boat, and it took me two days to get him interested in going bear hunting again. But, I think in the end he got the last word. We did shoot a bear. A nice one, he measured just a little over nine feet, which is quite a respectable trophy. And after the bear was down, he walked around that bear and looked at it very carefully.

Then he looked me right in the eye and said, "You sure that ain't a cub?"

2

Close Calls

I f a big grizzly goes through our place at Nabes-na, we don't bother him; he's no problem. But if a black bear is hangin' around, I'll kill it.—Lee Hancock, former big-game guide.

Like a monster out of the primeval past, the shaggy beast roared on hind legs to its full height. Towering over the lone hunter, the bear's hayhook claws flashed at the ends of its catcher-mitt front paws. Only six paces separated the two as each attempted to discern the danger facing him.

The bear hesitated only momentarily as the man instinctively raised his rifle and fired from the hip, as if in a trance. The echoing blast brought the hunter back to his senses. He retreated one step, working the bolt on his .30-caliber Winchester.

Too close to hear the bullet strike, the hunter wondered if he'd connected. He shot the bolt. Suddenly he realized the bolt had not caught. He'd pulled it nearly out of the rifle, and the bear was coming.

He jammed the bolt forward, pushing a fresh cartridge into firing position and squeezed the trigger.

The 220-grain, mushroom-tip bullet hammered the hulk as it edged forward. The bear did not go down, merely slapped its chest with one paw and popped its jaws together.

The hunter frantically worked the bolt, injecting a new shell and firing again.

The man's thoughts whirled. Was he hitting the bear? Did he have enough bullets to turn the charge? What if he didn't stop the bear before it reached him?

He had fired three times and readied his fourth. Just as he fired, the bear turned, looked at him and, amazingly, left.

Through the adrenaline rush that followed, the man tried to calm his shaking body. He fumbled for his ammunition, planning to follow and finish the animal. He was shaking so badly that he figured his chances of hitting a barn door were slim. Only then did he discover that his weapon was empty.

He distinctly recalled putting five bullets into the rifle before leaving camp. He could only recall shooting four times. Had the bear not turned and left, who knows what the hunter would have suffered. He would have had nothing for protection but an empty rifle and his fists.

At that point Earl Barnett decided to return to camp at Broad Pass, Alaska. It was the fall of 1932. When Earl reached camp, he and his hunting partner, Steve McCutcheon, formulated a plan to return to the scene and look for the bear.

The next day the men retraced Earl's steps. Then they discovered how Earl had come so close to the bear without seeing it; the animal had been lying in a depression hidden from Earl's view.

Not far away Steve and Earl found the bear lying as if it was asleep. Steve lined his gun up on the back of the bear's neck while Earl approached it cautiously. The bear was dead.

After spending several hours skinning the bear, the men found five holes in the beast. Earl had fired five times—evidently firing two shots initially on instinct. Now Earl's nine-foot, six-inch bear hide would always serve as a reminder of his brush with death.

The Volcano Bear

During my research for this book I interviewed many hunting guides, and several were somewhat embarrassed to mention that they had never had a close call with a bear, demonstrating how man's love for adventure often outweighs his regard for safety. However, some pros, mostly due to their constant exposure to the outdoors and the law of averages, have had hair-raising experiences. Among those who have survived a couple of close scrapes with Old Ursus is Bud Branham, one of Alaska's oldest living guides.

I met with Bud, and we discussed his colorful guiding career and close calls. "I think 90 percent of the so-called charges are not attacks," Bud commented. "Usually, the animal just wants to get out of a tight spot, and you happen to be in the way. But some charges are legitimate, especially if you get between a sow and a cub, or approach a bear on a kill. In those situations, bears can be dangerous, very dangerous. Especially grizzlies."

In his younger days Bud served as a guide for many well-known military men, including Admiral Fletcher, General Buckner, and General Twinning. "I also guided FDR," Bud said. "But we didn't go hunting . . . we went fishing because he couldn't walk."

On one occasion Bud guided Blackjack Fletcher, a

*four-star admiral, on a hunting trip on Uyak Bay in Ko-
diak. It was on this excursion that Bud discovered one
of the most unusual bears he had ever seen.*

Blackjack Fletcher, another hunter and I were
camping in an old house on the beach along Uyak Bay.
It rained almost constantly, but we still hunted in the
rain. Every night bears would come down to the beach,
feed on the salmon and walk on the trail that cut across
all the bends in the creek.

One rainy and misty morning, we left the cabin and
walked along the straight trail through the brush.
Suddenly, we ran right into a huge brown bear. I was
leading and jumped aside, saying, "Jack, there he is."
For days we had been seeing giant tracks on the muddy
beach, and I thought this must be the same bear that
made them. Jack shot. The bear had already turned,
and was getting ready to escape when the bullet hit him
in the chest. He disappeared in the brush and came out
again about thirty or forty feet down.

Then I took a shot, which hit the bear right across
his butt, just under his tail through the fat part. The
bullet didn't seem to faze him, but we still had a badly
wounded animal on our hands.

About three hundred yards across the flats, the
mountains began and there were alders up a thousand
feet or more. We waited awhile and then started
following the trail, which was clearly marked with
blood. I knew from the large amount of blood and the
bright color that Jack's shot must have hit the lung.

When we came to the base of the mountain, the
bear was moving up through the alders ahead. I
stopped there. I didn't want to take an admiral into that
sort of situation. My crew chief, whose name was Reynolds, was carrying a shotgun—a twelve-gauge pump—

loaded with buckshot, and I was carrying a rifle.

I put Admiral Fletcher on a nearby rock and told him to watch very carefully. Reynolds and I went in on the trail about a hundred feet. We could see where the bear had laid down. The alders were torn up, and blood covered the ground. After resting there for a few minutes, the bear had moved away on a parallel path. I knew he was badly wounded because a hurt animal will not climb; he goes parallel or comes down. I also knew he was very dangerous. We followed slowly and cautiously. In about a hundred, two hundred yards, I looked up and there he was waiting for us. He was standing up, and I shot him in the ear.

Well, the interesting part of this story is that the bear had no hair on his body. His whole back and head, and clear down on his side was all scar tissue. The hide wasn't any good, but the Admiral wanted it. We decided the bear must have been burned in the 1912 eruption of the Katmai volcano. There had never been another conflagration on Kodiak Island. But Katmai killed all of the wildlife on Kodiak except protected or mature animals. This bear must have been big in 1912 to have survived such a fire.

Alatna River

July 16

Wade Nolan and his wife, Hazel, have experienced as much excitement during their young lives as many people would in several lifetimes. Wade is a biologist, hunter and wildlife photographer. During a single year, it's not unusual for Wade to spend more than one hundred nights in a tent. He has filmed and observed bears extensively in Southcentral Alaska, Kodiak Island and the Alaska Peninsula.

When I asked Wade to share some bear stories with me, he gave me his journal and told me to use what I wished. In the following account from his journal, Wade describes a bear situation in which he used a handgun. Since that time, Wade says, "A handgun is better than no gun. I now carry a 12-gauge slug gun while adventuring in Alaska's backcountry."

In just a few minutes Hazel, Randy and I would be in the most remote place of our lives. The pilot revved the De Havilland Beaver's engines, and we soon left Circle Lake, flying to home base on the Koyukuk in Bettles.

We were 275 miles up the Alatna River in the west central Brooks Range. The nearest village was seven days away on the Koyukuk River. Our plan called for us to hike from Circle Lake up Arrigetch Creek into the Arrigetch Peaks and spend three days hiking and exploring. Then we would portage to the Alatna River and float for seven days downstream to Allakaket.

After assembling our Klepper Kayaks, we paddled across Circle Lake to a point where we'd be nearest to the river, pulled our kayaks out and walked the four hundred yards to the river. The Alatna was high, muddy and about fifty yards wide. We considered camping on the river bank, rather than at the lake where we'd left our kayaks. The mosquitoes were thick at the lake. But it was eight p.m., and by the time we could set up camp on the river, it would be especially late.

We returned to our kayaks, pitched our tents about fifteen yards apart and ate dinner. The lake was still, the temperature in the sixties and the sun low in the west while we cleaned the dishes. By midnight we were ready to hang the food in a tree and turn in.

Hazel was already in her sleeping bag, and Randy and I were getting ready to hang the food out of bear reach when there was a loud, splashing noise one hundred yards up the lake. It was so loud that I suspected a moose. Even above the Arctic Circle it gets somewhat dark around midnight in July, so we could barely see. Later, we heard more noise in some neck-high willows growing about fifty yards behind our tents.

Randy spotted him first and pointed him out to me. It was a black bear. We immediately began to make a ruckus to let him know we were people. As we expected, the bear dropped from sight. I told Hazel to get out of the tent, and I grabbed the gun—a .41-magnum pistol. I figured the bear might have left after identifying us. We peered into the scrubby willow and spruce, hoping not to see him. But then he broke out of the bush just behind us.

At this point I became concerned. There was going to be trouble. This bear wasn't afraid of people. He was an average-sized black bear, weighing 150–200 pounds. He eyed my pack sitting only eight yards away from where we stood. I couldn't believe my eyes when he grabbed my backpack in his mouth and shook it as he inched away from us. Randy threw two pots at him and we both yelled, but the bear had no fear of us. I leveled my gun above his head and fired a warning shot, hoping he was scared of guns. In the forest the shot seemed so loud the noise rang in my ear for a time, blocking out all other sound.

He dropped the pack and slowly ambled off toward the dense willow patch, ten yards away. He didn't charge off as I had hoped. The explosion at point-blank range hadn't really frightened him to any great extent. I knew I had to kill the bear if he came back.

Randy found my spare shells in the pack, and I reloaded, keeping six live shells in the gun. This time he circled camp and came in behind Randy's tent. He was moving fast. He swatted the tent and grabbed Randy's pack in his mouth and started for the brush with it. Equipment was falling from the pack and before he went ten yards, the pack caught on a snag and was pulled from his mouth.

This bear was not just casually inspecting our camp and equipment. He showed force in the way he grabbed the pack, and he was moving fast. At this point I resolved to kill him. We were in lots of danger and he left us no out. Randy and I advanced to his tent. The bear saw us coming.

I told Randy to grab a club, telling him that after I shot, a charge would be likely. If I didn't hit a vital spot, the bear could attack from close range, and I could lose control of the gun. In that case, I instructed Randy, grab the gun at any cost and finish the job.

The bear moved toward us. My gun was leveled. He wasn't offering much of a shot. Only a head and maybe spine shot were available—neither of which I wanted for stopping a bear only thirty feet away in dim light.

My trigger finger was tense as he approached. I noticed my gun and hands were steady. I aimed at his head, hoping for a split-second opportunity for a heart shot under his chin. But now we were only eight yards apart. The bear could cover that distance in one second if wounded, then there wouldn't be time for a second shot. Aloud, I said, "Get with me, God," and the bear lifted his head, exposing an area the size of a saucer over his heart.

Almost automatically, I leveled the sights on his heart and let go with my only chance at stopping him. The bullet crushed into the bear's chest and jarred him backward onto his haunches. He immediately leaped to my left behind some scrubby willows and the next jump took him out of sight. I had the hammer back ready for a second shot, but he was gone.

"The worst thing that could happen has," I said. "We've got a wounded bear!"

We all stood still listening. No sound. Then from twenty yards away, a long moan. He hadn't gone far. I told Haze and Randy to stand still, but to watch the brush. For ten minutes we waited. It seemed like ten hours.

We were facing a life-threatening situation. We were two hundred seventy-five miles from the nearest village, with one gun (a pistol), twilight in the forest and a wounded bear. I knew we had to wait and then go after him. I prayed he was dead.

Slowly, I inched along his exit route, gun poised in front of me, hammer back. I was ready for a charge. I saw something dark and low in the willows just ahead of me. I circled to the left for a more open view. It was the bear.

For the next five minutes, I worked my way forward. More of the bear's shape came into view. Finally, I could see his chest at ten yards away. No movement. I stepped in closer and looked for his eyes. They were open. I tossed my hat at him. No response. He was dead.

We gathered Randy's equipment which was strewn all over the place. The bear had thrown equipment over a twenty-square-foot area. We couldn't find Randy's telephoto lens, but we did find the case for the lens— with teeth holes in it. Randy's tin cup also had two punctures in it, and the cup was crushed.

We decided to postpone a decision on what we would do until morning. It was nearly two A.M. when we turned in. I was physically and mentally exhausted. Sleep came quickly.

July 17

As soon as I awoke the next morning, I began thinking of our situation. We had been on the lake only six hours before a life-threatening bear encounter occurred. According to our plan, we would now leave our kayaks, food and equipment cached on the lake and backpack up into the Arrigetch for three days. We were about to leave behind over four thousand dollars worth of equipment, including two boats—our only means of transportation out of the Brooks Range—and eight days of food. If we encountered a camper-wise bear in six hours on this lake, how long would it take for another to destroy our kayaks and our supply of food?

The only choice left was to scratch the Arrigetch trip and start downriver. I woke Haze and Randy and told them of my decision to leave the area. They agreed. We ate a hasty breakfast, portaged the kayaks and equipment to the river and began our river journey at four A.M.

July 21

We stopped in an area that had been burnt by a forest fire and picked blueberries. We found black bear prints on the bank. We paddled and floated for hours through the burn. The weather felt more like Arizona than the Arctic. Temperatures hung around seventy-five degrees all day. Randy and I didn't wear shirts and got nice tans underway.

By ten P.M. the sun was getting low and shone through high cirrus clouds, casting a peaceful evening light over the river. We had a destination in mind, a cabin across from a creek that was through the first set of meanders west of the Alatna Hills.

At eleven P.M. we picked a bare gravel island about two hundred yards wide, pulled out the boats and carried the sleeping gear and tent over to the far side to a patch of sand. A channel measuring about one hundred yards wide separated us from land on both sides of the island. I felt extremely safe here for some reason.

We opted to eat first and didn't pitch the tents. We were enjoying the quiet and the alpenglow sunset when I turned and saw a black bear step out of the burnt hillside onto the bank. We decided to leave, no matter what the bear did. We hollered, but the bear just stopped and looked. He sat back and I could see his long, red tongue lapping his snout.

We made more noise. I grabbed my gun and spare shells. Hazel began packing everything up. Randy and I walked toward the bear as he stepped into the channel. Our equipment was on his side of the island, only 120 yards away.

We kept moving toward the bear and our gear, yelling loudly. He stopped. We grabbed our gear and carried it back across to our boats. When I glanced back, the bear was swimming the channel, coming for our island. Only his head was visible in the swift, green channel.

The next time I looked he had aborted the crossing attempt and was on the bank. We quickly launched the kayaks and paddled out into the channel on the opposite side from the bear. He noticed we were leaving and began to head downstream, matching our progress. As the river braided back together he was still following us on the bank, now at a trot.

It was a bit unnerving to be chased by a bear at eleven o'clock at night, eighty miles from the nearest village. We wanted to camp and eat. So we floated for eight miles or so, and pulled onto another gravel bar. We ate, set up only one tent and hung the food in a small cottonwood tree. I didn't see any bear tracks on our island. We turned in under cloudy skies at half past one in the morning, dead tired. We had just spent fifteen and a half hours on the water.

A Midnight Walk with Bruin

Lee Miller, recently retired from the Alaska Department of Fish and Game, is another experienced outdoorsman and one of the most bear-wise men on earth. I asked him if he'd ever had any close calls with bruin, and he told be about his encounter on the McNeil River, an area known for its high populations of brown bears and photographers.

One of my scariest experiences with bears was a time in 1961 when I went down to the McNeil River to do some work for my supervisor, Al Erickson. Erickson wanted to conduct some night observations at the falls to learn about the bears' feeding habits—whether they fed all night or not. Unfortunately, Erickson had broken his leg and couldn't do the work, so he sent me.

From the cabin on the spit, the falls are about a mile or a mile and a quarter away. To get there, you follow a bear trail up through the alders. I left the cabin at about eleven o'clock, planning to be at the falls by midnight. Even though it was July, it was pitch black in the alders, and I had to take a flashlight.

As I walked, I could hear the bears all around me. Supposedly, there were sixty-five in that small area at one time. They were everywhere. I could hear them off the side of the trail fighting with each other and slurping up fish. I could barely see the end of my gun barrel, and I thought, "What the hell am I doing walking up through here in the middle of the night?"

When I finally reached the falls, I could still hear bears moving off the trail in front of me. I sat down in the dark and made my observation for Erickson. A group of big boars were feeding on salmon. I could barely see their outline, and they were growling at each other while they ate. I kept thinking, "This has got to be the craziest thing I ever did."

I waited until it got a little bit lighter, around half past one or two in the morning, and headed back for the cabin. That's enough of that. Anybody who wants another night observation can do it himself.

Bear Raid

I met Marshall D. Biser, Sr., aboard the Pacific Star, *a Quest Charters boat out of Seward, Alaska. Marshall works as the first mate on the* Pacific Star. *When the two of us began talking about bears, he told me about his close call.*

My son Marshall, Jr., who we call Buck, and I were on a moose hunting trip in September 1987. We had flown out of Fire Lake near Eagle River to a spot on the Yenlo River about 150 miles northwest of Anchorage.

Because of the regulations forbidding us from hunting on the same day of our flight, we occupied ourselves with setting up camp when we arrived and looked forward to the first legal day we could hunt. After a big breakfast the next morning, we decided to hunt on opposite sides of the river. We had a small inflatable boat, making it possible to cross back and forth. Buck hunted the west side and I took the Mount Yenlo side.

At about eleven o'clock I began to have this funny feeling that something was wrong, and I headed back down to camp. When I got to the bluff at the river side, I realized our camp had been raided by a bear. As I was straightening up, the bear appeared on the bluff above me. I shouted and made all kinds of noise, but he held his ground and just kept woofing and growling. Then he moved toward me, ducking under a blow-down tree and standing up. He growled again. Then he came down on all fours and charged toward me at full-speed. I shot him in the neck, and he died instantly. The bullet left his shoulder at the top of his spine.

Shortly afterwards, the game warden came by and told me to move to the other side of the river because several camps on our side had been raided. I showed him my bear, and he took it for someone that wanted a black bear rug.

Buck came into camp at dark with the news that he had shot a moose upstream. Once he had gutted the animal, he hiked out. The next day we went back to quarter the meat. The bull was lying in about a foot of water, making things tough. We backpacked the four quarters and the backstrap out a mile and a half that day. It took us all day to get the moose back to our camp.

On the fourth day, as we went to retrieve the remainder of the moose, we encountered a large brown bear that had taken over the carcass. The bear was a blonde-bodied, dark-legged animal that we judged to be about twelve hundred pounds. We didn't argue with him.

Next, we began looking for my moose. As we were making our way through the woods, we kept hearing brush break behind us. Buck said, "Dad, let's wait and maybe you'll get your moose right here."

We had just taken off our backpacks when I saw a bear looking at us through the brush about twenty yards away. His head looked as big as a bushel basket. At first, I hesitated to shoot because I didn't think that one bear could make as much noise as we had been hearing, but when he made a move at us, I fired the first shot. My .300 Weatherby magnum was zeroed in at three hundred yards and the 180-grain, soft-nose bullet hit him just above his nose. He reared on his hind legs and growled and screamed like nothing I had ever heard. He frantically batted at his face with both front paws and kept roaring.

Buck fired a shot, and I shot a second time. We both fired again, and he went down to stay. Between my rifle and Buck's 7mm Weatherby magnum, we'd stopped the male grizzly.

No sooner had the first bear gone down than a second one roared out of the brush. I said, "Oh, my God, here comes Big Momma." She was running in high gear. It only took her one to one and a quarter seconds to cover the twenty yards, and she was on top of us. I fired one shot when she was about five yards away. All I could see in my scope was brown. She rose on her hind feet in one motion and struck me, knocking me to the ground.

I heard a shot and rolled over to see what was happening. Buck was standing by a tree about two yards away. The bear was lying on the ground about eight feet away.

I then discovered that I had a cut on my left hand, between the index finger and the thumb. The bear's claw had ripped through the skin on the top side of my hand and nearly emerged through the skin underneath. I was mighty thankful that this was the only injury we received.

After gathering myself together, I got up and we just stood looking at each other. Suddenly, we heard teeth chomping and turned around in amazement. There were two more two-year-old bears staring at us from about fifty yards away.

My gun was a five-shot and Buck's was a four, so that left one load apiece to take care of two mad bears, jumping and growling at us. I covered Buck while he reloaded, and he covered me as I loaded, all the while watching for trouble from these animals. In about ten minutes they left the area, and we sighed with relief. As we got ready to skin the bears, Buck said, "You know, that was almost as exciting as sex."

I looked at him and said, "I never had sex scare the hell out of me."

The Clamming Caper

Chuck Lewis, Jr., skipper of a commercial fishing vessel, described one bear encounter that occurred while he was still on his boat.

We were over in Kukak. The skipper and another man were clam digging, and I was on the boat. They'd dug holes all along the beach. While I was watching them, I saw a bear come ambling down the beach. Every time he'd come to one of their clam-digging holes, he'd dig in it then go to the next one and inspect it curiously. He kept getting closer to those guys, so I started waving and hollering. But they were about a hundred yards away from me, and they couldn't figure out what I saying through the wind.

The skipper got in his skiff and puttered toward me

to see what I was yelling, leaving his partner on the beach. As he came closer, I kept pointing and hollering. Finally, he turned around and saw the bear, which had now moved just about thirty yards away from the guy on shore. The skipper turned the skiff around in a hurry and motored back to rescue his partner.

Hard-Won Horns

George Malekos, owner of the North Slope Restaurant in Eagle River, invited my wife and me to his restaurant to tell us about his nerve-racking encounters with bears. While we ate breakfast, George described how one deer hunting trip turned into an unforgettable challenge with a bear.

In November 1986, three friends and I decided to go deer hunting at Zachar Bay on Kodiak Island. Although we knew Zachar Bay was a heavily hunted area, we also knew it was heavily populated with deer—so we were anxious to set up our camp at the cabin belonging to a friend, Dr. Yassick.

Before we left on our trip, a woman at Peninsula Air had called and told us that we might want to avoid Zachar Bay and the Yassick cabin. She explained that hunters had been having lots of problems with bears there. One group had a bear come into the cabin while they were still inside. The men had hung a piece of deer meat high in the air, and the bear had hoisted himself up and pulled the meat down. The hunters nicknamed the bear Nadia Comaneci and wrote their story on the wall of the cabin, so groups that came later could have a good laugh.

Two other resident hunters had told us that 1986 was the first year bears in the area moved *toward* the sound of gunshots. To bears, the shots were supposedly just like the sound of a dinner bell.

But despite these warnings, we set out for Zachar Bay. I went with one of my cooks, Craig Kline, who did not have much hunting experience at the time, and Jack Danbury, who worked at Boondock Sporting Goods and is a proficient handgun expert and hunter. My regular hunting partner, Carl Johnson, made up the group of four.

I have a hunting partner with whom I hunt all the time. We both take two guns. When he carries a .378 Weatherby, I carry a .224 Weatherby, which is rather small. When I carry a .340 Weatherby, he carries a .257 Weatherby. We're not really stuck on Weatherby calibers, but we like the way the bullet shoots.

The first morning of our trip we spotted several deer high in the hills and decided to break off into pairs to track them. Because Craig had never hunted much before, he went with Carl. Jack came with me. As we climbed the hill, I walked very slowly. Jack is an older man with emphysema, and any strenuous exercise is difficult for him. By the time I reached the top of the hill, he was quite a way behind.

Right away I spotted a nice forked-horn, heavy-based deer. I called back to Jack, but he couldn't get to the top of the hill quickly enough. The deer was getting ready to take off, so I shot him.

As I gutted the deer and Jack kept guard for me, we spotted another buck running about three hundred yards away. "That animal looks huge," I said to Jack. Although I didn't have my binoculars, I knew the deer must have been massive if we could see his horns from that distance.

"Do you think you can hit him?" Jack asked.

"I think I can," I answered with assurance.

I pulled down on him, and sure enough I killed the deer with two shots. It took me about twenty-five minutes to hike over the top of the hill to retrieve him. When I reached the deer, I realized he had the ugliest horns I had ever seen; they were wide, but without points. The horns just looked like spindles.

Once Jack and I had field dressed both deer, we started downhill for the cabin. With about a quarter of a mile left to go, we stopped to rest—and that's when we probably made our first mistake. From our resting place, we could see some rocks sticking up from the bay in front of our cabin.

"I'm gonna' see how this pistol shoots," Jack said. He had carried a handgun with him, along with his large rifle—a .458 Sauer. Jack fired six shots, almost in a row, down into the rocks.

Meanwhile, I had grabbed the two deer and continued dragging them down the hill. We were walking along a bear trail that cut through the scattered alders and open areas. All the hunters used this trail to climb up and down the hill. Soon, we came to a large rock, and we stopped to rest again. With one deer on either side of me, I sat down with my back against the rock. As we rested, Jack and I admired the deer and commented that they could have been brothers with their white faces, dark spots and good-sized bodies.

I carried the .340 Weatherby and a .454 Casull with a 265-grain bullet—a very large handgun.

Just then, Jack heard some thumping on the ground. From where I was sitting I couldn't hear anything, so I was surprised when Jack stood up and yelled, "Bear, George!" As he yelled, Jack stepped away and slid down the shale on the side of the hill. I whipped around, and there was a huge bear no more than ten feet away. We both froze, and our eyes locked. I'll never forget those eyes. Little, brown, beady eyes in that skull, staring at me, almost saying, "Please go away."

The bear kept inching forward, looking from me to the deer. He just wanted me to leave, so that he could take the meat. But there was nowhere I could go. I couldn't turn and run down the hill because the ground was frozen on the trail, covered with five or six inches of snow. And I wasn't going to take my eyes of that bear. The only thing I could do was reach for my handgun. Everybody knows that you don't shoot a bear when he's above you. If you do, he'll fall down on top of you. As the bear inched closer, Jack yelled, "Don't shoot, George. Don't shoot him." But the bear kept coming closer, and I knew he was getting ready to jump on the deer. The deer were in front of me at my feet, and the loose shale was all around. I was stuck.

So I aimed for the bear's eye and squeezed the trigger. I'll never forget the sound he made—a giant roar. I cocked the gun again, thinking he was going to come tumbling down the hill. But instead, he disappeared off the trail. I turned and saw him about ten feet from the trail, spinning in circles and batting his head with his arm.

I had heard stories that .375s sometimes bounce off bears' heads. But I was sure that, at the angle the bear had been looking at me when I pulled the trigger, my shot had hit.

I fired another shot, and then another. The second bullet went wild. I had aimed for the bear's head, but he was turning and spinning. I wasn't sure where the third shot had hit, but by that time, Craig and Carl had heard the commotion and the three quick reports and appeared over the ridge of the hill.

Now, the bear was moving uphill. I hollered and told

them I had wounded a bear. I heard them yell, "Oh, shit!"

"Carl, I don't know which direction he went," I yelled.

In the meantime Jack had climbed back up to where I was standing. I grabbed my rifle. We knew we had to find the bear.

Jack asked me if I had hit the bear and I told him I had shot him in the eye.

"Then you'd have a dead bear," he said.

We looked around on the ground, and Jack insisted that I had hit him in the foot.

"Now, wait a minute," I answered. "How the hell could I have hit the bear in the foot? I never even saw his foot.

"Well, you hit him in the foot," he says. "There's a little bit of blood here, but not pools."

We followed the footprints up into the alders. While Jack and I searched up above, Carl and Craig went down below. Soon, we discovered the bear had moved into a steep gorge. It was starting to get dark, so I said, "I think we better take these deer down, hang 'em in the meat house and go back to the cabin and talk about this. Tomorrow we've got a job cut out for us—we've gotta go find this bear, or somebody here is gonna get hurt."

When we got back to the cabin and discussed the incident, the three others had me believing that maybe I missed the bear.

"You were scared. Maybe you were shakin'," Carl said.

"Maybe the second shot," I told him. "But the first shot, I put that bullet right on his eye. And he roared. I know I didn't miss him."

"Well, you're shooting eighteen hundred pounds of

energy at the muzzle with a .454. Maybe it was just the muzzle blast."

The argument went on and on.

Early the next morning we decided to pair off as we had the day before. Jack and I decided to search the gorge, while Carl and Craig hiked up above. This way, we would pedal-push the mountain until we found him.

When Jack and I got down to the beach, we counted four brown bear directly in front of us on the hill where we'd been hunting. We decided not to go up the mountain. Bears were all around us, just meandering in the brush.

When we got back to the cabin, we saw Craig and Carl coming. They had also run into brown bears—three, including a sow and cub. That made eight bears within a quarter of a mile of the cabin. To complicate matters, we discovered our meat house had been raided during the night. A bear had dragged away two deer. Which two? My big forked-horn and that ugly, spindly-horned deer.

We all decided to make another plan to find the wounded bear, but first we needed to eat breakfast. Craig, Carl and I went to get water for coffee, following the bear trail that led behind the cabin to the beach.

We had walked about seventy yards from the cabin when a strange pile of grass caught my eye. I should have left it alone, but instead I kicked it with my foot. Underneath the hump of grass was one deer hoof, a skull and the ugly, spindly horns, licked clean. There were teeth marks in the skull. Everything else was gone.

"Why couldn't it have been the big-based horns instead of these pitiful things?" I asked.

Carl made a smart comment. "Well, the bear must

have been a trophy hunter and took your big deer." We chuckled a little bit, and then I made my third mistake: I picked up the horns.

When I picked up the horns, a bear suddenly rose up above us. He had been lying on a little shale rock mound about fifteen feet up. As he stood there popping his teeth, we all bolted bullets quickly. The bear now had the option to escape and climb up the hill, but instead he came barreling down the shale with his teeth still gnashing and the hair raised along his spine.

I still held those stupid horns in my hand. The instant I dropped them, Carl shot the bear between the front shoulders with his .378 Weatherby. The bear rolled down the hill, almost falling on top of Craig and me. We stumbled over each other trying to get out of the way. When I turned back around, the bear had stood up on his hind legs.

I hit him in the chest with a .340 Weatherby at no more than twenty feet, and the bear fell backwards. "Now you put a round in him to make sure," I said to Craig. So he shot, and the bear was dead.

As we slowly walked up to the bear, I thought, "Oh, no. Now we've got two bear . . . this one and the one I wounded yesterday." We rolled him over, and lo and behold . . . above the bear's left eye was a fresh, three-inch crease along the skull. On his right front paw, there was a bullet hole that he had been licking. The wound was gray, but shiny, so you could tell it was fresh. Then, we found my pistol bullet lodged in the paw; I had hit it as the bear was spinning.

And he was big. But he was a *she*. She was eight and a half feet. We dragged the carcass to the bottom of the mountain, skinned it and took the hide to the Department of Fish and Game, leaving the body of the bear behind.

The next morning we decided to do a little more deer hunting. My intention was to swing over to the spot where the bear had been lying. In the back of my mind, I knew my trophy horns couldn't be far from that area. By the time we reached the top of the mountain, the fog had rolled in. We couldn't see fifteen feet in front of us.

I said to Jack, "Let's drop down and pick up the horns and go back to the cabin."

Jack didn't want to look for the horns, but as we walked down the mountain, I kept trying to inch over to the area where I thought they might be.

Soon, we reached the spot where we had left the carcass the day before. It was gone. With my binoculars, I scanned the area. I looked over in a little gray alder patch that ran down to the beach, and there was the biggest gray bear I had ever seen in my life. He had dragged the deer carcass into a little depression and was lying on top of it.

If I had come straight down the mountain to get my horns, I would have walked right into him, and there's no way I could have escaped that bear. That's the last time I hunted Zachar Bay.

The Beaver Dam Bear

George was glad to survive that deer-turned-bear hunt. But his adventures with bears were not over. In September 1987, George and a fellow named Chris Hurrsey went hunting near Movie Lake in the Susitna Flats and ran into a bear that meant business.

We had walked about two and a half or three miles that morning, stopping periodically to glass for moose, when Chris spotted a bear. The animal was about 150 yards away, feeding out in the open in a marshy spot.

Chris fired at the bear and missed. He took a breath, sat down, fired and missed again. The bear took off for the alders loudly splashing the water around him.

I had a clear shot and knew that a rear-end bullet, if placed well, could be deadly. I aimed for the bear's rear and pulled the trigger. At the time I was standing on an incline, and as I pulled the trigger, I slipped a bit. But still I heard the *pppiiiff* of the bullet report, and the shot slapping its target.

"I got him," I said.

"No, ya didn't," Chris yelled back. "You missed him. You never even. . . ."

"We're gonna have to go over there and see," I said. "I know I hit him. I heard it."

We argued on and on. In the meantime, the black bear had appeared again on a bluff two hundred yards directly in front of us.

When Chris fired two more times and missed, the bear dropped down and disappeared in a patch of alders. Chris wanted to walk across a nearby beaver dam, climb up the hill and find the bear. While I was warning him that he would get completely soaked, the bear popped out of the brush again, looked directly at us, then disappeared.

"What is this monkey up to?" I asked as I pulled out my binoculars.

"George," Chris said in a low voice, "That son of a bitch is in front of us. He's coming to get us."

I was just getting ready to walk forward a bit and investigate when I saw a blur of black, twenty feet below the little hill where we were standing.

"I'm out of bullets," Chris shouted. "Kill this son of a bitch."

I aimed and fired. The bear was so close I could actually hear him breathing and see his tongue hanging out. I hit him broadside with my .340 Weatherby and 250-grain Nosler—forty-eight hundred pounds of energy. But the bear never even broke his stride; he just twisted his head a little bit and kept running.

Now the bear was on top of the beaver dam—two bounds away. I shot again, and the bear fell down like a ton of bricks directly on top of the dam with his butt hanging over into the water. I'm still not sure who placed that last bullet in the bear's head, me or the Man upstairs.

No Snowshoes Allowed

An Athapascan native, Gust Jensen, who lives at Lake Iliamna on the Alaska Peninsula, told me about his near miss with bruin.

One December I went hunting for a giant of a bear that had been wounded by another hunter a long time ago. My uncle had told me, "Don't go after that bear. He's wounded and he's mean. Everybody's afraid to go and get him."

That only made me want to go after this bear more, so I started moving into the brush after him. There was quite a bit of snow, clear up to my knees, and I had snowshoes on. I was snowshoeing along, when I looked up and barely saw the bear's head through the brush. I didn't want to go any farther, so I shot and broke his jaw. The bear started coming through the bushes, flattening them as he ran by. I thought my time had come, and I got ready to jump to the side.

Only there was one major problem. I had forgot I had snowshoes on. When I tried to leap, I sat right down on my butt. My snowshoes were caught with a bear only ten feet away. Luckily, I had held on to my gun, and as the bear looked to one side a little bit, I shot him in the back of the ear. I made sure I didn't miss him or that would have been the end.

Close Call With a Denned Bear

Max Schwab, a registered guide from Talkeetna, has had enough thrilling outdoor adventures to last a lifetime. Max tells one special tale about a bear that he hunted for five years before he saw anything other than his tracks.

This mysterious bear lived just fifteen miles from Talkeetna, but to my knowledge no one ever saw him. He existed close to people without letting them know, by coming out only at night and keeping to salmon streams surrounded by giant alder patches and rugged country. I saw his tracks several times, and they were easily distinguishable by their size. I had never seen bigger ones anywhere else, including Kodiak. I tried tracking him in the fall a couple of times, after it snowed, but had no luck. He'd disappear just about the time of the first snow and as soon as all the salmon were gone. Several times I got close enough to hear him and smell him, but he hid himself in the dense alders, escaping as soon as he had wind of me.

In the fall of 1987, we had a late first snow, with a light covering higher in the mountains. By this time I had a good idea of the bear's territory. I landed my plane along the river, set up camp and went looking. I found his tracks just before dark, so I went back to camp to spend the night and get a fresh start early in the morning.

As usual the tracks were in a dense alder patch in a treacherous, steep-walled canyon. They were two, maybe three days old. I didn't have much hope of catching up to him, but I thought following his tracks would be a good chance to learn more of his habits. I followed them up and down through gullies, across draws and through dense hands-and-knees brush.

After about a half mile of this, I came upon a four-foot-diameter nest where he had spent several hours sleeping. The tracks leaving the nest were two, three days old. I walked just about two hundred yards from this spot when I saw an area that looked like it had been dug up by the bear. I figured he had found a dead moose and might still be nearby, so I chambered a round in my .375 and carefully took a few more steps. There was a movement in the brush.

It was the bear—not more that seven or eight steps away—waiting for me. Because of the dense bushes, I could only see his head, which appeared to be the size of a large beach ball. I was a lot closer to that giant than I cared to be, and I figured the shit was going to hit the fan any second. Without stopping to think, I fired, and he instantly dropped out of sight with no movement or sound.

The shot through the brain had killed the bear immediately. But my biggest surprise came when I realized the bear was still in his den. He was lying with his head poking out of the entrance and the rest of his body back in the den. I studied him for a few minutes and made sure he was dead by poking him in the eye with my .375 at arm's length. Then I pulled on his ears with the intent of dragging him out of his den. . . . No way.

After spending about an hour trying to wrestle a thousand or more pounds out of that hole, I decided the only solution was to skin him inside the den. The entrance was about three feet in diameter with a five-foot ceiling. Although a six-inch-deep nest of dry grass was the only thing in the den, there wasn't room to roll the bear over. I had to skin the hide away from each leg, then cut the skinned leg off and drag it outside. It was getting near dark, and it was completely dark inside the den. I gutted the bear and dragged the organs out of the hole to let the carcass cool as best I could to save the meat and hide from spoiling. I started a fire outside, cooked some bear liver and crawled into the den to sleep with my new companion. It was a long, cold, cramped night.

It took most of the next day to skin as much of the bear as I could inside the den, bone the ribs and remove the backstrap. I forgot my knife sharpener, so I had to whet my knife on small pieces of stone that were in the den. Finally, after grunting and straining for several minutes, I was able to shove the bear outside and finish skinning him. By this time, it was almost dark again and I didn't have a pack big enough for the hide, which measured ten feet even. The skull measured twenty-nine inches.

My plane was five rugged miles away, and it was well past dark when I arrived. Now, I was tired, wet, cold and hungry. But mainly, I wanted to fly to get a larger backpack and make it back to the den as quickly as possible to get that bear hide out before it spoiled. So I took some candles from my airplane survival kit and spaced them along the runway to light my take-off. There was enough starlight, so I could see to avoid the mountains. However, there were a few seconds of absolute darkness after I passed the last candle. The sound of the landing gear catching the top of a small spruce tree was a little frightening.

The next day I went back bright and early with a big-frame pack. After fleshing every ounce of fat off the hide, I was barely able to carry it those five miles down the slippery boulders of the canyon. I reached my plane just in time to avoid using the candles again.

"Your Roar is Bigger Than Mine"

I received the following letter from Gary Van Hine describing an unusual face-off with a bear.

Dear Mr. Kaniut:

I am a U.S. Forest Service employee, and in my work as a road recon and locator, I have had numerous encounters with brown bear. I run into about two to seven bears a year, usually surprising them as much as myself.

One day my crew and I were working on Catherine Island, cutting a trail for a survey line. We had been making considerable noise, talking loudly over our chainsaws and Sanviks. At one point I stopped to re-sharpen my saw, while my partner kept hacking brush with her Sanvik. As I finished the sharpening, I rose and told my partner, "Stand back, I'm going to cut that hemlock off-line."

At that moment a large brown bear came charging over the crest of a brushy depression. The bear had to cross a barrier of several blow-down logs to get at us, and instead of jumping over one, he simply ducked under and "bench pressed" the ten-inch-diameter log over his back and dropped it as he passed through. My partner and I had frozen in horror, but suddenly the bear stopped about ten feet from us.

The roar he had emitted as he charged scared me, but as he stopped, I reached down and picked up the Homelite chainsaw and pulled the starter cord twice, as quickly as I could. The second pull started it, and a bellow of white smoke blew towards the bear. Later, my partner described the look on the bear's face as "your roar is bigger than mine." The bear glanced over his shoulder as if to check whether he had any help coming. Then he turned and bounded over the log and was gone. A moment later, we heard him in the brush, circling us.

During the time of the attack my partner was behind me. I didn't realize she had run up the P-line and found our .375 H&H rifle. By the time I had started the saw, she was up on a rotten stump five feet over my head, covering me. When the bear ran away, I shut the saw off because she was trying to tell me something.

"You're white!" she yelled. "Van Hine, your face is really white!

I admit I was frightened. And to prove it, the hair on the area around my sideburns turned mottled white over the next few weeks.

Catherine Island is believed by some to be where bears take their cubs for "training" each year. I believe our survey crew, as well as others working in the area, disturbed the bear, who thought we were infringing on his territory. He treed another crew later on that month a few miles away. He also tore out our survey stakes as fast as we could put them in the ground. Needless to say, I was glad to move on to another area for surveying later in the season.

Sincerely,
Gary D. Van Hine

Quick Temper

Cecil Jones, big-game guide, lives near Homer, Alaska, and the homestead where he grew up. Cecil has been hunting since he "was big enough to start packing a .22 rifle" and guiding since 1969, after apprenticing under established guides Earl Stevens, Dennis and Chris Branham and Ray McNutt.

Cecil responded to my request for bear stories by sending several accounts of his close calls. Reading through his tales, I found a competent, cooperative and congenial guide—one I'd book for a hunt.

One of his most frightening experiences with a bear sow taught him how protective mothers of all species can be over their young.

For me, it had been a pretty uneventful day. After helping saddle horses and seeing my brother Troy and hunter Richard Chamberlain off to mountain goat country early that morning, I had taken my time cleaning up the cabin. There was no reason to hurry. I was not expecting them back before dusk anyway.

Richard, a coal-mine operator from Ohio, was here on a ten-day hunt for mountain goat and black bear. It was late October, our last hunt of the season, and Richard was the only hunter we had in camp. Troy and I would swap off if necessary, both taking turns as cook and guide, so it would be an easy hunt for both of us. This would be a welcome break for us after a long, hard season.

In the afternoon I cut up enough firewood to last through the hunt. By the time I finished cleaning my .300 and .44 magnums, it was a little before dusk. I decided to go fill the water bucket and maybe walk out on the gravel bar and see if I could see anything of Troy and Richard.

As a precaution against bears, I took my .300 along . . . not that I was really expecting any trouble, but you just never know. Some people spend a lifetime in the woods and never have a single bear encounter. But

then again you also hear every year of some unfortu-
nate soul being mauled or killed by bears. So around
here we never venture far away from camp without a
gun of some sort.

At the cabin, we get our water from a stream about
two hundred yards away. I went out and filled the
bucket, then set it on the bank to be picked up on my
return. Then I started walking up the stream bank,
planning to hike out about a quarter mile to where the
stream opens up into a wide gravel bar. I had made it
up the bank about three hundred feet when I saw a
brown bear sow and a single cub hit the stream just
ahead of me, maybe fifty feet away.

When the sow hit the water, she started looking for
fish. She would bound a few jumps then stop and stare
sharply into the stream. The cub was following behind,
imitating her. He was a spring cub and just a cute,
little, blonde ball of fur. He kept jumping to the spots
where the sow had just scared away any fish that might
have been there.

The bears started downstream and I started moving as quietly as possible away from the bank, trying to
keep a patch of alders between us. Even though their
leaves had fallen, the trees did offer some camouflage,
and I could see through them. But I could only move
away from the bank perhaps thirty feet without getting
into the brush and making noise. I wanted to just stand
back quietly and let the old girl move on down the
stream.

To my relief, the sow did move along about two
hundred yards—but her cub stopped about even with
me. To make matters worse, the cub then climbed up
on the bank just in front of me. Under the circumstances, he didn't look nearly as cute now as he had a
few seconds before.

Up to this point, I had avoided chambering a round into my .300 to prevent any unnecessary noise. When the cub saw me, I decided to go ahead and load my gun. I wasn't sure what would happen next, but whatever it was, I wanted to be prepared. I didn't have to wait long. The cub let out a little squeak and before the sound had even ended, the sow was up over the bank. Within three steps, her expression had changed from "What's going on?" to "I'll teach you a thing or two!"

And she probably would have taught me a real lesson about bears' tempers if I had not had my rifle. Now, I had a decision to make: I had to choose whether to shoot the ground in front of her and hope she turned, or drop her before she got to me. I didn't want to shoot her. The cub was too young to survive on his own. But on the other hand, I was not sure that I would have enough time to chamber another round if I shot in front of her and she didn't turn. I still decided to try it. As she roared toward me like a locomotive, I shot into the sand about fifteen feet in front of her. The shot didn't stop her, but it did make her swerve to the side. She went into the brush about thirty feet to my left, and much to my relief, the cub cut right across and went in behind her.

I've never seen an animal get any madder quicker than that old sow when she looked up and saw me standing close to her cub. I still don't know if I would have had time to chamber another round had she kept coming. But I'm still glad for the decision I made and the way it worked.

A Fourth of July Celebration

Black bears are notorious for making terrible nuisances of themselves. They've been known to ransack campgrounds and destroy cabin interiors. Cecil Jones recalls a terrorist bear that gave his family a Fourth of July they'll never forget.

It all started out sometime around three in the morning on a cloudy July 4, 1979. Our little blue dog woke us up from a sound sleep with a series of sharp barks. We tried to ignore him and go back to sleep, but he wouldn't quiet down. After listening to him for a few minutes, my wife Ina got up and scolded him and then lay back down. The barking promptly started again, so this time Ina got up, went out on the porch, swatted him a couple of times to show him she was serious and then jumped back into bed, hoping that this would be the end of it.

Well, the peace only lasted a few seconds. Obviously, he was not going to stop with just a scolding. This time Ina decided to lock him up in the outhouse so that we could get some sleep. At least there he would be farther from the house, and the outhouse would muffle the noise.

So back out the door she went, only this time Blue wasn't on the porch. He was hiding under the car. Ina assumed he was trying to escape another scolding. Reaching as far as she could under the car, she secured a firm grip on his collar and pulled him out, then packed him off to the outhouse and locked him inside. The barking stopped, and we went back to sleep, thinking nothing more about it until we rose at about seven. That's when we first realized that Blue hadn't just been barking at his shadow.

There, on our living room window, were a number of muddy pawprints obviously made by a medium-size black bear sometime during the night. He had come up on the porch and peeked through the window. However, the real surprise came when we looked out in the yard.

Our car had bear tracks all across the hood. It had rained some during the night, and the ground was muddy. On closer inspection, we could see where the bear had chased Blue around the car two or three laps. There were also marks where he had tried to get under the car to grab the pup but was too big to fit.

Apparently, the bear had been very close each time Ina had gone outside to scold the dog. He may well have been sitting on the car top and watching as she carried Blue out to the outhouse. The pup was definitely relieved to have four walls around him for the remainder of the night and even happier to see us that morning.

The bear, becoming bored with our place after the action slowed down, moved on, seeking greater excitement. He found it a half mile up the road at my brother's house. There, around five, Troy was awakened by someone banging around on the porch. Jumping up to see who was calling at such an early hour, he peeked out the window and in the entryway sat an average-sized black bear, licking up the food in the dog's food dish. The bear left the porch when he heard noises inside and strolled out into the weeds across the yard. Troy fired his .357 into the air, and the bear tore off through the woods toward a large, brushy canyon not too far away. The excitement died down and all was calm until the next day.

This time trouble surfaced on the other side of the canyon, about two miles away. Mom and Dad were sitting in their living room, enjoying a cup of coffee when they spotted a man coming across the field in front of their house. They could tell by the way the man was hurrying along that something wasn't right. Even from a distance they could sense an air of panic about him. He was obviously headed for help, so they went outside to meet him and see what the problem was.

As he came closer, they recognized him as a young man who had been living in a tent over on the canyon edge while helping his brother build a house. When he came into the yard, he was out of breath and very frightened. He asked Dad to call the police, saying, "There's a crazy man on the loose."

Mom and Dad finally got him calmed down and got the story out of him. As he related it, he had been snug in his sleeping bag inside his little pup tent, snoozing away, when suddenly someone jumped on top of his tent and began stabbing him with an ice pick.

When he started screaming, the attacker backed off and by the time he got his tent unzipped and stuck his head out, the maniac had vanished.

Being alone and without protection, he rushed to find help. He pulled up his sleeve and showed dad the "stab marks" on his arm. I suppose to a newcomer from the Lower 48, the marks would appear to have been made by an ice pick. But to anyone who has lived here any length of time, the wounds were recognizable as tooth marks from a bear. An inspection of the area around the tent revealed evidence that the attacker was an medium-sized black bear.

In all probability, the same bear was involved in all three incidents. Where he went after that, nobody knows. He had tried dogs, dog food and people without any satisfaction, so maybe he just decided he'd stick with blueberries. At least they don't scream when you grab 'em.

Of Bears and Biologists

*One of the responses I received regarding bear
stories was from Dave Athons in Soldotna, a tale by
Dave Nelson. The story captures an experience Dave
Nelson and some colleagues had.*

To many fishermen, the Russian River on Alaska's
Kenai Peninsula is synonymous with sockeye or red
salmon. Each year thousands of tourists and long-
term residents alike stand shoulder-to-shoulder on
this picturesque stream while tempting this finicky
species with coho or streamer flies. In addition to anglers, bears also flock to the stream in record numbers.
Fishermen report numerous black bear sightings at
the popular Russian River campground, where the primary attractions are the anglers' catches, garbage and
improperly stored food.

As a fisheries biologist with the Sport Fish Division
of the Alaska Department of Fish and Game, I have
spent hundreds of hours on Russian River during past
years. My encounters with black bears have been infre-
quent, and although these animals are potentially
dangerous, none have exhibited aggressive behavior.
Black bears were at Russian River before biologists, so
I always give them the right of way and am careful not
to provoke them.

Brown bears are not common on the Lower Russian
River, although sightings do occur. I observed my first
brown bear there in 1972 at the scenic Russian River
Falls, which is about a half mile below Lower Russian
Lake. The female with two small cubs sensed my presence, called the cubs and ambled off up the hill. It was
an interesting experience, but hardly one to chill the
blood when retold around the campfire.

My next encounter came in 1974 while counting salmon which spawn in the stream between Upper and Lower Russian Lake. On rounding a bend, I surprised two brown bear, feeding. At one time, I had been told or had read that shouting will send them on their way. "Nothing ventured, nothing gained" is an old, but true adage. Sure enough, one shout and they bolted into the brush. As far as my limited experience went, the ferocious Alaskan Brown Bear of song and story was not living up to his reputation. And that was just fine with me.

In 1976, Fisheries Biologist Al Havens and I were conducting escapement counts on Upper Russian Creek, which is the major tributary to Upper Russian Lake. This is the only area utilized by early-run sockeye, and brown bear activity was very evident. We saw a large brown bear leave the stream approximately 150 yards ahead of us. Assuming the bear had caught our scent and was on his way, we proceeded with our work. When we were adjacent to the area where the bear had left the stream, he suddenly reappeared. Shouting and splashing the water had no effect, and the animal charged from about fifty feet. He ignored a shot fired over his head. The animal closed the distance between us with amazing speed. At twenty feet we were a split second from firing in earnest when the animal broke his charge and returned to the bank. He stood on his hind legs surveying the situation for several seconds and then ambled off into the brush, leaving two white-knuckled biologists standing in the stream.

To say the least, this was an unnerving experience, and I vowed eternal vigilance while working in areas frequented by brown bears. For protection, I had chosen the Remington Model 870 Wingmaster, a 12-gauge shotgun with the short barrel designed specifically for slugs. I had used this particular model with the standard barrel for the past twenty years in pursuit of upland game as well as waterfowl, and felt quite comfortable with it.

October 3, 1978 again found me at Upper Russian Creek engaged in sockeye salmon egg sampling. All in all, 1978 was a banner year for Russian River sockeye salmon with the highest recorded run of over 130,000 salmon returning to their natal stream to spawn and perpetuate their fascinating life cycle.

Sampling enables the Department of Fish and Game to determine the survival of the sockeye eggs after they have been deposited in the gravel, as well as the total number of eggs in the stream. The record 1978 run had attracted bears and other predators in large numbers, but because the early-run spawning was complete and there were less than five hundred late-run fish in the stream, I didn't anticipate any problems. I was accompanied during this trip by temporary biologists Jim Browning and Rance Morrison as well as Jim Friedersdorff, a biologist with the Fish and Wildlife Service stationed in Kenai.

The stream was relatively low, and we elected to carry our gear and pull the boat as far upstream as we could, rather than leave it at the creek mouth. The shotgun was nothing but a nuisance at this point, so I laid it across the seat of the boat—something that I will not do again.

Jim Browning was in the lead pulling the boat by a short rope. Rance Morrison and Jim Friedersdorff were at the stern pushing while I was on the left side about ten feet behind Browning and five feet from the boat. As we rounded a bend, Jim let out a yell, turned and ran.

All I can recall is a split-second glimpse of the head and shoulders of a large brown bear as it broke through the grass and brush along the creek. As Jim raced past me, I turned and grabbed the shotgun from the boat. The bear passed within a few feet of me and was rapidly closing the distance between itself and Jim. The animal was now ten feet downstream from me at the stern of the boat. Rance Morrison was also at the rear of the boat about five feet from the bear. As the bear turned to pursue Jim across the creek, I fired . . . the shotgun never reaching my shoulder.

The first slug from the 12-gauge took the animal through the neck exiting the other side; the second struck the bear a few inches below the ear. It dropped immediately, rolled and tried to get up. A single shot from Rance's .44 magnum ended the drama as four very shaken biologists stood around the dead animal. It had been less than ten seconds from the time we saw the brown bear until it lay dead in the creek.

In retrospect, we don't know what provoked the bear. We had shouted several times going up the stream, kept up a constant conversation, and the noise made by an aluminum boat being dragged over the rocks must surely have been audible for an appreciable distance. On skinning the animal, we found it to be a mature female with no visible injury. There were no cubs. All we could guess was that this large animal had staked out its territory to harvest the few remaining fish in the stream, and no one was going to force her to relinquish her claim without a fight.

There were many lessons learned from this incident. Even though this particular animal remained on the stream after hearing our approach, frequent yells and other loud noises can't do any harm. It's sometimes very difficult to work or fish and watch for bears at the same time. If possible, one person should be responsible for overall supervision. The shotgun or similar weapon belongs with the supervisor and not in the boat, on the bunk or under the equipment. Weapons should receive periodic maintenance and all parties should be familiar with their use. Practicing prior to going into the field is more than warranted; it should be required. However, foremost in our minds is that individuals venturing into bear country should be prepared for any eventuality. Brown bears are unpredictable animals and well-deserving of everyone's respect.

Practice Pays

Steve Pavish, a resident of Anchorage for more than twenty years, had this eerie tale to tell about man's instinct for survival.

Seems that two men had left Petersburg to go moose hunting on the mainland. Since it was difficult to find dry wood in Southeast Alaska, the men took turns walking about five hundred yards from camp to fetch firewood from a dead tree.

One man was returning to camp, arms heavily laden with wood, barely able to see over his load. He wore a shoulder holster and pistol, which he had often used in the past to practice quick-drawing. About this time he stumbled onto a brown growler crossing the trail.

The bear roared and threw a punch at the hunter, striking the wood and sending the man flying. As he sailed back toward the tree he'd just left, lumber was dropping all around him like popcorn.

The next thing he knew the bear was lying on top of him, perfectly still. The man was greatly alarmed, but quickly noticed the reason for the bear's immobility.

The beast had blood running from its nostrils. Getting a grasp of the situation, the hunter suddenly realized he held a smoking revolver in his hand.

When he crawled from under the the bear, he discovered an extra hole up its nostril—a passageway for the bullet now lodged in the bruin's brain. The hunter had shot the bear in a subconscious reflex. Evidently, his fast-drawing practice had finally paid off.

Campground-Wise

Mike Dishnow, an educator from Wasilla, Alaska, sent me an account of a run-in his family had with a bear while staying at the Quartz Creek campground on the Kenai Peninsula during the summer of 1978.

I was doing grad work at the University of Alaska in Anchorage that summer. My wife, our one-year-old son Mickey and I decided to get out of the city for a Saturday night. At the campground we set up our Eureka Lightweight Mountaineering tent, which had room for two adults.

At about four that morning, I heard something knock over the instant coffee can we had left sitting on the picnic table. "Darn squirrel," I thought. Then we heard the most horrible, shearing sound of claws ripping through the tent over Ruth's head. A bear had torn through the rain fly and the wall of the tent.

We froze for what must have been minutes, but seemed like hours. Time stood still and everything seemed to move in slow motion. I whispered a plan for Ruth to leave the tent with Mickey and run to the truck. I would exit from the snow entrance at the other end of the tent and try to distract the bear.

The bear was gone. We ran to the truck. Ruth

became hysterical and broke down crying. I was shaky and could see myself trembling as I took down the tent. I was now carrying my .44-magnum revolver, which I had purposely left in the truck before because of the baby.

We packed quickly and by seven were back in our Anchorage apartment. My wife has not been in a tent since. I still have the tent with the claw marks. Mick and I continue to camp, but not without a rifle.

I'm still not sure what provoked the bear. We had a *clean* camp and left all of our food, except bottles of coffee creamer and instant coffee, in the pickup. We also had left the clothes that we cooked in that evening in the truck.

I've always felt that the bear was simply curious or "campground-wise." I've also watched a blackie in a British Columbia campground stick his nose in both ends of a tent, just like a curious dog. My wife still thinks that the bear was attracted by our son's crying, which had been going on most of the night.

Anyway, the incident was darn scary, and the effects still linger when family camping is discussed. Like I said, Ruth no longer participates.

Bear in the Bush

The wounded bear is a dangerous customer, as more than one person has discovered, some at the cost of their lives. Cecil Jones related another close call he had with a wounded animal.

Rain was pattering down on the roof when we rolled out of our bunks at five A.M. and kindled a fire in the little woodstove. By the time breakfast was over, the rain had stopped, so the four of us gathered our gear, jumped into the boat and headed down the bay. The water was calm and we made good time. At the first canyon we pulled onto the shore, and one of the hunters and I stepped out onto the beach. The other hunter and guide proceeded on down the bay to the next canyon around the point.

Jim and I walked up the canyon a short distance to a good observation point and sat down to glass for bear. It was the month of May, on the Pacific side of Kodiak Island. The alders were already starting to leaf out even though some snow still covered the mountains and the shady areas of stream bottoms. We had been glassing for about an hour when we spotted a bear about a quarter of a mile away and up the canyon from us. The bear had just risen from where he had bedded down. He was not a really large bear, but looking through the spotting scope, we discovered he didn't appear to have any rub marks that might mar his fur. We talked it over and decided to try for him.

The sky was overcast, and there was hardly any wind. Stalking would be tough. It was impossible to walk through the coarse grass without making noise. Bears have exceptionally good hearing, and I was wishing we had some rain or wind to help camouflage the noise. The bear was moving fast across the canyon, so we had to hurry along to get within shooting range. Finally, we came within fifty yards of the bear which had now moved out onto an open hillside above an alder patch. We were as close as we were going to get. Jim sat down, took a rest off his knee and touched off a round.

The solid thump from the impact of the 220-grain bullet was unmistakable. The bear went down, tumbled off the hillside and rolled out of sight into the alders. We circled around so we could see where he had hit the alders, hoping to find him there in the edge of the brush. We continued to circle the alder patch, but still failed to see any sign of the bear.

When I suggested that we would have to go into the alders and search for the bear, Jim claimed his feet were so sore that he couldn't go another step. I didn't push the issue; as guide, it was my responsibility to ensure that the bear was dead, or if only wounded, to end the suffering as quickly as possible.

Nevertheless, I didn't cherish the idea of going in alone. It is not a wise thing to do, but feeling confident the bear was dead by this time, I proceeded to follow the well-defined trail he had left when he rolled into the brush.

I soon came to the point where the bear would have stopped rolling. My heart sank. There was no carcass at the spot and a faint trail of blood led into the dense thicket. With a round in the chamber and a finger on the trigger, I started the slow, nerve-racking job of trying to follow the trail and at the same time keeping vigilant on all quarters. The lack of blood on the trail bothered me. It looked as though my impression of a solid hit was a false one. I stuck with the trail and it soon became apparent that the bear was circling. This indicated that the bear was still using all of his senses and could possibly attack at any time, from any angle.

I followed the track back to within ten feet of where I had entered the alders. Here was a plain imprint where the bear had laid down and watched as I passed by on his trail. The alder patch suddenly seemed a little stuffy. Moving carefully and looking in all directions, I worked my way to the edge of the brush and stepped out for a breath of fresh air.

I was not quite sure what to do at this point. It could be hazardous to continue following the bear alone. On the other hand, if I waited until evening for the other guide to return, the rain that was beginning to fall would obliterate the trail. Then I heard the welcome drone of an outboard down the bay. The other guys were returning with a nice nine-footer.

We hurried down to the beach and explained the situation. The other guide and I returned to the alder patch. We picked up the trail where I had left it and followed straight down the middle of the alder patch. Already the rain was fouling us up. The trail was getting hard to follow across the open places. Sometimes we would lose it completely and had to scout around until we found where the bear had crossed a snow patch. At least now, the bear was not playing any funny games, but traveling in one general direction.

For four hours we followed the trail in the steady rain. Finally, I saw the bear run across a small clearing up ahead. I got off two quick shots, neither connecting. Feeling terrible for not dropping the bear, I ran up the hill until I was above the alder patch he had entered. Then I side-hilled across until I came to a deep ravine. I stood on the rim, watching below and hoping to see him climbing out the back side. What I didn't realize at the time was that the bear was hiding behind a hummock, less than twenty feet from me.

The other guide appeared in the ravine about seventy-five yards below me. I had glanced over in his direction when the bear suddenly sprung up with a loud groan and leaped towards me. At fifteen feet I put a slug into his hump that spun him around, and he jumped off into the ravine.

This time the bear was dead when he stopped rolling. Skinning him, we found that Jim's shot had passed low through the chest, missing any vital organs. The hide squared eight and a half feet.

Fortunately, situations like this do not happen very often, but when they do, they have a way of planting themselves permanently in the back of your mind.

Bears as Bluffers

Chris Thompson is a former police officer who now lives in Anchorage and is an avid hunter. In the spring of 1987, he and his friend Doug went fishing on Grant Creek, near Moose Pass, about forty-five miles southeast of Hope. On the way in to the creek, Chris and Doug stopped at the ranger station at Moose Pass to ask for directions. There they happened to run into a fish and game biologist, who they questioned about bears in the area. Although the fishermen had brought along their .375s, the biologist urged them to leave their heavy guns behind, saying it was too early in the season to see bears. With that advice, Chris and Doug strapped on their .44 magnums and set out for Grant Creek.

To reach the creek, Doug and I walked about three and a half miles over tough country with a lot of short, steep hills covered in thick grass. Finally, we reached our destination and quickly began fishing for rainbow trout and grayling. I was using my favorite lure, a black- and gold-colored Panther-Martin, and Doug was using a Mepps. We had only been fishing a short time when I nailed about a two-and-a-half-pound rainbow. I asked Doug to take a picture of me with the fish, of course. A couple more casts and I had a grayling and then another rainbow. We fished a while longer, and suddenly, it seemed like the fish just died out. It was starting to get later in the evening, about eight o'clock, so we decided we'd better get out of there before it got dark.

As we reached the top of a knoll, I got my fly line caught in a tree. My buddy Doug walked on down the hill while I reached up and started untangling my line from the brush and trees. When I got it undone, I couldn't see Doug any longer and yelled out, "Doug, where ya at?"

"I'm down here," he called from the bottom of the hill.

I had taken about five steps, when I heard a noise in the brush. I immediately thought I'd scared up a moose. Then, out of the corner of my eye, I saw a large brown object hurling towards me from about forty or fifty yards away. I dropped my fly rod and spinning rod and drew my .44 Ruger Redhawk out of the holster. Within two blinks of an eye, the brown bear was within ten feet of me, fortunately putting on the brakes.

I had my handgun cocked and was aiming right at his head. The bear made a woofing sound. He was so close to me that I could actually see the pink in his lips when he barked. He stood there for ten or fifteen seconds, lifting his nose up in the air, trying to smell me. Luckily, the wind was blowing toward me.

The bear woofed another time or two, but I held my ground with my handgun cocked and aimed. He turned broadside and gave me the perfect shot. My lifelong dream had always been to take a brown bear. Now it was brown bear season, and I had my brown bear tag. But even though I'm a good shot, I didn't think it was wise to try and drop an eight-hundred-pound animal that close to me with a handgun. So, I just played it out and let him make the next move.

He began walking away, taking four or five steps at a time and then looking back over his shoulder at me. I held my ground until he was out of sight, then backed down the hill toward my buddy. I told Doug to cross the creek while I stood guard. Doug holstered his .44, which he had also drawn when he saw the bear. Once I had crossed the creek, we hurried back to our car as if the bear was following us all the way.

There really aren't words to describe the fear inside you when you're facing a bear at that close range, staring into his eyes, trying to guess his next move. I had worked as a police officer for eight years, so I drew my weapon naturally, without even realizing it. I remember looking down the barrel, into the sights and noticing that I wasn't even shaking. But after that bear turned and walked away, I couldn't have held a cup of coffee if I had tried.

3

Ursus Humorous

In the fall of the year when berries have had a hard frost, they get fermented. I've often wondered if a bear doesn't get a bit tipsy from eatin' too many berries. Berries do produce a certain amount of alcohol. You cut a bear's belly open, and there'll be 150 to 200 pounds of berries. I've never heard of any biological data on that, but that doesn't mean it doesn't happen, late in the fall.—Clark Engle, master guide

Not many bears are fastidious, but the one that showed up at the Engstrom home in Nome proved to be. It was June 1985 when Ron and Lorena heard noises outside. The stomping and shuffling that was coming from their new deck was a bit unusual. They looked out the window and discovered a thoroughly happy grizzly soaking up the suds in their hot tub. Ron fired a warning shot with his rifle, and the sad, but clean, bear sought soap somewhere else.

Unfortunately, the most well-known side of bear behavior is the one of destructive power, due in part to the public's seemingly insatiable hunger for bear stories. Whether due to some base instinct or the love of a tale, we tend to glamorize and sensationalize the grotesque, failing to realize bears are more than killers.

A bear's daily existence is consumed with procuring a meal, protecting itself and procreating, but a bear is not always "all business." In nearly all their activities, bears possess human-like qualities, namely their sense of fun and play. Bears have a sense of humor.

Guess Who's Coming To Dinner

When it comes to food, bears find it difficult to turn down a free meal. On Columbus Day in 1987, Ed Gurtler left his airplane, a Cessna 170, on a river bar near Cripple. The plane contained nearly five hundred pounds of moose meat from Ed's most recent hunting trip. Ed spent the night at his family's old homestead nearby.

During the night, he heard a terrible racket coming from across the river, exactly where his plane was parked. Wondering what could be creating such a noise and suspecting the wind as the culprit, he cranked up his outboard motor and eased out into the Innoko River. With the aid of his head lamp, Ed discovered a hungry grizzly on the far bank. This bruin had come to dinner, without an invitation, and quickly located a bear's culinary dream—a plane full of partially butchered moose meat.

Ed fired a warning shot over the grizzly's head, but the bear stared straight back into his head lamp, wondering why his meal had been so rudely interrupted. Ed maneuvered his boat a little closer to try to get a better look at his plane. It looked like it had crashed. The windows were smashed, the door was ripped off and the fuselage was bent. When he saw the damage, Ed decided to keep his distance and stay in the boat. Now he was stuck with a $5,000 to $10,000 repair bill, one less load of moose meat, and no way to get home.

Ed set off his emergency location transmitter beacon. For two days no one responded to the call. Finally, an orbiting satellite alerted officials at Elmendorf Air Force Base in Anchorage of the signal; Alaska Fish and Wildlife Trooper Charlie Beatty was dispatched from McGrath, about forty miles away, to check on the situation.

When Charlie flew over Ed's location, it seemed like all was well until he circled for a better look and saw the smashed plane. He flew down to rescue Ed, never guessing that a bear's dinner party had caused all the trouble.

Burned by Curiosity

Master Guide Leon Francisco of Kodiak has had a multitude of experiences in the hinterlands of Alaska. One interesting story he told me involved an "enlightened" grizzly.

I had this bear run-in when I first began guiding about 1965 or 1966. I was working for a guide in the north country, around Mount McKinley.

I'd been dropped off with a load of camp gear to prepare a camp for a hunter coming on a moose hunt. The outfitter made two trips in with a wheel plane. On the second trip I went in with him and stayed with the rest of the gear. I started carrying it all from the landing area into the spruce trees to make camp. The last thing on the ground was a small plastic pint bottle of Blazo. I stuffed it in my shirt pocket, grabbed everything else with hands and teeth and made the last load there.

As I set my load down, I looked over the top of the pile. A grizzly stood in an opening in the spruce in the muskeg. It was a pretty good sized boar, and he just kept eyeing me. I didn't have a rifle, and the outfitter hadn't left his.

I stood there, not moving, thinking it would go away, but it started coming towards me—not running, just ambling. It just looked curious about all the gear, the tent, food and meat.

In back of this pile of gear was a small lodgepole spruce about eight inches in diameter. As he started coming towards me, I climbed up the tree, leaving everything on the ground. All that was left of my load was that little bottle of Blazo in my pocket.

The darn bear came up to the tree and stood up against it. He started clawin' at the tree. It hadn't been aggressive at all, just seemed curious. But then the bear began shaking the tree pretty good. I was afraid that enough of that shaking and he might knock that tree over.

I was pretty young at the time and new at guiding. I didn't know what this bear was about to do. Then he started reaching way up into the tree, and I kept climbing. I finally climbed to the point to where I couldn't go much farther up the darn tree.

The bear just stayed there.

The outfitter was supposed to come back and drop the hunter in an hour and a half but this was only about fifteen minutes after he'd left. There I sat for another forty-five minutes or so. And the bear kept banging on that tree.

What still sticks in my mind was that he wasn't at all offensive or angry, just curious. Then he started

breaking the lower branches off. That's when I remembered the Blazo in my pocket. I had a box of matches
in my pocket, too.

I dropped that Blazo on him . . . *glug, glug, glug,
glug.* Then I started droppin' matches on him. I don't
know how long it took before one of 'em finally hit him.
He just ignited—he just went *whoosh!*

He took off running. He ran into the spruce and
started rolling in the muskeg, just roaring. He got the
fire out and he just kind of shook himself and wandered
off.

I stayed in the tree until the outfitter came back.

The Outhouse Bear

*Hank Taylor, an Anchorage attorney, shared a
number of interesting stories. After the fact, most are
humorous; at the time, none of those involved was
amused.*

There was a logging camp on Montague Island
which had a privy—a two-holer complete with a half-
moon and a door cut down for ventilation. Four or five
guys were stayin' at this camp, and one day they took
a few hours off from logging and went out to a ridge to
do a little casual shootin' with their .22s.

A guy from California decided to take a little break
and went down to the outhouse. He walked on down to
the toilet, leaving his friends on the ridge. He leaned his
rifle outside the door and sat down on one of those
holes, naturally leaving the door open to enjoy the
scenery, as all good Alaskans do. A few minutes later,
the boys on the ridge looked over and saw a pigeon-
toed, wobbly shouldered, rollin' boar coming down the
beach and headin' for the outhouse.

They started yellin', "Bear! Bear!" The Californian looked up and said, "Ahhh, go on," not understanding why they wouldn't leave a man in his peace when his pants were half-masted. The guys kept yellin' and he kept ignorin' their joking. Soon the bear had reached the outhouse, and he stuck his big bushel-basket head around the door to see what this feller was doin'. This apparition gave the Californian something of a fright, and he often has said it was fortunate he was sitting where he was sitting at the time.

Slam . . . the rickety outhouse door banged right in that bear's face, and the bear jumped back a little bit, startled by the rudeness of it all. Then, over the top of the toilet door, the bear saw a hand come out, followed by a forearm, followed by a bicep, right up to the armpit. These fingers were stretchin', tryin' to reach the top of the rifle barrel, exactly two inches too far down. The guys on the ridge swore that damned arm grew to an amazing length. And the bear was sitting there like a big dog, just watching that arm strainin' and growin' to reach the rifle barrel.

Finally, the old boar just shook his head and wandered off on down the beach.

By and by the door opened a crack and the Californian peeped out. The rifle went back inside. The door slammed. The friends on the hill rolled with laughter over that arm that grew.

The Big Bear with the Little Head

Four guys crossing from Hawkins Island out of Cordova to the mainland came upon a small brown bear swimming in the water. Somebody got a bright idea, "Hey, look at the little bear. Let's lasso him." They roped the bear, and much to their shock and chagrin, he turned out to be a big bear with a rather small head. To make matters worse, he decided to climb aboard, determined to wreak violence upon the annoying people in the skiff. The bear took off to the bow, running two guys over the side. Then he ran the others off the stern. With the boat to himself, he lumbered back and forth, roarin' and growlin' and draggin' the rope behind him.

The boaters were out treadin' water in Prince William Sound, feeling rather embarrassed. Finally, the bear decided he'd had enough of the yachting set so he jumped over the side and went on his merry way, trailing the piece of rope around his neck. The four wet guys waited until he was far away before they climbed back aboard. They say it took them a year to get enough courage to tell their story in Cordova.

The Toilet Paper Bear

Ed Bilderback was toodling along in his boat with his two boys, now grown. Ed was carrying his big cannon, a .375. He had one round left in it. He also had brought along his M-l carbine. All of a sudden he and his boys spotted a black bear sow and a cub on the beach. The boys challenged their father, "Hey, Dad, capture that bear for a pet."

Ed had no interest in carting a bear back to Cordova, but just on a dare, he said, "Sure thing, kids." So he whipped the boat onto the beach and jumped out, grabbing the cannon that held one round. Ed ran at the bears, barking. (Supposedly, if you bark at a black bear, he'll head up a tree.)

The sow chased the cub up a tree, and she took off into the woods. Ed climbed up after the cub. He got a hold of the little black bear, a feisty little guy that scratched him. Ed took his jacket off to try to catch the bear inside. When Ed got the cub on the ground, the critter started bawlin' and raisin' hell. With that, the old sow got mad and came roarin' out of the woods. Ed wasn't about to kill her. He didn't want to cause any trouble, so he aimed his big gun right between her ears and fired a bullet just barely over her head. This diversion only stopped her for a minute, then she came charging after Ed.

He was sure he was about to be killed by a black bear. He knew there was no more ammo, so he started runnin' around and around a big spruce tree. Around and around they went, and Ed kept feeling more and more humiliated and disgusted. . . . Imagine Ed Bilderback killed by a black bear. Finally, the older son yelled, "Hey, Dad. Do you want me to bring the carbine?"

Ed hollered back, "Hell, no, but you can bring me some toilet paper."

He made another lap around the tree and got ahead of the bear, then jumped off a bank and hit the beach, going like hell. He leaped into the boat and pushed off just as the sow reached the edge of the water.

"Well, boys," Ed said. "You didn't want that cub anyhow, did you?"

And the boys said, "No, Dad, we think not." And they got on back to Cordova.

The Headlight Bear

Greg Brown had water around his cabin that was barely palatable. Down the beach, about four miles to the east, was good, sweet water. Every now and then Greg would make a water run on his John Deere farm tractor and load enough water on his flatbed trailer to last a week or so.

One evening, he hopped on his tractor, rounded up

his great, big German shepherd King and made a water run. King weighed about 125 pounds and was one big, tough, intelligent dog. He had killed two wolverine in open combat—now that's a tough German shepherd.

After Greg had loaded his water and started back to the cabin, it was almost dark, but he hadn't turned his headlights on yet. King was lying on the trailer. Greg was motoring along when a big sow and two grown cubs walked into his path.Greg stopped the tractor, and King saw the bears. He figured he'd take care of them himself, thinking "I'll get them out of the road, Boss. You just hold on a minute."

Like a streak, King took off. The sow saw the dog coming and turned and ran for a nearby spruce. But the two cubs decided they wanted to see what the hell was chasing them. King sailed into one cub, while the other cub went after King. The dog was doing pretty good, dodging and weaving and bobbing. He'd bite one cub on the ass and dodge the other one. Round and round they went, while Greg stood on top of the tractor screaming, "King, you dumb son of a bitch! Get back here." When the old sow heard all that growling and roaring, she changed her mind about her retreat. She turned and attacked. Now it was three bears on one dog, and King figured he better get out of this mess.

He high-tailed it back to the tractor, but instead of jumping back on the flatbed, he jumped on the seat, put his front paws around Greg and held on tight. Of course, the three bears took out after him, with the sow in the lead, charging the tractor full-speed. Greg turned the engine on quickly when the sow reared up and knocked the hell out of the John Deere, hitting it right between the headlights.

Greg reached down and flipped on the lights, put the tractor in gear and drove at the sow, trying to see around King, still hanging around his neck.

Each time Greg ran at the bear, she stood up and tried to take a swat. But, as the full beam of the headlights shone into her face, she started backing up toward the woods. The cubs took off, leaving their mother to fight the rear-guard action. Finally, the old sow decided she'd had enough, too, and she turned and ran into the woods.

Mutt and Jeff and Tweet, Tweet, Tweet

As Hank Taylor was telling his wealth of funny bear stories, one topic that came up on several occasions was his annoyance with journalists and other people who frequently distort information about bears and refuse to look at bear-man encounters from the bear's point of view. Hank explains, "Have you ever noticed how those journalists who write up bear attacks always slant their stories strictly to the victim's side of things? I've never been able to resist the temptation to look at incidents from the standpoint of ursus horribilis."

In 1958, two Arkies, one tall one and one short one, had a run-in with a bear out at Tustumena Lake at a place called Humpy Creek. During that time in the Territory of Alaska the law didn't require people to pay guides to take them hunting for bear. So these two Arkansas hunters, Mutt and Jeff I call them, had gotten someone to dump them off at the Kasilof River, then they walked back in the hills near Humpy Creek and killed a couple of black bears. By the time they had skinned out the bears and loaded them on their packframes it was getting dark.

These two had heard that the way to protect yourself when you're covered with blood and smell like a black bear is to make lots of noise as you're walking. So they had brought along whistles that they blew with every step, convinced that any bears in the area would run away when they heard the noise. Jeff, the short Arkie, was ahead, giving his whistle a "Tweet, tweet, tweet," when he heard a *thud*. He looked up and saw his tall buddy flying through the air. His buddy went sailing over into the alders. Jeff said that was the last thing he remembered.

Next thing he knew he was laying in traction in a bed next to Mutt at Providence Hospital with bandages covering his body and his limbs in casts. The human interest reporter wrote the story up in the newspaper, stressing how horrible it was for these two guys to be so broken and caved in, when they had dutifully blown their whistles every step of the way.

But look at it from the bear's standpoint:

Here's Old Ursus, trying to make a living. It's late in the evening. The mosquitoes are gone. And he's got this little riffle, where the humpies come up, and it's just a simple matter of picking up the fish, walking over to the gravel, making a neat, little incision, ripping out the eggs, tossing the fish aside . . . ahhh, the caviar is great.

Mr. Bear is just enjoying the peace and solitude of his favorite riffle on this little creek, when down the canyon comes this racket, "Tweet, tweet, tweet." He checks his ears, pulls out the wax, shakes his head. But the "Tweet, tweet, tweet" just gets louder. Finally, he's had enough of this. The noise is hurting his ears and ruining the fishing, so he turns around and knocks the hell out of Mutt and then clobbers Jeff and goes on about his business. He's thinking, "Taught that son of a gun not to blow a whistle in the middle of dinner."

At Last Resort, Curse 'em

One day in November my son and I were shooting snowshoe hares up at Homestead Long Lake, ten to twelve miles from McCarthy. I love to eat those rabbits, and they were all over the place, so we were really giving our .22s a workout. Suddenly, my son Trey stopped and said in a breathless voice that means more than the loudest scream, "Dad, there's a bear!"

I looked over and not more than ten yards in front of him was one of those little brown bears, also known as grizzlies. He was a typical Wrangell Mountain bear with a fringe around his neck like a clown's collar. He was blonde, square-headed and had a pug nose that looked like he'd run into a wall wide open. He was a grown boar; you'd have to lie to get him into eight feet, but it wouldn't be a big lie.

The grizzly was standing there with his nose curled and his ears laid back, snarling. My son was right in front of him, holding his little .22 long rifle. In two jumps, the bear could have been on top of Trey. My first instinct was to blast the bear right in his temple. But then I thought, "Wait a minute. I shot a bear through the head once and it didn't do much good."

I didn't shoot, but started to get mad instead. Here I am out here flat-footed with a damned .22 Hornet, and this grizzly bear ain't acting like he's gonna' run in the right direction. He's shifting his weight and eyeing my son. I cursed and decided, "Over my dead body."

I yelled, "You son of a bitch!" and started running at the bear to get his attention. I veered in front of my son. "Move backward!" I yelled to Trey. "Get behind a tree. If he comes toward you, let him have it."

I cursed that bear for all I was worth, but he didn't run; he just turned sideways a little bit. Then I heard *crunch, crunch, crunch* in the snow. I was never so proud of my young man. Instead of climbing up a tree, there he was at my left shoulder with his little .22 rabbit gun, cussing like a Marine drill instructor.

Finally, the bear made a little sideways motion and stepped back one step, and we stepped back one step, sliding our heels. He stepped back again; we stepped. He took another; we took another. Then he turned, and we took off. We ran back to the car. Out came the shotgun, and we went on with our rabbit huntin'.

The Case of the Police Chief and the Bear

Hank Taylor once defended a friend who was charged with killing a bear.

The local constable was arrested. The powers that be had put out a decree, saying that charges would be brought and offenders prosecuted for shooting a bear. The state policy at that time stated that any individual shooting a bear even in self defense could be charged with wanton destruction of wildlife and was liable to face prosecution.

The police chief in Yakutat called me. "Hank, come down. I've got troubles."

"What's the matter?"

"Well, they're prosecutin' me for shootin' a bear."

"What happened?"

I didn't believe the chief had deliberately killed a bear. I thought through what I knew of the man. He lived out of town, less than a mile from Fish and Game. He was an experienced man who had been in on all kind of bear tales. He didn't have any of that cheechaker, "Let me shoot the first bear I see."

He had an extensive supply of guns in his double-wide mobile home. He had .300 H & H magnums, a .30-06, a shotgun; he had a veritable arsenal of weapons.

He'd built his smoke house and smoked his salmon on his property. He was experimenting and making a little money on smoked salmon. He was also gaining quite the reputation with the local bear population. At one time he ended up with eight bears in his yard.

The chief kept calling the Fish and Game asking them to come over: "Hey, the bears are tearin' up my garbage cans. They're tryin' to get in the house." He had a great big commercial-type pumphouse, and they were even trying to tear it up.

He kept calling, and the Fish and Game would come over and shoot Roman candles at the bears, run them off, but the bears would come back. Then one big boar came in and chased the kids. The children barely made it to the house, and the chief and his wife were very upset. "These other bears are bad enough, but I'm not putting up with one chasin' my kids."

The Fish and Game didn't do anything about it. Then, in the middle of the night a bear was out front tearing up something. The constable got up out of bed with his shorts on and grabbed his pistol from right by the head of his bed—a .38 snubnosed Smith and Wesson, five-shot revolver. A business gun; not a bear weapon. He walked right by the bear guns, his cannons; he opened the door and a bear was standing there. He wasn't a big bear, just a bear bear.

The chief aimed over the bear's head and yelled, "Get the hell outta here!" and fired. One, two, three, four shots, and on the fifth shot the bear stood up. The officer shot him in the ear and killed him, not ten feet from his front door.

So he called Fish and Game, "Come on over here and get your bear."

They came over with steel tape, took some eight-by-ten-inch glossies and made a case out of it. What were they supposed to do? They didn't want to prosecute him, but the Fish and Game warden was forced to bring charges by the powers that be in Juneau.

I then learned that they'd had some trouble over at the Fish and Game. The warden had personally had enough of it and took a twenty-gauge loaded with shot and shot a bear in the ass. It sounded suspiciously like the *corpus delicti* I knew to be frozen in the freezer at the magistrate's house. I also knew the warden to be an honest man who wouldn't perjure himself in court.

The police chief demanded a jury trial.

While preparing for the trial, I asked if I could view the evidence before we had began selecting the jury. I went over and unfolded the frozen bear hide. I got down to the bear's backside. When I pulled back the fat in his butt: *rattle, rattle, rattle* . . . all over the district attorney's desk. Little, round pellets fell out, whether or not they came out of the warden's twenty-gauge automatic, I don't know. But this bear's ass was loaded with shot.

Shot was raining all over the floor, and I turned to the DA from Juneau and said, "I think I'd like to speak to the court and counsel in chambers." We stepped into a back room where I said, "This trial is a farce, and here's what I'm gonna do. Prosecutor, your witness shot that bear in the ass with a twenty-gauge shotgun because he was afraid for his kids. And I know that he knows that it's the same bear 'cause he's a sharp dude. He knows bears, and he's not gonna lie.

"You're gonna prosecute the police chief who wasn't trying to kill that bear with a .38 snubnosed. The son of a bitch committed suicide—he stood up and caught it in the ear."

The judge looked at the DA and, "What do you say about that?"

The DA said, "I want to talk to the game warden."

I said, "Fine, go out there and ask him if he ever shot a bear in the butt with a twenty-gauge."

As soon as the warden admitted he had, the DA came back, folded his briefcase and went back to Juneau. Case dismissed.

Salad

Told by Chuck Lewis, Jr., a commercial fisherman living on Washington State's Olympic Pensula.

One summer my dad hired a guy to cook on our fishing boat. He was a college-type know-it-all from the East Coast. Although his attitude was pretty annoying, the biggest problem was that this cook wouldn't fix meat. After a whole summer of vegetables, we all got a little disgusted with him and said, "Look, you fix us some sausage in the morning, and we want a hamburger once in a while." He kept arguing that eating meat made you violent, and whenever I got mad at him about his theories, he said I was just proving his point.

This guy also wanted to go ashore all the time. He wanted to get off the boat and go meditate. He would commune with the trees. He'd put his head against the tree and go, "*hmmmmmm ... hhmmmm.*" Anyway, each time he'd go ashore to meditate, Dad would say, "We've seen bears here earlier. You better take a gun just in case." But our cook insisted that bears wouldn't bother him because he was a vegetarian. He claimed the reason bears attack was because they sensed people were meat-eaters and felt threatened by carnivores. We would argue and argue about this stupid idea.

"Use logic," Dad would say. "What about deer and cow. They're grass-eaters, but bears eat them."

But he wouldn't listen. Each time he went ashore and came back safely, he returned with a big smirk on his face . . . point proven.

The year after he worked with us, this cook signed on with Red Netufsky on the *Wayward Wind*. One time when Red's boat was in Kukak Bay, where the bears are thick, the cook played his same old trick; he went ashore to meditate. Well, sure enough, a bear attacked him and ran him down to the beach. The bear caught up with him fast enough and worked him over, biting him on his butt, back and his legs.

He finally got away by taking his day pack off and throwing it to divert the bear. Then he climbed into the skiff and escaped. The crew on the boat called the Coast Guard and got him to the hospital. Soon, the whole fleet heard about this guy getting mauled. When dad and I found out it was the vegetarian, we got a big chuckle out of the story, knowing exactly what had happened.

It wasn't too much later when Dad and I bumped into our old cook in the small boat harbor in Kodiak. As we walked up the ramp, he was walking down, hanging his head like he was embarrassed and trying not to notice us.

Dad didn't say anything about the incident except, "Hey, chief cook, you don't suppose that bear was in the mood for a salad that day do you?"

In the spring of 1984 a contest was held by The Anchorage Times *(Sunday, May 20, pp. M-1 and M-8), soliciting the best bear stories from the public. I contacted Elaine Atwood, associate editor of the* Times, *requesting permission to use two of the winning stories, and she graciously consented.*

One On Maul

William R. Evans of Chignik

This one is on old Maul Ewitt, who used to super-
vise the salmon weir on the river between here and the
lagoon. I was new to Alaska then, and Maul was one of
my first friends. He sort of took me under his wing and
showed me the ropes. He probably did it because he
was afraid I'd accidentally kill myself if he didn't.

Well anyway, it was the middle of the salmon run,
and all the natives had gone fishing. There were a few
of Bobbie O's pigs running around loose, living off what
was on the beach. And of course the bears came
through to clean up on it, too. Most of the houses were
boarded up, and a few times a day one of the big
brownies on his way around the lake would wander
through like a stray dog looking for a bone. I was in the
village, putting a new roof on the school that first
summer, and at the end of the day I couldn't wait to get
out there and tie into those silvers. I remember the first
time out one broke my pole. I kept right on fishing and
landed two more on half a pole in twenty minutes.

Anyway, following Maul's advice I never went fishing without a 12-gauge shotgun slung over my shoulder. "You ain't never gonna need it," he'd said. "But go
out there without it once, and that's the time you're
gonna wish you had it." He never let the fact that bears
were around keep him from doing something he wanted
to do. He had a healthy respect for 'em. And I think his
advice was about as good as any a newcomer is likely
to get. Even in and out of the skiff all day tending the
weir, he kept a big .44 magnum strapped on, though
I'm sure he had long since grown tired of the weight.

The morning of the day I'm télling you about, we

had both seen a huge bear coming around the point toward us and hightailed it on out of there. Maul and I were bunking in one of the empty classrooms that summer, and this particular day Maul had promised to bring some liquid refreshment back up with him from the cannery. You know what summers are like up here. It doesn't seem to get dark in front of you until the sun's about to come up in back of you. Maul and I both were putting in pretty long days, but it finally got dark enough for me to quit so I went inside and started shaving potatoes and cutting up salmon steaks. Soon everything was cooked and my stomach was grinding, so I figured Maul was going to be late and dug in.

I forget if it was root beer or coca-cola that Maul had promised to bring back with him, but a half-hour later I was sitting around burping quietly into my hands, thinking about how good it was going to taste if he ever got there with it, when all of a sudden, down on the beach, there was quite a clatter—as if the Marines were landing.

Before I could get my boots on here Maul came, flying in through the door. His face was red and his eyes were bugged out, and as soon as he came in the room and closed the door, he pulled a bookcase in front of it and started piling kids' desks on top of the bookcase.

"It was a bear," he said. "Biggest dang bear you ever did see and it nearly got me!" When he figured there was enough junk piled in front of the door he stopped and reloaded the .44. He was shaking pretty bad, and the shells kept dropping to the floor.

I shoved a cup of coffee in his hands. The six pack of pop or whatever was still in the skiff down on the beach, and from what Maul said, neither one of us was thirsty enough to go back down after it.

"I'd just revved 'er up to drive the bow up onto the

sand," Maul said, "when I started thinking about that big brownie we'd seen this morning. It was blacker 'n pitch and I had to guess where the beach was and feel for the line. I jumped out into the dark and pulled 'er up when I started hearing a gawd-awful snorting and snuffing. Best thing I could have done was jump back in the skiff, but I wasn't about to turn my back on the bear. I whipped out the .44."

At this point Maul started acting it out and I feared for the old wood-burner we cooked our suppers on. "The snorting got closer but I couldn't see to shoot. Then he shoved his snout into the front of my trousers." Maul had emptied his big handgun into the dark and then hightailed it up to the school. By the time he quieted down we'd both drank so much coffee that neither one of us ever did get much sleep, and in the morning, bright and early, skipping breakfast, we headed down to the beach together to see what was there.

There was a big lump lying there in the mist, but it wasn't big enough to be the bear we'd seen the day before. "Must have been a cub with her," Maul guessed. "She's probably behind the skiff."

But there wasn't a thing on the other side, and as the mist cleared and the light got better we got a close look at what it was that Maul had shot. It was one of Bobbie O's pigs. It was probably the most expensive pig the State of Alaska ever had to buy. To hear Bobbie O talk about it, the pig was like a brother to him. From what we could find out, the meat of any animal shot belonged to the Department of Fish and Game, and of course that was Maul himself.

We ate darn well that summer, between the salmon and the pork and the bacon. And old Maul became more of a local legend than he already was. It helps make a legend more believable if you can laugh at him once in a while, and it helps make him more likable if he can laugh along with you.

And old Maul, God rest his soul, could sure do that. He liked a good laugh as much as the rest of us even if the laugh was on him.

Another story from The Anchorage Times *told from a different point of view:*

Just Like Uncle Albert Said

Mark Hickok of Anchorage

I'm getting tired of bear stories myself, but if you want a bear story, I'll tell you one nobody in our family will ever forget. Uncle Albert was a big, burly feller, a mite taciturn and given to dark moods, but a great hunter and trapper. Like most mountain folks he lived alone, didn't ask help from anyone and went his way peaceable enough unless put upon. He lived over the ridge from Cold Bay. He used to say he kept away from village folks ever since he was a little feller. He learnt they couldn't be trusted.

Early spring, he crossed over to our place to set a spell with Aunt Serapta. She was lonely with her young'in almost growed and on the roam. I was slippin' around in the brush and come upon him, unexpected like. I didn't give him no warnin' and got me a cuff that sent me rolling. "Girl," he growled, reared up like, "you'll get yourself kilt sneakn' around like that. Hmm, you must be one of Thistle's get—you got that reddish hair he had when he was just a little feller. Well, he didn't have no sense and got hisself kilt quick enough, and your Maw, too."

I backed away 'cause I could see he was in no mood for young'ins. It made me purty sad, too, having him talk about Maw and Paw that-a-way. But he was right, and all our kin knowed it. He started to set back down. "Now Girlie, it's mighty hard learnin' without your Maw to teach you. Some things you don't get a chance at learnin' twicet. Since we're kin, I'll tell you—don't never trust them village folks that come out here. They are just natural nervous about us and skeered 'cause they don't know our mountain ways. Keep out of their sight and don't make no noise. But if'en they do come upon you—it's them or you. Move fast and get to 'em quick. There ain't no mercy in 'em and once'st you try runnin' away, they'll never give up 'til they get you. Drive you plumb crazy, chasin' you."

That was the last time I seen Uncle Albert. He finished his business with Aunt Serapta and clambered back up over them mountains to his place. My kissin' cousin Jug trailed him 'cause he'd heard what a great hunter Uncle Albert was and hoped to get a few pointers just a-watchin' him. As I heard it, Uncle Albert was a-trotting down the back trail home when he came upon a tent set up right over his road. Now that road had been in our family maybe three hundred years— Great-great-great-grandpaw even used it.

Jug says Uncle Albert stood there a mite, swaying on his two feet, a-gazing at that sight, when this village feller jumps out of the bushes and starts shooting flashes from a black box hung 'round his neck. Uncle Albert didn't ask no questions. He just ate that feller up, shirt, pants, black box and all, just like he was a salmon, only a sight bigger. Well, Jug hung around for a spell to see what Uncle Albert done next. Jug was a-laying back in the brush, so's not to give himself away, when he heard more village-folk sounds. And there they was, buzzin' 'round that tent like bees 'round a honey-comb. Then they took out after Uncle Albert like he done something wrong, instead of him protecting what was his'n. They got him, too.

Jug said Uncle Albert pulled some mighty fine tricks trying to keep 'em off his tracks, but being as how he was a prime, big grizzly, his tracks was hard to hide. Once'st he came upon Jug, and stopped and told Jug to head out fast for home 'cause them village folk can't tell one grizzly bear from another and that they'd get him too. Uncle Albert was pure wore out by then.

Jug and I have our own cub now. We headed way over the mountains to make our place. There are no village folk 'round here, yet. But I'm teaching Little Albert every trick I kin think of to keep him safe from them village folk—just like Uncle Albert told me.

"Shall I Shoot?"

In 1946 Bob and Donna Huff arrived in Alaska and decided to make it their permanent home. Their three years mining and tenting at the head of Knik River and the Knik Glacier provided them a sound basis for their sourdough existence, which has lasted over forty-two years. They sluiced for gold and were able to keep the wolves away from the door before moving into a permanent residence in south Anchorage. During their days at the mine, they lived thirty miles from Palmer, which made it difficult to travel back and forth for food. So they subsisted on wild game. In three years at the Knik River, they shot twenty-five sweet-berry bears.

The Huffs told me some of the humorous bear encounters they experienced during their mining days when they lived in an abandoned cabin and later in a tent.

Our funniest bear experience was the time I crawled into a hole after the critter. We went out hunting one day, and I saw something black out of the corner of my eye. It looked like a black cat jumping up and disappearing behind the weeds. I asked my brother Dick what kind of animal was as black as can be and the size of a cat. Dick figured it was a marten.

We went up to look around and discovered a hole. While examining the area, Bea, Dick's wife, said, "There's a bear down there." Sure enough, one eye was lookin' up at me, about ten feet back in the hole. I drew a bead and shot him. We waited a while, then I crawled in, poked the bear with a finger and found no movement. The hole was not very big and I had to lie flat to get in. I grubbed around, found a paw, grabbed it and started pulling the bear out of the hole. My sister-in-law Bea, not taking time to rationalize, shouted, "He's moving. Shall I shoot him?"

I put everything in reverse and skidded out, bumping my head several times and skinning my elbows and back. We discovered what she thought was a bear movin' was me. I told my brother Dick to take Bea away from the hole so I could retrieve the bear without getting shot. The bear turned out to be a 125-pound glacier bear, the only blue bear we shot and ate for subsistence during our three years on the Knik River. At the end of our season, we nailed the salted hide flesh-side-up; when we returned in the spring, the shrew-mice had eaten off the flesh and fat and cured the hide beautifully.

The BB Gun and the Bear

One day our son Dickie came running into the tent to let us know that there was a bear outside. He grabbed his BB gun and ran out with us on his heels. I had grabbed my .270 and raced along behind him until we reached a point in the trail near the tent where Dickie stopped and pointed.

"There's the bear," he said as he raised his BB gun and pinged off a shot. Dickie had hardly fired when my .270 roared from my shoulder and the bear dropped. The bear fell on the edge of a cliff. I ran down, pulled him back from the edge and cut his throat. When the knife cut through, the bear came alive, making a horrible noise through his cut wind pipe.

I fell backwards over a dead tree while the bear bled to death on the other side of the log. My bullet had hit the bear in the mouth, blown out a couple of teeth and just knocked him out temporarily.

The moral is: don't go close to them until you are sure they are dead.

The Three Bears

One day Bea saw a bear up on the hill. My brother Dick and I looked for the bear but couldn't see him through the sarvis berries. Then the bear stood up to look at us, and I quickly shot him in the head. He dropped. I came to the point where I thought he had fallen, but no bear.

Suddenly, Dick shouted, "There he goes!" and shot twice.

But just then, I found my bear, dead.

Suddenly, another bear popped out of the brush and Dick hollered, "There he is again!" and fired a straight shot.

With the one I'd found and the two Dick shot, we ended up with three bears, but no big, bad wolf.

Jack Murrington Tells a Tale

One day at Merrill Field Jack Murrington told us a story about two couples that had left Anchorage in the early '30s and driven up to see him on the Little Susitna River. They drove a Model T up the Little Su as far as they could go then started walking the rest of the way to his cabin.

Jack was busy around the place when he heard some yelling. He grabbed his gun and went to investigate. He hadn't gone far when he came upon a man and two women on the ground telling him to shoot the bear in a cottonwood nearby. They were watching the other man trying to scoot a little higher, a few feet above the bear.

As the four people had approached Jack's cabin, they had stumbled onto the bear, which promptly ran up the tree. Not wanting to disappoint his friends who wanted pictures, the man cut a switch and went up the tree behind the bruin. He came to a fork, climbed opposite the bear on his fork and started switching it on the snout to drive it down the tree so his companions could get better pictures. That was a mistake.The bear climbed down the tree, all right. But once it got to the fork in the tree, the bear started up the opposite fork for his antagonist—thus the pursuer became the pursued.

Catchin' Bears Alive

Several years ago we were on our way home from Palmer on the Old Palmer Highway, the only road connecting Anchorage then. Just this side of Goat Creek, we ran into a traffic jam and thought there had been a terrible automobile accident. We got out of the car and noticed people staring across the brush and up into a cottonwood at a little black bear.

Moments later two guys showed up, one carrying a chainsaw and the other packing an axe. It turned out that they wanted to capture the critter alive. We heard one of the men say he wanted to get his hands on the bear, and I said, "You better leave it alone. Those bears are all covered with teeth and claws."

Meanwhile, the little bruin was up the tree looking down at those funny animals in colored fur on the ground making strange noises. One guy climbed up to the bear, but when the bear growled, he scampered back down in a hurry. Next, they cut the tree down. When the tree hit the ground, the bear jumped and took off with one of the men in hot pursuit. The guy dived for the animal, tackling a tree head on as the bear dodged and slipped away. The man was lucky he got K O'd by the tree instead of the bear.

Canned Bear

The predicaments bears can get themselves into is astonishing. Although bears seem to be curious by nature, their curiosity often gets them into trouble. Take the one-hundred-pound black bear cub that visited the Girl Scout camp near Cooper Landing on the Kenai in August 1976. It seemed only a matter of time before the little guy stuck his head into a five-pound Folger's coffee can from which he could not escape.

With Girls Scouts peering from behind trees and outhouses, Forest Service firefighters arrived on the scene armed with rope and tin snips. Meanwhile the Alaska State Troopers had sent out two of their men to help with the problem.

They lassoed the bear's paws, tying each to four

trees. Then they snipped away the metallic hat, cautiously taking care not to injure the critter. At that point the cub began snapping at his rescuers. They cut loose the rope a leg at a time, and the yelling girls scared the bear away.

Not a Single One

As he watched the water run off the floats of the bush plane and the aircraft vanish in the distance, the lone man savored a week's fishing on Wolverine Lake. Bill McGregor unrolled his bedroll and prepared a quick meal of canned stew and brown bread, eagerly anticipating morning.

At five he was up and sorting through his flies, looking for a tempting morsel for the rainbows or silver salmon that inhabited the waters. By eight he had caught and released two dozen 'bows, saving some for breakfast.

Each day Bill tempted the trout, and each day was equally rewarding, except there were no silvers. While engrossed in his sport, Bill continually experienced a nagging feeling that someone or something was watching him from the lakeside landscape. Bill sneaked peeks and even modified his fly casting style in an effort to get a glimpse of his surroundings, but he never saw anything out of the ordinary.

For a number of days Bill exulted in his activity . . . and wondered what wandered the shoreline. On his last day he resumed where he'd left off the night before, fishing from a small spit of land. Finally a silver struck. Exploding from the depths, it cartwheeled and tail-walked. Bill's pole bent double as the coho fought. Fifteen minutes elapsed before the fish was within his grasp.

At that point the mystery of the past few days was solved. Thirty feet away, a brown bear emerged from the brush. It snorted, gaining Bill's attention. The man whirled to face the bear. The bear rose to peer down at the mere man.

What could he do? He was trapped on the spit. Sweat spread across his brow. He rapidly considered his options—should he swim out into the lake? Running was futile, and what about the silver?

Then an escape plan suddenly formulated in Bill's mind. He raised his hard-won fish ever so gently and in a fluid, slow motion tossed it off to one side of the beast. The bear shot the fisherman a hurried glance, then snapped up the bribe and leaped into the undergrowth.

Bill was astonished. That bear had just watched and waited for a silver until the right time came. A rainbow wasn't good enough. Bill hustled back to camp and spent some anxious moments during the night awaiting the return of his pilot. The next morning the pilot touched down onto the mirror-like waters of the lake and taxied up to Bill's camp. Unable to contain his curiosity, the pilot excitedly asked Bill if he'd caught any silvers; the fisherman replied, "Nope, not a single one."

No Room at the Inn

While some people have trouble with bears in their fishing holes, others confront bruin in their cabins, creating quite a bit of pandemonium. The two sourdoughs returned to their cabin after a long, hard day of exhausting work. Leaning their rifles near the door and completing their chores, they went to sleep.

During the night a grizzly entered their quaint abode. The excitement began when the door closed behind the bear. Frantically searching for a way out, the bear headed for the window, which, unfortunately, was halfway between the top and lower bunk, just above the man's head in the lower bunk.

As the bear lunged toward the window and onto the bed, the entire bunk collapsed, the top half collapsing on the tenant below. Grunts, roars and shouts emanated from the crude shelter as the confused occupants fought to escape.

After a wild struggle, the man who had been sleeping on the top bunk finally broke free and grabbed a rifle. His partner was still caught somewhere in the dark shambles with the bear. The old-timer suddenly spotted the bear's ears silhouetted in the window. Realizing the shot had to be quick and accurate, he fired. Luck was with him.

The bear died atop the shaken partner and the remains of the bunk bed, his head sticking out of the broken window.

Roping a Griz

Have you heard the one about the Texas cowboy who wanted a grizzly? He worked at a construction camp in the North country where bears frequently raided the trash bins at night. The Texan decided to rope himself one of these bears.

His plan was to tie one end of his lasso to a twelve-inch spruce log. He figured he could drop his loop over a bear's head from the roof of the camp bunkhouse and count on the log to hold his bear. The bunkhouse was built over a drop off, its back side suspended above the ground on pilings.

One night, while his bunkmates slept, the cowboy climbed up on top of the bunkhouse and set up a watch on the roof. Before long Mr. Bear appeared, cautiously approaching the dump. When it was ten yards away, the Texan gracefully threw his loop over the bear's neck. Like a rocket, the bruin was launched!

Trailing a length of rope and a hunk of spruce log, the beast circled the pilings supporting the bunkhouse. The rope wrapped tighter and tighter, until the legs of the not-too-sturdy bunkhouse began to wobble. The dwelling toppled to the ground in a cloud of dust, burying the men inside under piles of logs.

The men pulled themselves from the wreckage. One had managed to find a rifle and he quickly dispatched the frenzied bear. The Texan decided roping one bear in a lifetime was enough.

4

No Escape

 nything that will flip over a three-hundred-pound boulder to lick bugs off the bottom is nothing to take lightly.—Steve Augustin

The only predictable thing about a brown bear is that he ain't!—Jack Naus

What constitutes a mauling? If a person is bitten by a bear, is the incident considered a mauling or must one suffer to the point of death before a man-bear encounter qualifies as a mauling? Some people have been mauled unmercifully and lived while others were bitten once and died.

Bear maulings occur throughout the state and involve every kind of bear—black, brown/grizzly and polar. Bears attack for a number of reasons, but their primary reason for attacking man is to protect themselves, mates, cubs, territory or a food source.

Mauling statistics are difficult to obtain, as no single agency in Alaska has coordinated efforts to compile a composite list of maulings. And while conclusive evidence is hard to acquire, due to unreported bear maulings, minimal information or undetected mauling information, my research shows there have been over 180 maulings in Alaska in the last ninety-three years— an average of almost two people mauled each year.

Forty-four of those victims died, roughly 25 percent. The greatest danger involved the person alone, as 15 percent or twenty-seven persons who were alone during the attack died. Although a recent fatality involved a bear which attacked a search party of seven, there is safety in numbers. Eighteen percent of those attacked in the woods were rescued by a partner while 2.7 percent were saved by a dog. Nearly 9 percent lived by feigning death, and the bear left.

My Partner Saves the Day

The entire episode could not have lasted more than twenty to thirty seconds, and Jack Naus became another statistic in the annals of bear maulings.

In 1981, I read of Jack's mauling in both Anchorage newspapers. At the time Jack Naus was a thirty-nine-year-old chief warrant officer with the Coast Guard. He went hunting with six friends and encountered a brown bear, and his letter tells his story best.

Dear Mr. Kaniut,

Just received your letter in regards to your forthcoming book and request for my story. I'll try to relate to you all I can recall, but because the incident occurred back in 1981, my memories are rather blurred.

In late September about seven of us went over to the Mansfield Peninsula of Admiralty Island for a day of deer hunting. We had hunted the island, which is located in Southeast Alaska, just west of Juneau, on many other occasions and had been very successful.

Approximately halfway through the hunt, I was walking down a well-worn path when I saw a brown-bear sow and two cubs coming toward me. I quickly moved off the path to give the sow and her cubs room to pass, but she still caught my scent and false charged, holding her ears up and woofing. She charged to within twenty yards of me, then turned and strolled back to her cubs. I retreated to high ground and informed several members of our hunting party about the bear. We waited until we were sure she had passed before continuing the hunt.

Later, about two miles down the trail, my partner Dave and I came into a large clearing. Hearing a noise in the blueberry bushes in front of us, we both halted. As Dave cried, "It's big, whatever it is!" a medium-sized brown/grizzly bear, weighing three hundred to four hundred pounds, broke through brush and charged from approximately thirty yards away.

Dave jumped to his right and I to my left, allowing room for the bear to escape. About ten yards into its charge, the bear made a sudden ninety-degree turn toward me. I immediately snapped off a shot—using a .300 Winchester magnum, 180-grain factory loads—hitting the bear between the head and the left shoulder. He was so close that I saw the dust fly. He bowled over.

As I fired, I had a feeling my bullet wouldn't stop him, and sure enough, the bear made a forward roll and bounced back onto his feet. Although Dave later told me that I fired in rapid succession, the next few seconds seemed to take place in slow motion. When I reloaded, I thought the round was never going to chamber. My next shot must have hit his skull as I tripped and fell backwards. I still carry lead in my right arm from where the bullet fragmented and ricocheted into my arm. That's how close he was!

Next thing I knew, I had a large brown bear with his jaws wrapped around my hip. At that point, things got hazy. Dave shouted at me to lay down and take it easy. He shot the bear twice, and the animal false charged Dave and then ran back into the woods.

I sustained about five half-inch round puncture wounds spread below my navel and around my left hip to my buttocks; a five-inch gash on the inner left leg and groin; a gash from the mid-cheek of my face to the top of my ear; and four to six entry wounds on my left arm from my own bullet. Fortunately, no arteries or veins were damaged and very little bleeding occurred. I've always kept my rifle as a reminder of the ordeal; a half-inch deep section of the forestock is missing and a point on the barrel looks as if someone rolled the metal off with center punch.

When I reflected back on the accident and ways that I might have prevented the mauling, I came to the conclusion that we probably arrived at the hunting site too early in the year, when too much underbrush was still present. And, perhaps we should have called it a day after the first bear encounter. But Monday mornings supply all answers.

Sincerely,

Jack D. Naus

The Beach Bear

Jim Hunter is another man with considerable experience outdoors, but as most of the stories in this volume show, even the most avid and knowledgable outdoorsmen are not immune to bear attacks. At the time of his encounter, Jim had worked as a National Weather Service technician and lived in Cold Bay (about 650 miles southwest of Anchorage on the Alaska Peninsula) for four and a half years with his wife and two young daughters. Brown bears were not new to Jim; he had once chased one from the steps of his weather service station when returning home from work one night.

In August 1983, Jim had planned a few days of beachcombing across from his home on Izembek Lagoon, planning to be afield from Sunday through Tuesday. Jim did not foresee any problems during his vacation and certainly did not expect bears in the area, so he chose to go unarmed.

He hadn't been ashore long, when he spotted a bear twenty feet away and coming toward him at a gallop. Jim knew that bears often bluffed and began shouting, thinking the animal would stop. When the bear kept charging, Jim threw a quart bottle full of water at him, hitting him squarely on the nose. In response, the bear grabbed Jim by the knee and slapped down with his paw, then picked him up in his mouth and dropped him. Jim heard the sound of his ribs cracking.

Recalling stories and protocol for such situations, Hunter made a decision to play dead. The bear soon lost interest in the motionless body and halted his attack. For twenty minutes Jim lay still on the ground, praying that the bear had gone away. Finally, he rose cautiously, saw the bear had departed and headed for his kayak on the beach.

As he felt the pain begin in his side and the strong winds blowing across the lagoon, Jim abandoned all thoughts of paddling back to Cold Bay. Instead, he returned to his camp and moved his tent from a grassy area to a sandpit. Knowing that his wife would eventually begin to worry and inform the authorities of his whereabouts, Jim, wet and aching, settled down to wait for help. Two nights and three days passed. On Tuesday, he had decided to paddle home despite his injuries, when a Peninsula Airways plane picked him up.

Jim was fortunate. His only injuries were gouges in his back and side, puncture wounds on his right elbow and knee and three cracked ribs.

A Rare Point of View

During an age when many want to destroy bears, I always appreciate hearing about or meeting people who understand these animals and acknowledge that people, rather than the bears, are the invaders. Jack Danielson is one of those who believes in this philosophy.

I read Jack Danielson's story in the *Anchorage Daily News* in November 1986. While following up on his story, I was also given a copy of the Alaska Department of Fish and Game report compiled by Area Management Biologist Roger Smith of the Kodiak office. Management Coordinator Greg Bos completed the report after interviewing Jack and his partner Lloyd Oler.

Jack and Lloyd, both data processing operators from Elmendorf Air Base in Anchorage, were deer hunting on the west side of Kazakof on Afognak Island. The partners had downed two deer, gutted them and were in the process of packing the meat down to the beach when they noticed they had company—a sow and twin cubs.

Although the bears were more interested in the deer meat than the hunters, unfortunately the men were in the way.

Later, Jack recalled, "It happened so fast. . . . The

mother bear was on me in a heartbeat. I kicked her. I was trying to get the gun that was about five feet away. She kept biting me. She didn't take huge pieces out of me. It was more like a dog, just bite and bite and bite. . . . I was kicking and screaming." (*Anchorage Daily News*)

After the struggle continued for about a minute, Jack decided to try a new strategy and play dead. But when the bear calmed, he again tried to crawl away, and the sow "'mouthed' him several times on the right leg and buttocks. . . . When she finally got a grip on his buttocks she carried him a short ways from the deer carcass and left him." (ADFG report)

In the meantime, Lloyd had disappeared. When he saw the three bears—the first live brownies in his experience—it was too much for him, and he admitted, "I jumped up, exclaimed a few words—not exactly printable—and ran as fast as I could, about a hundred yards. I was afraid.

"I heard Jack yelling and screaming, and all of a sudden the bear went to the deer carcass and [Jack] just laid there still. I thought he was dead or paralyzed. I was up there watching the whole deal and she looked up at me and I said, 'Oh God, I'm next.'"

When Lloyd saw Jack moving, he joined him. They rounded up their weapons and gear, and headed for the beach, arriving in two hours. The hunters then set up camp and awaited rescue, shooting flares, making large markings on the beach and starting fires. No rescue team materialized.

The next day four other hunters landed a short distance away, but before Jack or Lloyd could get their attention, the pilot who dropped them had left. The new hunters shared their first aid supplies with Jack. On the following day a pilot, spotting their distress signal, landed and flew Jack and Lloyd to Kodiak.

Jack held no animosity towards the bear and, in fact, planned to return to hunt after his wounds healed, stating, "That bear did nothing wrong. She was very clear that this was her land and 'if you're coming on my land, you're going to have to share it with me.'

"I was in the bear's country and the bear wasn't after me. She was just getting me out of the way. I feel if you're hunting on Afognak, that's part of the game. The bears are not out there to hurt people, they're there to get deer meat. . . . People just got to be careful."

In Desperation

Alaska Department of Fish and Game workers have had numerous close calls with bears and with death. The June 1981 issue of Alaska Fish Tales and Game Trails *relates an amazing account of one technician's desperate effort to escape.*

Two Alaska Department of Fish and Game technicians, Paul Kissner and Bruce Milenbach, set out to survey Dolly Varden trout on Admiralty Island in July 1967. After deciding it was too early for bears to be on the stream, Bruce left his rifle behind in the truck and Paul carried only a .38 revolver.

Giving his weapon to his partner, Paul ran ahead quickly to scout the trail. As he hiked along briskly, he heard a sound like a hog grunting. There was no other warning. In a split second, a bear leaped from the alder brush, grabbed Paul in its mouth and began shaking him.

When the animal released his grip, Paul stood upright and staggered backwards, stepping over the edge of a twenty-foot cliff. He landed face-down on a ledge, but even this fall could not save him from more harm. The bear found Paul and began biting him viciously in the buttocks, under the arms and in the back.

The pain was so extreme that Paul intentionally rolled away from the bear and plummeted down an almost vertical avalance chute, rolling and bouncing for about a hundred yards before he dropped over another twenty-foot cliff and landed in a patch of snow.

No sooner had Paul come to rest than the bear landed next to him, his nose jammed into the snow. Apparently dazed from the fall, the bear lumbered away. Paul had decided to roll again if the bear renewed his attack, which would have meant an almost certainly fatal drop of one thousand feet.

In a few minutes Bruce found Paul who insisted he pack the mangled leg in snow before rushing down the mountain to secure help via the radio-telephone. Kissner spent three weeks in the hospital and one year in therapy, with only one lasting injury—a partially stiff leg—to remind him of his ordeal.

A Chain of Rescue

What began as an Alaska wilderness trek turned into a fight for survival for a trio of hikers on Alaska's North Slope the first week of August 1979.

Chad Hansen and the husband-wife team of Quinn and Patricia Whiting-O'Keefe were hiking in the Arctic National Wildlife Refuge. Chad was a professor of Chinese philosophy from Vermont, and Quinn, a medical doctor on staff at the University of San Francisco. They were camping in the Schrader Lake country on the North Slope. Rolling, tundra-covered hills surrounded their camp. Sparse brush intermittently punctuated the terrain.

The group set out that morning of August 4, hoping to spot wildlife. They hadn't anticipated any problems and had no reason for alarm. Even though they had observed other game, they hadn't so much as seen a bear or other dangerous animals.

Though unarmed, they had taken precautions against bears. Patricia was wearing bells on her pack to alert any bears in the area of the party's presence.

Patricia was hiking several yards ahead of Chad and Quinn. Just after she disappeared over a knoll fifty yards from the men, her husband heard her scream.

Patricia had stumbled onto a grizzly mother with three cubs. The bear immediately charged Patricia and struck her with a front paw. There was absolutely nothing the hiker could have done. Even had she been holding a weapon with a bullet in the chamber, she couldn't have gotten off a shot. She didn't even have time to cover her face before the bear was upon her.

The men ran to her aid. Within seconds of Patricia's scream the men saw a sow with three cubs leaving the area. And then they saw another mother with twin cubs beginning to charge in their direction. They backed away and began searching for Patricia. When they finally found her, they knew they had an extreme emergency.

The bear's single swat had inflicted severe damage. The injuries, at first glance, included the loss of Pat's nose, right eye and the right side of her scalp. It is almost inconceivable that such damage could be wrought so quickly and so effortlessly.

Quinn began first aid immediately and attended her while Chad went for help. Quinn did what he could for his wife. Then they waited and wondered.

In the meantime Chad had his own problems. He had eighteen miles to cover to the nearest human habitation, eighteen miles of tundra, swamp and low hills. Five hours later he arrived at the U.S. Fish and Wildlife Service research station at Peters Lake.

Pat needed immediate emergency medical attention, and her hopes depended on a helicopter medivac. Since no such aircraft was available at the research station, Dr. Paul Fisher risked his life by flying a small plane into the deteriorating weather conditions. It was necessary for him to gain an altitude for possible radio contact with Prudhoe Bay. He was successful, and a chopper was sent from Prudhoe.

The pilot was unable to spot the couple and went to get Chad, who directed him to their location. When the helicopter neared their position, ground visibility was only twenty-five feet, and he was still unable to find them. Quinn hurried to start a signal fire. The pilot told them later that he would never have found them in the fog had he not seen the fire.

Patricia was flown immediately to Fairbanks where a team of surgeons awaited her. Dr. Glen Straatsma was assisted by Dr. Bill Wennen, Dr. Sam A. McConkey, Dr. Nobuhiro Tokita and Dr. Perry A. Mead. They worked on her for ten hours. In time it was discovered that her left eye also sustained damage. Although the doctors assessed her condition as very good, extensive plastic surgery was necessary.

Two days after her arrival in Fairbanks, she was flown to the San Francisco Bay Area for hospitalization.

Her rescue took longer than they had expected, but in retrospect all the elements had worked like clockwork. Quinn's administration of first aid, Chad's rescue run, Dr. Fisher's daring flight into bad weather to hazard a radio call, the signal fire and the helicopter airlift, the team of doctors in Fairbanks . . . any broken link in this chain of rescue would likely have spelled death for Pat. Her survival required all the rescue efforts to go like clockwork. And they did.

The experience has not dimmed Pat's desire to get back into the outdoors. Patricia and Quinn continue to camp and hike the backcountry.

Handgun for a Grizzly

Ben Moore, a carpenter in the civil engineering field and an enthusiastic hunter, hated to end the 1985 hunting season on an unsuccessful note. He had started out hunting in the Blair Lakes area with his usual partners but had returned home without a single trophy. So when his friend Richard Napoleane invited Ben and his fourteen-year-old son Ty to go hunting in Ferry, they eagerly accepted. However, the trip that began as an exciting challenge to turn his hunting season around ended in a nightmare encounter with a brown/grizzly.

Ben said he wanted to tell me his story so he could leave behind a truthful version for his children. He commented that he has been very irritated with the audacity of the media's attempts to get his story and with the misinformation that has been printed without his permission. For example, Ben's "exclusive" story and quotes have appeared in many magazines and newspapers, despite the fact that he only talked with one reporter from the Fairbanks News-Miner.

Richard already had set up his camper-trailer off the railroad tracks at Ferry. Since you can't drive from the Parks Highway to that hunting spot, we had shipped our vehicles ahead on Alaska Railroad flatcars. Richard, his two friends Del and Chin, Ty and I then drove the highway to an area across the river from our vehicle drop-off point. We arrived at the trailer at about seven o'clock in the evening, had a light dinner and hit the hay early.

The next morning we got up at five and took three-wheelers across the river bridge to our Jeep and station wagon. There was only enough room in the Jeep for two people, so I rode with Richard, and my boy rode in the station wagon with the other two hunters. At a fork in the road we separated, heading into the rolling hill country covered with thick brush. It was a typical Alaskan fall day—no precipitation, clear sky, gold and red splashed the surrounding hills.

At about seven in the morning we pulled out on a little ridge, looking for a place to park the vehicle and to glass the ridges without standing in the thirty- to forty-mile-per-hour winds.

"I'm just gonna run over here to the right to check for a place to park," I said, leaving my rifle in the vehicle.

I was aware of bears in the area, so I tried to avoid the brushy areas, where I knew bears could hide. Soon, I came to a wide, open clearing, and I lifted my binoculars to glass for animals. Suddenly, I noticed a bear through the glasses, and my heart skipped a beat. The image was so close it was fuzzy. The bear was on the same ridge where I was standing, about one hundred feet away. At about the same time I put the binoculars down, the bear stood up on his hind legs with his head above the brush. It bobbed its head, opened its mouth and looked at me for several seconds, then dropped out of sight.

I was a little startled, but not too concerned about being in danger. I've read quite a bit about bears and figured if I didn't react, the bear would move on. I relaxed, standing perfectly still. As I was glancing around, the brush exploded and I saw a ball of fur hurling toward me like it had been shot out of the bushes. I reached down and pulled out my revolver, a .357 Ruger single-action. By the time I drew and cocked my gun, the bear had practically reached the end of the barrel. I pulled the trigger, hitting the bear somewhere in the chest.

Still the bear charged forward, grabbing me by my lower right leg as he ran by. He picked me up, swung me over his head and actually threw me like I was a feather pillow. I landed on a rock several feet away, barely hitting the ground before the bear was on top of me, chewing my upper right leg.

Miraculously, I hadn't dropped my revolver and managed to get off another shot; but I was shaking so uncontrollably that I completely missed the bear. I struggled to cock the gun again, fired and hit the animal in the stomach, about a foot from my face. A huge hole opened up in its abdomen and blood poured from the wound, but the injury only angered the bear more. It grabbed me by the head, picked me up and shook. As I heard the bones in my face cracking, the bear dropped me. I fell on my back, staring up at the bear directly over me with its mouth open. The grizzly saw me move and came down for my head again. But as the bear lowered its head, I lifted my right arm, cocked the gun and jammed the pistol clear into its mouth. I pulled the trigger. The timing was perfect. When I fired that final shot, the pistol and my hands were in the bear's mouth.

The bear shook its head and shuddered. It reared back and took a powerful swing at me with its paw. And, almost as if the bear knew what had caused the hurt, it tried to knock the gun out of the way, but I clasped it tightly with both hands. Then the bear staggered over the ridge and down into the brush.

I decided if the bear came back, the worst thing would be to be lying down. But when I stood up, my leg buckled, and I fell back down. Instead of being scared, I was completely irritated, and stood back up, jamming my leg down hard. My eyes were bleeding so badly that, as hard as I tried, I couldn't see to reload the revolver. Later, when they opened up the gun, they had to use a rod to jam the cartridges out, since they were covered with blood. At first when the bear charged me, I was overcome with fear, but now I was mad. I had one live round left. I yelled out at the bear, challenging him to come back.

After about five minutes Richard appeared up on the ridge. Of all the shots I fired, he only heard one over the strong winds.

As he walked over the ridge, he hollered down, "Did you get a moose?"

"No, a bear got me," I said.

He looked down. "What?"

"A bear got me."

When he saw my face and condition, Richard understandably became upset and nervous. He helped me up to the Jeep, and we headed for the trailer five miles away. We had driven no more than one hundred feet when the Jeep quit. Richard crawled under the vehicle, anxiously keeping his eye out for the bear, and pounded on the electric fuel pump that had been giving us trouble. Finally, we got the Jeep running and unsuccessfully tried to contact the others on our CB.

But someone was watching out for me. Two paramedics happened to be down by the railroad bridge where our trailer was located; they had heard our message on the CB and called ahead for help. Shortly after we reached the trailer, three more paramedics showed up in an ambulance and tried to make some quick repairs before we headed for town.

My nose was actually hanging off, so they pushed it back to the proper place, then bandaged my whole face, including my eyes. After they put an inflatable splint on my leg, they loaded me into the ambulance.

The ride to the airport was torture. We stopped numerous times for the paramedics to insert an IV, but with no luck. Apparently, my veins were collapsed from the shock. When I tried to lay down, the blood ran from my nose cavity into my throat and choked me, so I had to sit up all the way to the airport. And my leg was swelling so badly that they had to take the splint off, which meant my leg bounced up and down each time we hit a rut or bump.

The paramedics wouldn't give me anything for pain because they thought I was going into shock. But I have to say that my face never hurt. I think the pain in my leg was so intense that it overrode the feeling in my face. Strangely enough, for the first hour or two after the mauling, the worst problem was a pain in my thumb. Richard was completely baffled each time he looked at my mangled face and heard me complain about a pain in my finger. Later, we discovered the cause of the pain when the doctor cut his finger on my thumb—a hunk of bear claw had broken off and embedded itself in my finger, extending a quarter of an inch through the opposite side.

It took four to five hours to get to the Fairbanks Memorial Hospital from Richard's trailer. I still think I could have been medivaced in with just a phone call and would have received medical attention faster. However, I am not criticizing the paramedics. They had never been involved in any incidents of this kind, and I think they just wanted to be part of the rescue.

About six miles from the hospital, we radioed in to notify the staff of our arrival. Once we reached the hospital, they X-rayed me and went into surgery for a little over four hours. Then I remained in the hospital for about two weeks and had to take two months off of work. Within two years of leaving the hospital I had many surgeries, so many I can't even count the number.

Dr. Parry, plastic and reconstructive surgeon, worked on my nose many times to rebuild it. For the first two months he couldn't make any progress because all the facial bones were shattered, and they needed to heal back together. Now my nose looks great, but I have no feeling in it. When the cold air hits it, the membranes swell. I feel like I have a cold twenty-four hours a day.

When I look back, I thank God that my son Ty was not with me when the mauling occurred. He wanted to go with me, but I persuaded him that there wasn't enough room in the Jeep. If he had ridden with Richard and me, he would have been about two feet behind me when the bear charged.

For the first six months after the mauling, I had nightmares all the time. I would wake up and the bed would be wet with sweat. Actually, I had one about a month ago, but prior to that, I hadn't had one for a long time. It's like anything else—the memory fortunately fades.

Grizzly Attacks Park Ranger

No one—neither experienced outdoorsmen, avid hunters nor even park rangers—are ever safe from bear attacks. During the summer of 1967, Jim Magowan, who worked as a ranger in Mount McKinley National

Park and lived on the premises with his family, learned this frightening lesson the hard way. Jim had just received a report of a nuisance bear in the area and set out in the park to investigate, when he had a much closer encounter with a mother grizzly than he could have ever imagined.

She hit me with her head, plowing straight into me and knocking me off my feet. Lying flat on my back looking at the sky, I tried to remain motionless. Then the sow started chewing on my head, and I could hear her teeth grating on my skull.

I thought, "At this rate, I'm not gonna have very long to play." Hoping to protect my stomach and vital organs, I curled into a ball and put my hands over my head. She chewed my shoulders and my arm, and bit me in the eye.

When the bear abruptly stopped chewing and quieted, I peeked out from underneath my arm to look for the sow. She had disappeared. Sighing with relief, I stood up and looked over my shoulder. To my dismay, there she was, sitting with her two cubs about fifty yards away. They were staring at me like kids at a circus.

As soon as I looked at her, she jumped off her haunches and charged again. I was wearing heavy climbing boots at the time, and when she got to me, I dropped onto my back and stuck my feet up into her face, hoping she'd chew on my shoes instead of me. No such luck! She simply brushed my feet out of the way, lunged, grabbed me by the leg, flipped me and threw me around. She grabbed me by the butt and threw me again.

When I hit the ground, I rolled, trying to curl up with my elbows out and stop with my belly down. I huddled there watching from under my arm, although I could hardly see. My glasses had been knocked off and my forehead was split open, causing blood to pour down my face. All I could see was brown blurs darting by. I waited. Nothing happened.

"If I don't get up now," I thought, "I'll never be able to get up."

It had all started when I was called to investigate reports of nuisance bears in the park. One man had even reported a bear chasing his car down the road. My wife Ellie had decided to come with me, and we had just jumped into our Suburban, when a woman staying at the campground asked to come with us. She had heard the talk of bears and was worried about her husband who was walking out on the grounds. We picked up her husband about a half a mile from camp and continued out toward Stoney Pass, looking for bears.

From the road, you couldn't see any animals that might be lurking on the ledges above. At one point I parked the car to check the elevated areas. When I returned, another car had pulled up, behind ours. The driver said he had spotted three bears out on the hillside about five miles down the road. I thought, "Gee, all I need is a mad bear to come tearing through this campground. We'll have bodies all over the place."

We drove to the area that the fellow had indicated, and I got out to look around. I had brought along a camera. Anytime an animal incident occurs, rangers are instructed to take pictures just in case identification is needed later on. Since I didn't have binoculars, I scanned the nearby mountainsides using the camera lens. Through the lens, I spotted the bears. From that distance I couldn't even distinguish the size differences between them, so I wanted to stay and observe a bit longer. Although I was paying special attention to maintaining my distance, ironically, my mauling was blamed on my supposed attempt to get close-up photographs of the bears.

Although on a slide, the bears would be no larger than a match head, I took two pictures of the animals grazing. As I turned to leave, a third bear appeared over the hill. All three stood up on their hind legs to sniff the air. As soon as the "late-comer bear" stood up, I thought, "Oh, no!" I realized I was looking at a sow and two cubs.

When I turned to leave, the sow growled and started to charge. I stopped; she stopped. As long as I stood still, she would turn and move back to the cubs. I tried moving at least twice, and each time, she charged. I froze while she led the cubs up and across the hillside. During this time, the wind had been blowing from the bears to me, but now that the animals had circled, they could smell my scent clearly. The sow began to charge again, and this time she meant business. I tried waving my arms, but it was useless. She charged within several feet of me and stopped. I put my hands up, and she faced me on all fours and lunged. The next thing I knew I was staring up at the sky.

When I finally stood up, the bears were gone. I called to my wife Ellie who was about a half a mile back. When she heard my yells, she ran for help. Ellie says she heard me scream each time I was hit, but I have no memory of crying out. As I caught my bearings and looked around for the bears, I realized the extent of my injuries for the first time. My right arm was so badly mangled and the shoulder so chewed up, that I couldn't do anything with them. I lifted up my bad arm with my other hand and stuffed it into my pocket, using it as a sling. My head and my buttocks were a mass of punctures and cuts, all from the sow's teeth. And I had one cut on my left calf that was about three inches long and an inch deep, and a hole punctured in my thigh clear down to the fascia. One of my boots was full of blood.

I walked back toward the car, yelling, "Ellie, I've been mauled." Soon, I saw my wife coming back down the trail to meet me. Meanwhile, the man we had picked up along the road took off in my Suburban to get help at a road camp about a quarter of a mile behind our campground. The foreman of the camp grabbed his rifle and hopped in his pickup. He didn't even realize what had happened until he saw me sitting in the middle of the road covered with blood.

The others helped me into the Suburban and we started out on the sixty-mile drive to park headquarters. Although the woman Ellie and I had picked up was a nurse, she got into the truck with the road foreman, maybe because she was too shocked by my injuries. Her husband, a psychologist, had totally panicked and was no help at all. To make matters worse, we met a convoy of semis, lowboys and tractors along the road. The driver of the lead truck pulled beside us, saying, "Hey, you'll have to get off the road. We've got a bunch of lowboys comin' through."

Of course, I naturally expected the driver of our car to reply, "Well, we've got a medivac here, and you better get the trucks out of the way." But instead, he pulled off the road and waited ten or fifteen minutes for the convoy to drive by.

When we arrived at park headquarters, the prospects of getting medical attention quickly began to look worse. By now it was about eight o'clock in the evening, and the fog and rain clouds had rolled in, preventing planes from landing or taking off. In 1967 much of the highway through McKinley park had been finished, but the bridges had not been built, and the road between the park and Healy was not open. The only way to drive out was on the railroad tracks.

The ranger on duty put in an emergency call to Healy and located the operators of a Power Wagon which had special wheels allowing the vehicle to drive on the rails or on the road. However, we interrupted the two operators in the middle of a night of partying. When they arrived at headquarters, they were very obviously still "under the influence."

At Healy they transferred me to a station wagon to take me to Fairbanks. Until that point I had too much adrenalin pumping to feel much pain. But the bedside manner of my rescue team was not too comforting. When the basket stretcher was loaded, the end still stuck out from the back of the car, so I got a real jar when they slammed the tailgate.

I began to relax as we rolled out of Healy, but just then the guys up front began to discuss the condition of their vehicle.

"Say," says the co-poilot, "This thing is really running nice!"

"Yeah! I tuned it up—put in new spark plugs and points."

"Wow, a week ago you couldn't have driven this thing a mile without breaking down."

"Well, it seems to run okay now, maybe it just needed a tune up."

It all became clear. I was going to die in a broken-down station wagon, halfway between Healy and Fairbanks.

But hope was not far away. Farther down the road, we saw flashing lights up ahead through the fog and rain. It was the beacon of an HH-2l helicopter, waiting to whisk us to Fairbanks International Airport. In minutes men in flight suits and helmets were loading me into the chopper. After a bumpy, bone-jarring, forty-five minute flight, we landed at the airport, only to find that the officials there had not called the ambulance.

"We weren't sure whether you'd need an ambulance or a hearse," they said.

At three o'clock that morning, almost eight hours after the mauling, I was loaded into the ambulance— the fifth vehicle I had ridden in since my rescue began.

It was between eight and half past that morning when they finally finished with me in the operating room. Five people had worked on me for three hours, using more than six hundred stitches to sew up my wounds. I was in the hospital fifteen days.

Physically, I feel very lucky about the outcome of the attack. I did end up with a lot of scars (at one time we counted sixty-three), but I just let my sideburns grow and wear my hair a little longer to cover some of them.

And, it may sound funny, but I also feel good about some of the psychological effects of the attack. During the mauling, I had to face the concept of what appeared to be certain death. As simple as it may seem, it was a revelation when I realized that I was vulnerable and death was inevitable. Since I've accepted this, I now live each day to the fullest, as though it might be my last.

It Came Out of Nowhere

In September 1988 Lawrence "L. W." Jones was mauled by a 650- to 750-pound blonde grizzly in the Skwentna area about fifteen miles upriver on the Yentna. I interviewed L.W. at Humana Hospital-Alaska where he was recovering from severe injuries sustained at the claws and jaws of the bear. His brother Troy and his friend Pat Merrill, who had accompanied him on the hunt, were also at the hospital and were very helpful in providing information. Recalling his experience in vivid detail, L.W. commented that the bear mauling had given him a greater adrenalin rush than any other incident in his life—and this is nothing to scoff at, considering Lawrence Jones fought in Viet Nam, was listed as "killed in action" after a grenade exploded at his feet, and spent four and a half months in a coma from his war wounds.

About nine feet in front of me an alder bush came to life with the fury of something I've never quite witnessed. I knew immediately it was a grizzly. He charged directly at me making a pig-like, grunting sound. As the bear lunged, I pointed the barrel of my Weatherby rifle directly at him.

The bear ran into the barrel, slapped it aside, then moved to my left about four feet away. I caught my balance and pointed the barrel at the bear again, this time aiming into his mouth. As he bit the barrel, pawed it and slammed it down again, he was charging and pushing. With all of the confusion, I couldn't release the safety, or every time I got it off, the jar would force the gun back on safety 'cause I couldn't squeeze the trigger. For whatever reason, fate was with the bear at that point.

Eventually, he slapped the rifle barrel back out of his mouth and moved to my left. He had me turned around 180 degrees; my back was at the bush that he sprung from. My only chance now was to shoot, so I pulled the trigger at point-blank range; and by the time the gun exploded, the bear had lunged again. I don't think he ever touched ground between the time the rifle fired and the time he was on top of me.

I also had a .44-magnum Redhawk in a shoulder holster. I was struggling to reach that gun, but as I rolled onto my stomach, the bear bit into my left shoulder and the holster, breaking the harness and jerking the pistol out of my reach.

The bear then bit through my left shoulder, picked me up, shook me and threw me back down. He began mauling my head from the rear on the left side all the way around to my left eye, lacerating the entire length of my scalp. My ear, I understand, wound up in three pieces.

Almost instantly, he grabbed me by my left hip area on the back side of my thigh, picked me up in the air and started shaking again. When he threw me back down, I landed on my left side where all the damage had been done. The bear then reached down with one paw, apparently in an effort to spin me over, hooked my stomach and ripped it open fairly well. Luckily, the claws did not puncture the stomach cavity.

Now, the bear was standing over me breathing, but I didn't turn around to check his position. Of course, I would have given anything if one of my hunting partners was nearby, but they were all downriver and out of earshot.

We had all come in to hunt three days earlier. There were five of us in the party—my brother Troy, Pat Merrill, our camp nurse, her brother-in-law Frosty Walters from down around Kenai and another friend, Ernie Hudson, from the Palmer-Wasilla area, like the rest of us.

That particular morning the four others set out for an old, established camp we had set up, that lies at the base of the Yenlo Hills and is about twenty minutes away by boat. I decided to stay in the new campsite area, on the west side of the Yentna River in the Hewitt-Whiskey subdivision.

It was a nice, sunny day, so I cleaned up the camp a little bit, then headed for the southwest area of the property in the general direction of Hewitt Lake. I had been following a relatively fresh moose track when I came to a path known as "the cat trail." As I followed the trail, the brush became a little denser. I walked at a slow, cautious pace, looking for moose and resting every now and then so I wouldn't become winded—you normally only get one shot in that sort of thick brush.

I was sneaking along quietly when the grizzly charged. In the past I had read to "play dead." But I had always sworn that I would never be attacked without fighting back. However, as the bear sat behind me, I truly believe this strategy saved my life.

It's hard to say how long I lay there, listening to his heavy breathing. After a few minutes, the woods grew silent. I wiped the blood out of my left eye and raised my head. I had to strain to see and hear. My left ear had been torn loose and filled with blood. When I didn't spot the bear, I rose up on my hands and knees. I put my baseball hat on to hold my scalp and my ear. I left my shoulder holster on as a light tourniquet, just in case the bear had severed some arteries in that arm.

Then I reloaded the rifle and stood up. I took a quick survey and didn't see anything anywhere, so I started backtracking my way down the trail. Once I started moving, I never stopped longer than a couple of minutes to catch my wind. I couldn't take the chance of lingering; the bear could be tracking me. It took forty-five minutes to get back to our hunting camp.

By the time I reached the cabin, I was exhausted. I sat down in a chair and thought I could walk down to the boat, but there was no way. I was losing my strength rapidly. I splashed water on my face and neck to cool down a little bit and help stabilize my system. I had just tried to radio for help on the CB without any luck, when I heard a resident of the area call on the radio. I interrupted his transmission and told him that I needed help—quickly. He indicated he'd come right over.

Within the next two or three minutes my brother called on the boat CB, and I informed him of my injury. Troy and Pat stopped what they were doing, left the other two partners on a sandbar and rushed to the cabin to get me ready for transport to a medivac down to Skwentna.

I wasn't sure how Pat and Troy would react to my trauma. I was sitting in the cabin with my good side to the door when they walked in.

"Don't panic," I said. "Everything will be alright."

After recovering from the first seconds of shock, Troy and Pat took forty-five minutes to cut off my upper clothes and bandage my injuries. They loaded me into a three-wheeler and slowly drove me nine hundred to a thousand feet down to the river. Just as we arrived at the river, the man I had contacted earlier on the CB was pulling up in his boat. We sped into Skwentna, and it was all downhill from there. A construction worker with a plane was waiting to take me into Humana Hospital-Alaska. The surgery took about four hours. Now, it's just a matter of healing, both physically and mentally.

"How Am I Gonna Get Out of This?"

In the fall of 1981, Fred Roberts answered a local newspaper ad for an assistant bear guide, thinking the job would be great way to go hunting and get paid for it. Since the hunt was on Kodiak Island and Fred was the only applicant from the area, he got the job. I first met

"Sky," who acquired his nickname from his home state of Montana or "Big Sky Country," in June 1988, and he told me of his ordeal in frightening detail.

Our party consisted of the hunter Bob Tatsch, from La Verne, California, the guide and me. Bob is an excellent hunter and a good storyteller. He kept us entertained with one tale after another.

The bear season started on October 25, but we were unable to make it to camp because of the high winds. Our plan was to fly out to Spiridon Lake, about sixty air-miles due west of the town of Kodiak. After we waited a couple of days, the winds died down enough for safe flying conditions, and we received a call from the air service requesting that we be on the float dock as soon as possible. We couldn't fit all of our gear in the Cessna 206 on the first trip, so I waited until the following day.

When I reached the camp, I spent half of the day getting the equipment squared away. I had brought in a raft and an outboard motor, which we would use to hunt Spiridon Lake, the third largest lake on Kodiak. In the afternoon, we went hunting about three or four miles from camp in the rolling hills, overlooking some valleys and mountainsides. It was sunny and cold, maybe ten to twenty degrees, with a strong wind. On the first day we didn't see any activity.

On my second day we took the raft and motored down to the southeast end of the lake. We were having some problems with the outboard motor, so I dropped off the hunters and arranged to meet them later, after I had taken care of the problem.

It was after lunch when I caught up with them a mile or two beyond the lake. They had shot a deer, boned the meat and were ready for me to pack it in to the boat. We stopped and chatted a bit, and I gave them their lunch—apples, cheese and granola. They pointed me in the direction of the deer carcass and then set out over the top of the hill to hunt one of the valleys on the other side.

As I walked toward the deer through the alders, each step I took through the dead grass and brush crackled like I was walking on dry corn flakes. I never reached the deer. I heard noises that sounded like something was sneaking through the brush. When I looked up, I saw a bear barreling down on me from sixty to seventy feet away. She was chocolate brown, fairly good-sized, and coming at me flat out.

At a time like that most people think that your life flashes before your eyes. My first reaction was, "How am I going to get out of this?" But there was no time. The bear, which seemed to stand eye-level with me on all fours, hooked around the back of me and grabbed my right arm. (I still have the knot where she tore the membrane all to hell.) She lifted me and slammed me onto the ground, then picked me up by my right thigh and dropped me again. This happened several times, and I even remember being upside down in the air. Sometimes I fell to ground, and sometimes she tossed me high enough that I turned a semi-somersault.

At one point the bear happened to throw me down on my face. I landed in the fetal position; fortunately my head lay in a depression in the ground. The bear began to bite me, from one end of my body to the other. Fortunately, the pack, which was secured tightly around my waist and shoulders, spared my back and my head a lot of injuries. For quite a while, the bear took bites out of the pack and picked me up by the straps.

Then the bear ran off, and I thought, "Oh, boy, let's get outta here." But in a moment she was back. When she returned, the bear took a bite out of the left side of my head, above the pack extension. I think the bear would have swallowed my whole head if the extension hadn't been there. Her top left canine pierced my left eyebrow, splitting it open and damaging the lower part of my eye socket.

Now, I couldn't see at all. Both eyes were swollen shut, and my left eye was totally hanging loose. I lay motionless, listening to the bear. I could hear her perfectly, trotting away, returning and leaving again. I propped one eyelid open with my finger to check what was happening and saw two cubs run by. Then I understood why the attack had occurred. I don't think the bear would have challenged me and gone to such extremes just for some deer meat. The sow was trying to protect her cubs.

Finally, the bear was gone. The wind had picked up, so I knew the hunters couldn't hear me from the spot where I had fallen. I half-hobbled and half-crawled about fifty yards to an open area closer to the ridge. I called out their names, knowing they would realize I was in trouble if I shouted while serious hunting was going on.

When the hunters came to find me, they spotted the sow and two cubs, maybe 250 yards away. I suppose they could have shot them, but I don't think that thought entered their minds. Now I had to make it back to camp. Fortunately, my injuries were not bleeding much, and I was not experiencing shock or massive trauma. However, I did have a lot of ripped and exposed flesh, which made getting antibiotics crucial. In some places, my flesh was torn right off the bone. We had no sterile bandages, just a dirty T-shirt, band-aids, vitamins and aspirin. Other than covering my wounds with a T-shirt, there was not too much the others could do.

Because of the terrain and the distance, the hunters could have been hurt if they tried to carry me. And it would have been extremely uncomfortable to be carried. I could only bend one leg. When we came to brush, they had to break branches and limbs or move them out of the way. To make matters worse, my right arm was useless, dangling from my shoulder. The two and a half hours it took to reach the boat seemed like days.

We finally reached our camp on the lake. Regulations require hunting guides to have radio communication of some sort, but for some reason, our senior guide did not have any emergency locater transmitters, hand-held radio or side band radio communicatons like most camps have. The guide was also thinking about setting out for the end of the peninsula and trying to flag down a passing boat (a crab boat) from the beach. I remember thinking that would be like climbing to the top of a mountain and trying to signal a 747 flying at forty-thousand feet. It was darn near impossible.

I was shocked. The guide obviously didn't know that country, even though he had been hunting there for fifteen years.

I said, "Well, first of all, crab season ended over a month ago; there aren't gonna be too many crab boats out there right now." I told him the best bet was to take the boat across the lake and hike three or four miles over to Village Island, which is on Uganik Bay on the north side of Spiridon Peninsula. People live there year round, and I knew that the town was large enough to have a mail stop and send out weather reports.

While the guide set out for Village Island, Bob arranged a distress signal on the beach with some bright orange sleeping pads. Then he prepared a smoke fire. I think it was about one or two o'clock in the afternoon when we heard an airplane. Bob rushed out and tried to light the fire, but couldn't get it going. He grabbed a can of gas and doused the brush and garbage. From fifty yards away, I could hear the *whoosh* of the wood catching. Bob returned a little later with singed eyebrows.

The airplane was the same one that had dropped us off. Complying with Alaskan bush custom, the pilot was flying over our camp to check if everything was okay. With the clear and sunny weather, he spotted our distress signal immediately and dropped to two hundred feet to see what was going on. Bob was in a panic, and as the plane passed over the tent, he almost shot it down with an emergency flare.

As soon as the pilot had landed, he and Bob debated whether or not I should fly back in the airplane. I decided I had better wait for the Coast Guard. Even if they could remove the seats and get me into the 206, I didn't think I would be able to ride safely and comfortably. So the pilot took off again, increasing his altitude to call the Kodiak tower. By chance, a Coast Guard surgeon, Dr. Martin Nemeroff, happened to be listening to his scanner. He grabbed his bag and was on the flight deck in four minutes. They had trouble finding a pilot, but the H-3 reached us less than an hour after the pilot radioed the tower. I think I made it to the base airport before the guide had even returned to camp with help.

An ambulance met us at the airport to rush me to the hospital. Dr. Ron Brockman, an old army doctor, was on duty. Dr. Brockman had operated on several mauling victims before, and I felt very confident in his abilities. Now, you can hardly see the scars on my face. It's pretty hard for me to imagine that my lower face was ever split wide open. I was in the hospital two days, and it probably took another two months to recuperate to the point where I could move around comfortably. However, my desire to be in the woods remains as strong as ever.

My advice for others going into the woods is to always expect the unexpected. You need to be prepared for any type of accident. Should something like that ever happen, you should be prepared to respond by carrying first aid supplies and a radio. Now I always carry a hand-held VHF and a personal ELT. The hand-held radio will reach any aircraft overhead.

During the entire trip in from Kodiak, I thought about my girlfriend, Kathy Byington. This was her first year in Alaska. She's from Boston and was teaching elementary school here in Kodiak. Now she meets a guy that goes out and gets chewed up by a bear. I knew she would be completely shocked.

I was curious to know Kathy's reaction to Sky's experience. When the mauling occurred, she had lived in Kodiak for only several months, after moving from Boston to work as a teacher. They are now married. I asked Kathy how this frightening incident had affected her outlook toward her new boyfriend and her new home.

Funnily enough, it was Halloween when I found out about the accident. At the time, I was cleaning up after a chimney fire that had started in the oil stove. Soot and smoke filled the house, and I was covered with black. Then, I got this phone call about Sky.

It was Fly Right Air Service. A woman asked me if there was anything they could do in regards to "the Mr. Roberts emergency." I just couldn't grasp the situation, and she had to repeat the story three times.

The woman said that Sky had been mauled by a bear and medivaced to the hospital. I was so new to

Kodiak, having been here only three months, that I didn't even know what medivac meant. Everything was completely foreign. I can remember thinking, "What's a bear mauling?"

As soon as I had cleaned off some of the soot, I rushed to the hospital and found out Sky had been there three and a half hours. I had to wait another half an hour before I was permitted to see him. At that point, I was glad I hadn't known about the mauling any earlier, or I would have had to wait and worry for four hours.

When I first saw Sky, I was relieved, although he looked awful. He was bandaged up. His eye was closed. Tears were coming out, and he was very pale. But I knew he was going to be all right.

One day after school I went to see him at the hospital and was told that Sky had checked out. It was pouring rain like it can rain only in Kodiak. I went home and waited for him. Finally, Sky showed up about six that evening. He was soaked and said he was tired of being cooped up in the hospital and had to get some fresh air.

Sky's recovery period was a very trying time, because he was on pain killers and would say things that were out of character. I was concerned about him having nightmares. But Sky is a tough guy and won't let anything stop him. Despite my worrying, I knew he'd be just fine.

Sky has been bombarded with questions about his mauling. The answers he's come up with reflect a great deal about his sense of humor and his personal philosophy.

Sky Roberts' List of the Ten Most Asked Mauling Questions

1. Question: How do you feel?
   Answer: I feel fine, but the bear feels better.

2. Question: Was the bear big?
   Answer: In comparison, it was smaller than a service station, but bigger than a tow truck.

3. Question: Weren't you really scared,?
   Answer: Not really—it was quite reassuring knowing the bear was ten times my size and there was nothing I could do.

4. Question: What were you thinking when the bear was chewing you up?
   Answer: She was ripping my brand new Pendleton hunting shirt and had tore my lucky suspenders.

5. Question: Did the bear do much damage?
   Answer: Other than ruining my shirt and suspenders, my back pack is full of holes and small items such as granola bars fall out.

6. Question: Were you in a lot of pain?
   Answer: Actually it was a warm sensation similar to being dragged over cactus bushes.

7. Question: I'll bet that you never want to go through that again.
   Answer: It was quite rewarding. I learned a lot from the experience and I would recommend it to any outdoorsman.

8. Question: When you feel better are you going to go out and get the bear?
    Answer: No, I have a system where the bears get me.

9. Question: Are you afraid to go out in the woods again?
    Answer: I get flashbacks as soon as I step off the pavement. I am considering moving to Detroit, where I can walk around without fear of being harmed.

10. Question: Will you ever get over this traumatic experience?
    Answer: What experience?

After interviewing Sky Roberts, I wanted to learn more about U.S. Coast Guard rescue procedures. I spoke with Chief Cook in Kodiak, who explained the rudimentary aspects of air rescue.

We have two U.S. Coast Guard Search and Rescue centers in Alaska. We coordinate our search and rescue with the Sitka-based contingent, which handles the Southeast portion as far north as Cape Yakataga. While we coordinate our efforts with Sitka, the district office in Juneau handles extended searches or those involving several units.

On rescue missions we fly a helicopter or a C-130 Hercules, which is a cargo plane. We can go out to Cold Bay, or farther if we refuel. The choppers will fly different speeds depending on the weather. Choppers fly at one hundred knots; the C-130 flies at 350–380 miles per hour.

Our operations center is on watch twenty-four

hours a day. We maintain two people on watch during the work day. When we receive a report of an injury in the field, we confirm the report. The operations center notifies us. If it's an extreme emergency, we set the beepers off for both the maintenance crew, who will get the helicopter ready, and the pilots who will be flying it. We also call the flight surgeon on all emergencies.

We have two procedures on emergencies: 1) for extreme emergencies we start the launch right away; 2) for minor incidents, we call the flight surgeon, a medical doctor with flying experience. We get as much information as possible so the flight surgeon can make the best judgement possible—will it further compound the injury if we put a patient in an aircraft? What's the best thing to do for a heart attack victim or one who may have the bends? In the most extreme cases the flight surgeon usually says to get the guy to the hospital right away.

We make necessary arrangements with medical facilities, notify family members and try to get a medical background on the victim. We arrange for ambulance transportation from the Kodiak airport or the municipal airport downtown because it's closer to the hospital, for extreme emergencies.

A normal flight includes a crew of five in the H-3 helicopter—a pilot, co-pilot and three crewmen (avionics man, flight mechanic and corpsman). We have EMT-trained crew members also.

The normal time for launch is less than thirty minutes. Generally twenty minutes is a fast launch. During the day we get off quicker than a night launch—in fifteen to twenty minutes, as opposed to thirty.

Face to Face with Two Brownies

Soldotna businessman Rollin Braden is an avid outdoorsman, but he had no way of anticipating or warding off an attack by two brown bears on a moose-hunting trip.

In September 1984, my Dad, my brother Wayne, my friend Darrel and I were hunting in the Caribou Hills. Our moose camp is located twenty miles off the Sterling Highway east of Ninilchick, Alaska. A summer-maintained gravel road gets you fifteen miles into the Caribou Hills. From that point, you can only travel by all-terrain vehicles along the six more miles of seismograph trails that lead near our cabin. There are many steep hills and bottomless mudholes, but the fantastic hunting and scenery make it all worthwhile.

Our camp sits among thick timber at about two-thousand-feet elevation. The surrounding mountains rise up over the tree line about thirty-two hundred feet. Winter comes early. Usually by mid-September, we have our first snowfall and by mid-October, winter is there to stay.

Our hunting camp differs from most in that area. Some would consider it very crude, but it provides us with a safe and comfortable shelter. The cabin is made from an old eight-by-ten-foot camp trailer, which has a bed and food storage cabinets, attached to an eight-foot-square living room and an eight-foot-square bunk room that sleeps four. At the entrance to the cabin we have a sixteen-foot-square metal roof, open on three sides and supported with wood poles. Under the roof in one corner, we dug a hole in the ground and circled it with flat rocks for a fire pit. Everyone does their own cooking, and each frying pan hangs from the ceiling.

Once we reached our cabin and got situated, we all went hunting in our favorite spot—a place we called the moose pasture where we had been hunting since 1968. Moose roam freely through this area. There are usually enough bulls so that we all get one or at least enough to share.

Within a few days of our arrival, Dad and Wayne dropped bulls, with racks ranging in size from thirty to forty inches. After this success, they both decided to take a break from hunting one day and drive their four-wheelers up to Lou Clarke's dinner. Lou is a neighbor who lives about two miles away, and he puts on a big spaghetti feed every year. Since Darrel and I only had a day and a half before the season ended, we opted to stay at the camp and hunt.

We didn't waste any time. We only took breaks from hunting long enough to rush to the cabin, a half mile away, grab a bite to eat and get right back to looking for a bull. Darrel was hunting from a tree stand. At about five o'clock he dropped his bull. I let out a Comanche yell of celebration and threw my hat up into the air. Then I made my way over to Darrel to help him dress the moose. Because it was getting late, we decided to wait until the next day to completely quarter the bull and haul it out. As we started to walk along the the willowed trail to the cabin, we spotted my Dad and brother about a mile away, returning from supper.

Just then we heard brush cracking and noises in the grass. I was itching to get my bull, since I'd be the only one skunked if I didn't fill my tag. I asked Darrel to stay on the trail and watch, so if I spooked the moose and couldn't get a shot, he could do the job for me.

Cautiously, I picked my way through the alders and spruce trees. I had to sneak through grass that grew over my head and every few steps, I'd stop . . . look

. . . listen. First I'd hear noise in one area, then I'd hear it in a different direction. For about ten minutes I stalked the noises; my binoculars hung from my neck and I gripped my rifle, tense and alert to each sound and movement. I kept looking for signs of moose—droppings or a smell. Usually I can smell a moose before I see it.

I held my gun with the barrel pointing to my left, just as ready as I could be for any kind of confrontation. I was creeping around a large spruce tree when two brown bears broke out of the grass, tearing toward me at full speed. I figured I could gain a second or two if I backed around the tree. As I stepped back, I whipped my gun around and fired at one of the bears.

The shot was futile. They kept on coming. The next thing I knew they had hit me, knocked me to the ground, and both were on top of me, chewing at my body. At first I tried to resist the attack by moving my arms or legs, but every time I'd move a limb, they'd bite at it. I decided it was no good to try to defend myself, and I forced my body to relax.

I turned my face and stomach down into the moss, trying to protect my head and abdomen from their canines. At one point the bears stopped chewing. I waited a few seconds, but when I raised my head, both bears were steadily watching from about ten feet away. They saw me move and bolted back to chew on me some more. Their bites were furious. I could hear their grunting and blowing and feel their breath on my face, as they licked and slurped. Now I had a dozen bites all over my body—on my hand, shoulder, butt, leg.

I kept thinking, "Is this the way I was going to go?" When I thought of death, I started to panic and felt this overpowering urge to run, but I knew better than to move again.

I decided to keep my face down, until they had left for a long period of time. When they did stop chewing, I had to force myself to lie quietly. Had the bears left? Could I be so lucky? Finally, I couldn't stand it any longer. I got up and looked around. I didn't see them. As I glanced around me, blood poured into my eyes. A part of my scalp hung down in my face, and I touched the top of my head to check the damage. The scalp was ripped four or five different ways, and in some spots, I could even feel my skull. One tear ran straight over my head from ear to ear, and another tear ran down the back of my head from the tear on the top of my head.

Once I had pushed my scalp back into place again, I took off my outer heavy wool shirt and wrapped it around my head. I kept looking around frantically for the bears. I didn't see them, so I started backing away and then turned and jogged through the trees. I whispered a prayer, "Dear Lord, help me find the right direction out of here." I was disoriented and yelled Darrel's name, hoping that his shouts would show me the right direction.

I had to yell about three times before he answered me. When Darrel heard the shot and the noise in the woods, he thought I had dropped my moose. Then he heard me yelling and thought I was just calling out in excitement over my kill.

Finally, Darrel detected something wrong in my voice and answered me through the thick, high grass. As I jogged in his direction, he ran toward me. Seeing me holding the shirt on my head and the blood running down my face, he knew what had happened.

By then, my brother had caught up with him. I didn't even stop running as I told them I had been mauled by bears. I knew that I was losing a lot of blood and had to get to a doctor quickly.

Darrel and Wayne had a hard time keeping up with me. Once we got back to the cabin, I told them I had to get to town as soon as possible. They were both completely stunned, with pale faces and mouths hanging wide open. I had to tell Darrel and Wayne what to do. We decided to rig up one of the four-wheelers with a trailer to take me out. But that turned out to be an ordeal in itself. The trailer was no more than a school-bus seat with two wheels on it.

To complicate matters, Wayne had decided he was going to drive. His own machine was down the trail about a mile, where he had left it to run to us after hearing the shots. My four-wheeler and Darrel's were next to the cabin, but Wayne didn't know how to drive either one of them very well.

I finally went over to my four-wheeler and started it for my brother, saying, "Take this one." He jumped on it and rode down the trail to the spot where the trailer was parked. After hooking up the vehicles, he headed back to the cabin to get me and in his rush to return, broke the axle underneath the trailer.

While Darrel and I waited for Wayne to return, my Dad showed up. He had also come to check on us when he heard the shots, but couldn't catch up with us on the trail. When Dad saw me, he turned white and looked absolutely petrified. After hearing the gun and seeing the blood, he said his first thought was that I had shot myself.

Now our main concern was to rig up another device to carry me. We had another trailer that we sometimes used for hauling meat. After the others had hooked it up and laid a mattress on top, I got in and sat down. Someone wrapped a towel around my head and laid a heavy parka over me, then I braced myself for the six-mile ride over the bumpy trail to our pickup truck.

While Wayne drove, my Dad rode on the back of the machine, periodically glancing down at me in the trailer. Fortunately, the blood had almost stopped running by the time we left the cabin. Although the pain of the bear bites was dulled by shock and excitement, one deep wound in my butt was hurting badly. I had a Copenhagen can in my back pocket and all during the hour-long ride to the pickup, I bounced up and down on that hard can. When we reached the truck, I threw it as hard as I could into the woods.

Our luck did not improve once we reached the truck. The pickup had a flat tire. While I lay on the trailer, Dad and Wayne made record time changing it. Then we got in the truck and drove fifteen miles down the chuck-holed backroad, which led out to the highway. I kept telling Wayne to go faster, but he stubbornly kept his speed, saying it would be better to go slow and make sure we made it.

When we got to the highway at Ninilchik an hour later, we decided to stop at a restaurant and call ahead to Soldotna so the hospital would be prepared for my arrival. The people at the hospital talked my Dad into waiting for a Ninilchick ambulance. In ten minutes, an old Suburban arrived. It was cold as ice inside and the windows were frozen up. After they loaded me in the back, three women that I knew personally started cutting my clothes off with scissors. They stripped me right down to my skivvies and my legs were shaking uncontrollably with the cold. Then they placed heat packs under me to bring my temperature back up.

In Clam Gulch another ambulance met us to take me to the Soldotna hospital. However, the Soldotna hospital isn't equipped to take care of the type of wounds I had, so they packed my injuries with ice and planned to medivac me to Anchorage.

At the time North Pacific Air was contracted to fly all emergency cases from Soldotna to Anchorage. Supposedly, the company was on beeper-call twenty-four hours a day. But the hospital staff tried to reach the flight people for an amazing three and a half hours with no luck. Finally, they decided to call the Anchorage Air Medivac, which flew to Soldotna and picked me up. It was probably two o'clock in the morning when I reached Providence Hospital in Anchorage—nearly seven hours after my mauling.

My attending physician Dr. Scully asked me if it would bother me to tell about the attack one more time, and I assured him it was okay. While he took pictures and cleaned my wounds, I told him the entire story. Although I lost a tremendous amount of blood, I never did lose consciousness during the ordeal.

I was kept in the intensive care unit four days and remained in the hospital four more. It took more than two hundred staples to repair my scalp. My medication knocked me out for the first three days of my stay. Dr. Scully came in almost every day to check on me. He wasn't concerned about the wounds as much as he was worried about the possibility of infection. My left hand did become infected, and an infection specialist came in at least once a day to monitor my progress. He told me that I had eight different bugs, two of which he couldn't identify.

The pain began as soon as I arrived at the hospital. Every time the nurses would come to clean my wounds, the blood would leave my face and go all the way to my toes. They were so rough, and I definitely got no sympathy.

The dirt all over my body didn't make me feel too much better. I had been hunting for nine days when the attack occurred and had spent two days in the hospital before I was cleaned. Although blood was caked in my beard and everywhere, the nurses never did wash my face or clean anywhere besides the wounds. When Kathy came up from Soldotna to the hospital, she washed me up, and I felt 100 percent better.

After I left the hospital, Kathy, who I was just dating at the time, came over to clean all my wounds three times a day. Some of the bear bites were three inches deep and had to be attended almost constantly in order to heal properly.

Considering my injuries, I healed very rapidly. Several people have come into my store—even those from Outside, who have read the story—and asked, "Isn't this the place where a guy was mauled by a bear?" When I tell them it was me, they look a little disappointed because they don't see an ear missing or disfiguring scars.

I haven't stopped hunting since the accident, but I'm much more cautious. In the past, I've split off from my partners to hunt by myself. I rarely hunt by myself anymore, and if I am alone, I stick to a tree stand.

My attitude toward life in general has also changed. Things that used to seem like big burdens or problems are not as important to me anymore. Now that I've had a second chance, I like to take life a little bit easier.

A Nightmare and a Burial

In November 1988, I bumped into Jim Derks, a retired colleague, who asked if I had heard about the most recent bear maulings. I hadn't, but sure enough, when I went home to check the daily newspaper, the frightening story was splashed across the front page.

Two men on unrelated hunting trips had been mauled by bears—one was injured, the other killed.

Duane Christensen of Fairbanks and a partner were deer hunting on Kodiak. Harley Sievenpiper of Juneau and two friends were also deer hunting, but they were hunting the southern end of Baranof Island in Southeast Alaska.

Christensen was gutting a deer near Uganik Lake, when he discovered a bear, forty feet away in full charge. He waved to avert the attack, but the bear kept coming. The hunter shot his .338 Winchester magnum from the hip and hit, but the bullet seemed to have no effect.

In seconds the bear had knocked Christensen onto his back. When Christensen realized that he wouldn't be able to reload his gun, he rolled onto his belly to protect his vital organs and hollered to his partner, Bill Burgess.

As the brown grizzly sow began chewing on her victim's buttocks, Burgess came running and saw what appeared to be a bear jumping up and down. While the angry mother brown/grizzly chewed on Christensen's buttocks, Burgess risked a shot from eighty yards; the shot struck the bear in the head.

The bear rolled off Christensen and lay four to five feet away. Her breathing stopped briefly, but then resumed. Burgess shot the bear three more times. What became of the sow's cubs remained a mystery to the hunters, but they wasted no time leaving the area.

Christensen could walk, and the hunters were able to reach camp. They spent two days awaiting rescue. Christensen's injuries, including infected bear bites on his back, legs and buttocks, were treated close to home at Fairbanks Memorial Hospital.

Christensen believes the bear was conditioned to their gunshots and followed fresh, deer-blood spoor to him.

*Another deer hunter, Harley Sievenpiper of Juneau,
was not as fortunate as Duane Christensen.*

*Don Kluting of Sitka led the search for Sievenpiper,
whose partners reported him missing on Friday, November 4. When I called and asked Don if he'd be willing to
share his experience, he was very helpful. Born and
raised in Sitka, Don worked as an EMT with the Sitka
Volunteer Fire Department, served as a team leader
with the Sitka Search and Rescue Team and has been
trained in tracking. In addition, Don has hunted since he
was twelve years old, so he was well-prepared for the
demanding job on Baranof Island.*

Friday night I received a phone call from Rollin
Young, a state trooper. He told me that there had been
a bear attack down at Port Alexander and asked me to
come with him and check it out. Harley Sievenpiper's
two partners, both in their mid-thirties and experienced hunters, had reported him missing. Their story
sounded pretty dismal, so we figured we were setting
out on a body recovery rather than a rescue attempt.

I gathered all of my normal gear and met Rollin
down at Bell Air, a charter service, on Saturday morning at a quarter past seven. We flew to Port Conclusion
on the south end of Baranof Island, where the mauling
had occurred. We arrived on the scene at eight o'clock
and talked to the skipper of one of the fishing vessels
that was to serve as our command post from the bay.

Ten to twelve volunteers were already in the field.
We radioed ahead and told them to stay put because we
wanted to catch up and get organized before we proceeded.

Rollin and I then went straight to the beach and
started up the trail. We had barely begun hiking when
I noticed something blue in a patch of muskeg off the

side of the trail. I went over to investigate and found a pack, a rifle, glasses, gloves, a hat, a lighter and a watch all lying in this area. The other members of the search team had missed this spot, which was about two hundred yards from the beach and what we believed to be the actual scene of the mauling.

I called Rollin over. Sievenpiper had obviously been sitting under a spruce tree, near some blueberry brush, looking across the muskeg and waiting for a deer to show. His rifle was on safety, and the scope covers were off.

We could see where the bear had run down a little knob rising up behind the victim and charged him from thirty yards away. The tracks in the muck on the side of the muskeg knob were pressed in deeply, which leads me to believe that the bear was on the run and charging hard. At that speed I don't think Harley would have even known the bear was coming. He might have heard something, but by the time he was able to turn around, the bear would have had him.

At that point we proceeded up the hill, following the trail that the bear had left from dragging the body. The path was wide and covered with blood. It paralleled the beach for half a mile, bordered with patches of thick blueberry brush.

The rest of the search party from Port Alexander was waiting about two hundred yards up the trail. The two hunters that had been with Harley started on the search with us, but quickly turned back when we reached areas where there was a lot of blood and gore. Understandably, they were really upset.

Apparently, the hunters had been about three quarters of a mile from Harley, when they heard him scream. They fired three shots in the air, hoping that their partner would respond. But the scream was the last sound they heard. Harley never fired back. When the men rushed over to see what was wrong, they found the bloody trail and torn clothing. I believe that if they had followed the path immediately, they might have gotten hurt themselves.

We split the team into two groups. Six members stayed with Rollin, and I headed up the trail with the other six. Since I have had training in tracking, I went ahead with my group, and Rollin's followed. According to normal procedure, each time I found a clue—torn clothing, blood or bone chips—I would radio back to Rollin, and he would hike to that point and log any data.

The bear's path switched from one game trail to the next and then went off in its own direction. We continued to find more clothing—bits of pants, a wool shirt, boots, long Johns and socks. About a mile up the trail, we lost the traces of bone and blood spoor, but I could still make out spots where the body had been dragged.

That's when we heard the bear growl. I quickly radioed Rollin and told him we had a bear in the area. Rollin was about two hundred yards down the hill and gave me instructions to kill the bear if I got a good, open shot.

I left three of my men on the ridgeline and took the other three with me. We veered to the left for about twenty yards. Two members of the party became a little bit nervous, so they stayed behind at that point, while Jim Lange and I climbed up the hill another twenty yards to see if we could get a clear shot at the bear.

Suddenly, we saw him. At the same instant we spotted the bear, he took off charging full-force for the three guys I'd left on the ridge. The bear definitely knew all seven of us were there, but he made the decision to go directly for the three men.

The bear came down that hill like a freight train. It all happened so fast, it was just unbelievable. I'd hate to say how much time it took for the bear to cover the seventy yards, but I swear it was just a second of two. That bear was just a blur.

He started through the brush, knocking down dead trees that were two and three inches in diameter like they were toothpicks. Jim and I each fired a round at fifty yards through the brush. We hit the bear through the ribs, but the bear didn't even slow down. I was working the bolt on my Ruger as fast as I could. I've always heard stories about bears not being able to run downhill fast, but that wasn't true this time!

By the time we each chambered another round, the bear was within twenty yards of the three men on the ridge. I knew I only had time for one more shot before he would be on top of them. I ran closer to get a better shot and fired. Jim fired right after me. Luckily, the bear stopped charging and turned toward us. Just by the stare in his eyes, you could tell that the bear knew we had shot him and that if he reached us, he would kill.

When Jim and I fired, we both hit the animal in the shoulder. As he whipped toward us, the bear flipped and landed upside down. That was it. I put one more insurance shot through his head. Then it took me exactly eleven steps to walk over to the bear. The three guys on the ridge were within two steps of the bear.

During the charge, one man had taken a step backwards, slipped and was hanging onto a tree over a twenty-foot drop-off. Another had misfired; when he went to take the shell out of the chamber, he had bent the casing and jammed his rifle. The third guy had taken a step backwards and fallen into a hole up to his waist. He panicked during the attack and began firing in the air, managing to hit the bear in the foot one time with a .30-30.

We were all armed. I was using a .338 magnum. Jim was using a .338-06, basically a .30-06 shell dressed up to a .33-caliber.

We radioed Rollin and told him everything was okay; the search party was alive, and we had killed the bear. Although I was completely calm during the charge, I had begun shaking as soon as the bear dropped. I was realizing that if our shots hadn't hit the bear in the right spot, we could have had three or four bodies on our hands.

Now we continued up the hill seventy yards to the point where the bear had first growled at us. There, we found the body. It was half-buried; the back of the body was exposed, with sticks and dirt piled around. We could see clearly where the bear had laid on top of the mound. Rollin took his pictures, and we proceeded to roll the body over and move it into the bag. I took a better look than I should have at the body. It was in very bad shape.

We skinned the bear. The skull was twenty-four inches, and the hide squared roughly nine-and-a-half or ten feet. It was a big bear. When I talked to the game biologist here in town, he told me the animal was in excellent physical shape. The bear was very strong, with no body fat whatsoever, although bears at that time of the year usually carry a bit of fat. The hide was also in perfect condition.

Don was beginning to regain his composure by the time I spoke with him, but searching for the missing hunter and recovering his remains was definitely a grisly and unforgettable task.

Now I'm much calmer. When I returned to Sitka the day we shot the bear, I realized what had just happened, and it was like reliving a horror movie. It amazed me how the bear dragged the body an entire mile or so and then moved up fifteen to sixteen hundred feet in elevation into the spruce and hemlock. It's also unusual to encounter a man-eating bear. That animal charged his victim, knocked him down and then proceeded to feed on him. Then, the bear charged us. He was completely wild.

People need to know more about the bear's power and speed so they can respect the animal more. Perhaps this whole situation could have been avoided if Harley had kept a partner with him. The bear would have charged him, but they might have had a chance. Now that I've seen this, I'm going to be a hell of a lot more cautious in the woods. I plan to watch my back and listen to sounds much more closely from now on.

Nearly a Statistic

Research for this book brought a multitude of letters and phone calls. One letter led to several stories from Ben Forbes of Sitka. Ben is a registered guide who has worked extensively with Search and Rescue operations. One story was of an unusual and eerie discovery in a drifting boat.

When I was working at Excursion Inlet, one of my men owned a cruiser, and every chance we got we would go out and look the country over for bear sign. One time we went over to Mud Bay, across Icy Straits from Excursion Inlet. As we came into the river mouth and anchored, we saw another fishing boat there. There was no skiff around so we assumed that the man was ashore. It was in the fall; deer season was open, so it was very likely he was hunting. And just as we anchored, a skiff drifted down the river, out into the ocean where the fishing boat was anchored.

While we thought the hunter had probably forgotten to tie up his skiff securely, something may have gone wrong. We decided to rescue it and see if we couldn't take it up the river and give it back to him. I rowed over to intercept this skiff. When I got over to it, I looked in it; a man lay unconscious in the bottom of the boat, in a big pool of blood. I tied a line on it real quick and rowed it back to the cruiser.

We got him aboard, dried off and undressed and found that he had been mauled by a bear. He had been bitten through the leg in the thigh, and the leg was broken. The leg was badly lacerated from the bear's teeth. And the bear had also clawed him on the back, ripped his back open a little bit, tried to bite him on the head and tore part of his scalp loose. He was a real mess to look at.

So we cleaned him up, dried him off, got him warmed up and bandaged. He regained consciousness after a while and told us about what had happened. And as we pieced the story together, we filled in some of the details that were pretty obvious.

He said he'd shot two deer up on the mountainside. One fell right where he hit it, and the other one ran down the mountain and into the brush and timber. So he dressed the first one out and started down the mountain to get the second one. He found the deer down in thick brush, and as he was going down the hillside to it, he stumbled onto a bear that had claimed it.

As he came through the brush to the deer, the bear jumped him, grabbed him by the leg and just shook him like a cat would shake a mouse. The bear broke his leg, dropped him, and clawed him on the back with his paw and tried to bite his head. The bear's teeth just snapped across his head, and then he picked up the deer and left.

The man lay there for a while, and then managed to crawl down to his boat. He had pulled the boat up on the beach. The tide had gone out, and the boat was tied up to a tree. So he untied the line, crawled over the side and got in the boat, knowing the tide would come in after a while and float the boat and then the river current would take him out the river. He figured when he got out close to his boat, he could row over to it and get on board and probably take care of himself.

As it happened, he passed out, and if we hadn't been there to see his drifting skiff when he went out the river mouth, he would have been another mysteriously missing fisherman; the tide would have taken him out to the ocean, and he'd have probably never been seen again.

Rather than waste time towing the stranger's boat, we split up. The owner of our boat took him into Hoonah to catch a plane into Juneau. I rowed over to his fishing boat, picked up the anchor and took it into Hoonah and left it with the U.S. Marshall. Then we went right back to Excursion Inlet and back to work.

Later we heard the man was in the hospital for about seven weeks before returning to Hoonah to re-claim his boat. And he apparently got along okay. Too bad, I don't remember his name at all; in fact, I'm not so sure I even knew what his name was, and none of us over at Excursion Inlet ever did hear from him. I don't think he even knew who picked him up and brought him into Hoonah.

This table of bear maulings lists over 170 recorded mauling incidents. Not all bear maulings in Alaska are recorded here, as no single state agency compiles mauling statistics. Also, this list does not include maulings that involved polar bears.

Bear Maulings in Alaska

Victim	Place	Date	Type of Bear	Apparent Reason for Attack	Details of Attack and Outcome	Fatal
1. Captain Healy	Sitka	Pre-1895				
2. A prospector	Lower Yukon River	c. 1900 or before	"glacier"	Mistook man for sheep or hunger	Shot once, used knife, grappled, tumbled over cliff.	
3. Archie Park James Leroy Anton Eide	Valdez diggings?	1901	"glacier"	Hunting-wounded bear	Archie was mauled, played dead. Mongrel dog intervened. Bear chased dog. Bear left. Partners sewed him up with an old sail needle and snowshoe lacings.	
4. Harry Johnson	Kern Creek, Seward (mile 72)	1908	brown	Surprised sow and cubs	Yelled, hit her, didn't fight anymore.	
5. Bill Riordan	Baranof Island	Fall 1908	brown	Surprised sow and cubs	Fought, kicked. Tried to leave after initial mauling, mauled worse.	
6. Man	Valdez Trail	c. 1909	brown	Surprised		X
7. U.S. Deputy Marshal	Mole Harbor, Admiralty Island	1909	brown			X
8. Two native boys	Cold Bay	1910	2 brown		Boys followed wounded bear; second bear struck boys from behind.	XX
9. Farmer	Seward	1911	brown	Surprised	Backed up, ran, tried to stay on stomach, was knocked unconscious, walked to help.	

Bear Maulings in Alaska (cont.)

Victim	Place	Date	Type of Bear	Apparent Reason for Attack	Details of Attack and Outcome	Fatal
10. Allen Hassleborg	Admiralty Island	1912	brown	Wounded	Played dead; bear left.	
11. Otto Bergstrom	Seward	Fall 1913	brown	Surprised; too close	Mauled.	
12. Moose hunter (partner of George Clyde)	Chickaloon Flats	Fall 1913	brown	Wounded	Cheechako tried to trail bear; was killed.	X
13. King Thurman	Chickaloon Flats	1914	brown		King found dead with pistol on chest; bullet hole in head.	X
14. A miner	Prince William Sound	c. 1915	brown			X
15. H. E. Peterson	Hope	November 2, 1915		Hunter-wounded bear	Followed bear, which turned on him and tore him to pieces.	X
16. Pete Kivian	Paramanof Bay, Afognak Island	c. 1916	brown	Surprised a previously wounded bear	Got off one shot, moved after initial mauling (conjecture); bear died of wounds.	X
17. Mr. Stockman	Beluga River	Fall 1916	brown?			X
18. Earl Hirst and partner	Valdez, Cordova	1917	large brownie	Surprised	Pack-saddling horses. Partner shot bear; bear attacked him; Hirst shot bear six times, killing it.	
19. Guen, the brown bear hunter	Paramanof Bay	c. 1918	brown	Wounded?		X

	Location	Date	Bear	Circumstance	Details	
20. Clarence Thompson	Falcon Bay, Chichagof Island	April 22, 1920	brown	Hunting. Surprised bear on deer kill.	Thompson fired two unaimed shots; bear bit him and tore his clothes off; Thompason crawled two miles to water and was found next morning. He never lost consciousness.	X
21. Two prospectors	Hoonah Sound	August 1921	female bear	Prospectors tried to dissuade bear from eating their provisions. Bear charged.	One climbed tree. She mauled the other. Tree climber got down and hit bear on the nose with a pick. She thumped him and left them for dead. They crawled for two days to Hoonah. One prospector later went insane from tooth wound that penetrated brain.	
22. Native	Baranof Island	Fall 1921			Two natives were charged. One escaped and returned later to find mangled partner.	X
23. Sam Fedderson Henry Knight	Chitsia Mountain	November 1921	brown sow by den	Hunter mistook bear for moose.	Knight wounded bear. Returned with Fedderson and was mauled. Fedderson shot bear off.	
24. Jess Sethington	Unuk River	1923	brown	Wounded?	Probably killed by Old Groaner	X
25. James Orr	Ugashik	November 10, 1925	brown bear (1,400 pounds)	Wounded bear charged	Hunting. Shot bear four times with .30-30, and bear fled to brush; bear attacked Orr; Orr died an hour and a half later. Bear died also.	X
26. Dick Wroworth	Klutina River	October–November 1927	brown		Bear knocked man into campfire, where he remained for fifteen hours before crawling to his trapping cabin; help arrived later.	

Bear Maulings in Alaska (cont.)

Victim	Place	Date	Type of Bear	Apparent Reason for Attack	Details of Attack and Outcome	Fatal
27. Peter Jorgensen	Forty-Mile country	August 1929	grizzly		Hand-to-hand; bear knocked him down and fled.	
28. Jack Thayer	Admiralty Island	October 1929	brown	Surprised	Shot once, bear mauled and left. His partner survived by scaling a tree.	X
29. Titus Demidoff	Indian River, Sitka	1936	brown	Following bear	No time to use gun. Bear attacked him, shook him unconscious; bear left.	
30. Man	Southeastern	Between 1930-1941	brown			X
31. Mike Kalmanof	Kodiak	Fall 1930	brown		Hunting.	
32. Fred Zanoff	Kanatak	November 1930	brown	Ambushed from behind woodpile	Bear struck boy's chest, knocking him into stream. Boy died two days later.	X
33. Harry Lance	Chichagof Island	August 1931	brown sow and cubs	Got off one shot, feigned death; bear left and later died.		
34. Greg Brown	Chulitna Bay, Alaska Peninsula	1932 or 1933	brown	Wounded	Bear mauled Brown and left. Brown regained consciousness and killed bear. Brother rescued him and returned him to a cabin where Greg sewed himself up with a sail needle.	
35. Wayne Phillips Art Hoefer	Chichagof Island	September 1935	brown	Surprised	Deer hunting. Shot once, tried to get pocket knife, yelled, partner (teenager) ran from 50 yards and scared bear away.	
36. Eli Metrokin	Rainy Pass	1935			Shot, wounded, killed bear.	

Name	Location	Date	Bear	Situation	Description	
37. H.A. Dahl	Hood Bay, Baranof Island	c. 1936	brown	Surprised	Deer hunting. No time to fire, fought, fell, drew knees up, covered face with arms, yelled. Bear left. Dahl moved, shoved fists down bear's throat, shot and killed bear.	
38. W. M. Nutter	Skilak Lake	Fall 1936	black	Surprised sow with cubs	Bear treed him, clawed his legs. He shot and killed it with a .22 pistol.	
39. Alvin Denis	Cordova area (Copper River & N.W. Railway)	November 1937	brown	Sow with cubs	Chesapeake dog drove bear off.	
40. Bruce Johnstone	Southeastern	c. 1939	brown	Wounded bear	Shot, wrestled, held bear's jaws; client shot bear off.	
41. Alexis Ungyak	Chignik	November 6, 1939	brown	Surprised	Stabbed bear to death with a knife.	
42. Rade Peckovich	Admiralty Island	Pre-1940	brown	Surprised	Grabbed bear, jammed head under bear's jaw, poked fingers into bear's nose. Partner shot bear off.	
43. "Wild Bill" Matilla	Nakwasina Passage, Sitka	December 12, c. 1940s–1950s	4 brown	Bears protecting kill.	Played dead; bears left.	
44. Charley Wells	Fish Bay, S.E.	c. 1940s–1950s?	brown?	Surprised	Charley, with a brace on his leg, shot deer. Bear mauled. When partner Phil Williams arrived, bear was gone.	X
45. Assistant guide	Southeastern	c. 1940s–1950s	brown	Sow with cub	Victim ran and was decapitated by bear's swipe.	X
46. Ed Younkey		1940s–1950s				X

Bear Maulings in Alaska (cont.)

Victim	Place	Date	Type of Bear	Apparent Reason for Attack	Details of Attack and Outcome	Fatal
47. Nick Lean	Upper Russian Lake, Kenai Peninsula	c. 1940s	brown	Surprised	Hunting. Victim had no time to shoot. Dove into brush on stomach. The guide, Nelson, shot bear, but momentum carried it onto Nick on slope below; bear mauled pack board. Partner shot bear off.	
48. John Gregg	Chena Hot Springs	November 1940	grizzly	Surprised at man's cache	Bear jumped Gregg, who shot it. Dog intervened. Bear fled. Gregg shot twice more and killed bear.	
49. Frank Barnes	Stikine River	October 6, 1940	brown	Surprised sow with cubs		X
50. Big Jim Kasko and son	Fishermen's Point, Tenakee Inlet	c. Fall 1940	brown	Surprised	Fired once, grappled, shot and killed bear.	
51. Man	Southeastern	Pre-1941	brown		Played dead; bear left.	
52. Army sergeant		Pre-October 1943	black		Blackie approached swimmer. They traded blows, bear swam away; man taken to hospital.	
53. Lawrence Swensen	Steele Creek, Forty Mile Country	c. 1943			Swensen may have died of natural causes.	X
54. Olaf Heller	Lisianski Strait	c. 1943	brown		Fired once; hit bear with gun; bear left.	
55. Robert Boyd Eddie Wilhelmy	Kodiak	Pre-1943	brown cubs		Hiking. Encountered bears. Men climbed a tree. Bear chewed on one; the other jumped out to distract her and was bitten.	

Name	Location	Date	Bear	Circumstance	Notes	
56. Ivanovitch	Malina Bay, Afognak Island	c. 1945	brown			X
57. Bud Thayer	Eagle Creek	July 1946	"brown"	Wounded	Wrestled in water; partner shot bear off.	
58. A. F. Blaine	Minto, Fort Selkirk	August 1946	grizzly		Tried to fire; safety on. Bear knocked him down, bit him; dog diverted bear, and Blaine fired. Blaine had been mauled three times previously.	X
59. Oscar Larson	Unuk River	October 23, 1947	brown	Sow with cubs	No time to use gun. Bear knocked him down; he stayed still. She bit him several times, then left. Larson has had three other near-maulings.	
60. George Harju	Juneau	Fall 1947		Too close?	Deer hunting. Bear knocked him down and chewed his foot. Partner shot and killed bear.	
61. Lee Ellis	Gambier Bay	1948	brown	Wounded	Guiding. He fired once. Bear shot off by client.	
62. "Pappy" Walker	Whitney Cannery, Kenai	July 1948	brown		No gun; Walker kicked her, fell to the ground, covered head with arm. Dog diverted bear; bear left.	
63. Fred Barmore	Kodiak Island	Fall 1948	brown	Sow with cub	Protected self; bear left.	
64. Gregory J. Hildebrand	Southeastern	1949	"grizzly"	Surprised	Yelled, shot bear; dog diverted bear; bear left and later died.	
65. Dan Gillis	Dome Creek	c. 1949	black	Bear followed him on trail	No gun; waved switch at it; fought with knife; bear left.	
66. Hardy Trefger	Alsek River	June 19, 1949	brown	Surprised sow with 2 cubs	Shot bear as she hit him, lay still; she left.	
67. Jack Reed	Ewe Creek, Denali National Park	July 21, 1949	grizzly	Sow with 3 cubs	No gun; ran, jumped off 20-foot cliff; bear left.	

Bear Maulings in Alaska (cont.)

Victim	Place	Date	Type of Bear	Apparent Reason for Attack	Details of Attack and Outcome	Fatal
68. Knut Peterson	Slana River	August 31, 1949	grizzly		Ran for river; bear mauled. Peterson lay still; bear left.	
69. Highway worker	Teklanika, Denali National Park	September, 1949	grizzly cub	Releasing cub from trap	No gun; man walked to front of truck; cub exited trap and mauled his arm. Man later lost use of it.	
70. Mark Rigling	Salisbury Sound, Chichagof Island	Christmas 1950–55?	brown?		Mark's remains found. Bear may have jumped and killed him as he packed out deer.	X
71. Indian woman and girl	Nabesna Village	c. 1950s	grizzly			X X
72. Ralph Reischl	Admiralty Island	1950s	brown			
73. Ray Deardorf	Taku River	c. 1950s	brown			X
74. Alexie Pitka	Khotol River	May 1950	black	Wounded	Fought with knife, talked to bear; bear left, later died.	
75. Mike Fuller	Denali National Park	1951	grizzly			
76. Man	Eagle River	Pre-1952		Bear came into camp.	Man shot, then wrestled with bear until it died.	
77. Ed Wagoner	Peters Creek	Pre-1952			Kicked bear in face while on his back.	
78. Ed Lovedahl		Pre-1952	brownie	Wounded	Approached "dead" bear; companion shot bear off.	
79. Henry Knackstedt	Kenai River	1952-53	brown	Surprised sow with cubs	Held up gun, did not fight back; when he was unconscious, bear left.	

80. Ralph H. Gaier	Skwentna River	Winter 1952-53	black	Hunger?		X
81. Boat skipper	Prince William Sound. Southeast	1953-4	brown		Poked bear in eye, tried to crawl away after initial mauling; he stayed put after second mauling and was "buried"alive. Man later escaped.	
82. Jesse Hatch	Kenai	September 13, 1954	brown		Bear bit, hit. Hatch got off one shot, wounded bear; bear thrashed as Hatch inched away.	
83. Bill Brody	Ninilchik River	August 25, 1955	brown	Surprised sow with cubs	Hit bear with gun, grabbed bear, fought her; she left.	X
84. Willis S. McBride	Big Oshetna River (50 miles N. of Eureka)	September 1955	grizzly			
85. Forest H. Young, Jr.	Chilkat River	September 1955	grizzly	Protecting meat	Yelled, tried to climb tree, fought, played dead; bear left and returned. Partner brought a weapon and light and went for help.	
86. Lloyd Pennington Everett A. Kendall	Snowshoe Lake (mile 150 Glenn Highway)	April 17, 1956	grizzly	Protect den?	Both guide and client were killed.	XX
87. Herman Oergel	Maclaren River	September 7, 1957	grizzly			
88. Rod Darnell	Whitestone Harbor, Admiralty Island	September 29, 1957	brown	Surprised sow with cubs	Shot, then threw self to ground; partner shot bear off.	X
89. Walter Johnson	Fritz Cove, Juneau	April 27, 1958	black (young)		Grabbed and twisted bear's ears, kicked it in the rear; it left.	

Bear Maulings in Alaska (cont.)

Victim	Place	Date	Type of Bear	Apparent Reason for Attack	Details of Attack and Outcome	Fatal
90. William M. Faulkner John Lowe	Tustumena Lake	September 6, 1958	brown		Bear mauled them and left.	
91. Lee Hagemeier	Montana Creek, Auke Bay, Juneau	July 27, 1959	brown	Surprised	Rolled into ball; bear left.	
92. Dan Luddington	Summit Lake, Paxson	October 1959	grizzly	Sow with cub	Fought, shot and killed bear.	
93. Doug Olson	Russian River	May 27, 1960	black			
94. David Norton	Lower Taku River	July 20, 1960	brown	Surprised	Partner shot bear off and killed it.	
95. Mrs. Frances Johnson	A lake north of Minto	August 9, 1960	black	Hunger?	One male companion fought bear with stick while other got pistol and killed bear.	
96. Bruce Johnstone	Behm Canal, Ketchikan	September 16, 1960	brown	Wounded	Client shot bear off and killed it.	
97. Henry W. Jones	Rodman Bay, Baranof Island	July 12, 1961	brown		Jones had been whistling and singing to alert bear but was mauled. Bear left.	
98. Napier Shelton	Igloo Mountain, Denali National Park	August 4, 1961	grizzly	Possibly attracted by squeaky sounds.	No gun; climbed tree, kicked bear; bear pulled him from tree, mauled him and left.	
99. Harold Tuttle	Mile 90, Glenn Highway	September 15, 1962	grizzly		Tuttle got off one shot, rolled into ball; bear left him for dead.	
100. Don Hymes	Fox	July 21, 1963	black			

	Location	Date	Color	Hunger?	Description	
101. George Roberts	Tatlanika River	August 7, 1963	black		Sleeping, fled tent. Roberts fought with hands, grabbed bear's jaws, shot it off; Partners killed it. Bear in good condition.	
102. C. Wayne Majors	Minto	August 7, 1963	black		Asleep; bear bit head; Majors yelled; a friend scared bear off and killed it.	
103. J. William Strandberg	Manley Hot Springs (160 miles west of Fairbanks)	August 18, 1963	black			X
104. Larry Bidlake	Porcupine River, Fort Yukon	August 19, 1963	black		Ran, climbed tree, kicked at bear, tried to divert it with stuff from pack. Friend scared bear off.	
105. Man	Baranof Island	1964	brown			X
106. Jack Lee	Alaska Peninsula	April 1964	brown	Surprised	Bear mauled, fled.	
107. Fred Lewis	Nakwasina Passage, Sitka	Fall 1964	brown		Got off one shot, protected self; bear was wounded and driven off by companions.	
108. Joe Want	Olga Bay, Kodiak Island	c. November 25, 1964	brown	Sow with cubs?	Bear bit Want and left.	
109. Elvin Hess	Mile 26, Haines	May 13, 1965	brown		Timber cruising. No time to use gun; bear mauled and left.	
110. Paul Kissner Bruce Millenbach	Hood Bay, Admiralty Island	July 19, 1967	brown	Surprised	No gun; jumped behind alders, yelled to partner, was mauled, rolled off cliff; bear left.	
111. Scott MacInnes Mike Moerlein	Resurrection Creek Trail, Hope	August 5, 1967	brown		Ran, fell into fetal position; bear bit and left.	

Bear Maulings in Alaska (cont.)

Victim	Place	Date	Type of Bear	Apparent Reason for Attack	Details of Attack and Outcome	Fatal
112. James L. Magowan	Denali National Park, Mile 56	August 8, 1967	grizzly	Sow with 2 cubs	No gun; bear charged from 200-300 yards; Magowan played dead, protected self, rose after initial mauling, fell into fetal position on knees; bear left.	
113. Charlie Wells	Fish Bay	October 19, 1968			Got off one shot; bear left.	X
114. Leo Beeks	Admiralty Island	1970	brown	Sow with cubs	Slugged, kicked, fought; bear left.	
115. Mrs. Dave Gratias	Denali Highway, Mile 82, Paxson	April 1970	grizzly	Sow with cubs	No gun; ran, and bear bit arm; dog diverted bear; Gratias escaped into cabin.	
116. Dave Norton	Taku River	July 1970	brown	Surprised	Knocked down; partner shot and killed bear.	
117. Husband and wife	Byron Peak, Portage Glacier	September 1971	grizzly	Cornered?	Husband knocked to ground; wife went over cliff with bear; bear left.	
118. Chris Cauble	Toklat River, Denali National Park	July 21, 1972	grizzly	Sow with 2 cubs	No gun; tried to hike around single bear, discovered three; sow charged from 120 yards, bit, mauled and left.	
119. Ray J. Capossela Nelson Stimaker	Tazlina Lake	September 5, 1972	grizzly	Protecting kill, wounded	Guiding. Bear charged. Capossela fired, ran, hit bear with gun. Stimaker killed bear after Capossela was dead.	X
120. John Minifee	Glenallen area	September 6, 1972	grizzly		Escaped into a tree.	

						X	
121. Al and Joyce Thompson	Funny River Trail	September 6, 1972	brown	Sow with cubs	Awakened and punched by bear; fought, played dead; bear left.		
122. Leland Collins	Funny River area	October 29, 1972	brown	Sow with cubs	Moose hunting. Shot and wounded bear, reached trail and help.		
123. Dick Jensen	Naknek	July 21, 1973	brown	Surprised sow with cubs	Fought her, kicked, moved after initial attack. Bear returned and mauled Jensen worse.		
124. Mark V. Carey, Roger L. Pearson	Big Creek, Denali National Park	July 23, 1973	grizzly	Sow with cubs	No gun; sow bluffed then charged Carey, who tried to flee in sleeping bag then played dead. Bear attacked Pearson, who also played dead: bear left.		
125. Al Johnson	Mile 7, Denali National Park Road	September 11, 1973	grizzly	Sow with 3 cubs	No gun; bear pulled Johnson from tree; he fell into a fetal position, got up as soon as bear left and walked to road.		
126. Richard Bennett	Haines	July 1974					
127. Robert Thompson	Santa Flavia Bay, Kodiak Island	Sept. 1974	brown	3 cubs	Deer hunting. Bear knocked him down and mauled him; bear left.		
128. Jay B.L. Reeves	Frosty Creek, Cold Bay	August 2, 1974	brown				
129. Ron Cole	Lake Creek, Skwentna	May 27, 1975	2 brown	Mating	Fought, got up after initial attack, tried to climb tree, played dead during second mauling; bears left.		
130. Peter Stys	Girdwood	July 22, 1975	brown		Yelled; bear left.		

Bear Maulings in Alaska (cont.)

Victim	Place	Date	Type of Bear	Apparent Reason for Attack	Details of Attack and Outcome	Fatal
131. Michael Bishop	Igloo Mountain, Denali National Park	August 6, 1975	grizzly	Surprised sow with cubs?	No gun; ran, fell, protected self; bear bit and left.	
132. Forest Roberts	Burma Road, Big Lake	September 8, 1975	brown	Wounded	Hunting. Mauled by a wounded bear.	X
133. Alan Lee Precup	Glacier Bay National Monument	September 12, 1975	brown	Hunger?		X
134. Major William Carlock	Big-Little Oshetna River confluence, Eureka	September 18, 1975	grizzly	Surprised a sleeping bear?	Got off shot, wounded bear, and it left.	
135. Jim and Julie Carlson	Richardson Highway	October 25, 1975	brown	Sow with cubs	Yelled, hit bear with thermos; bear left.	
136. Ray Hose	Livengood	Summer 1976			Friend killed bear.	
137. Robert L. MacGregor	Slate Creek, Forty Mile Country	July 22, 1976	black	Hunger?	Tried to climb tree?	X
138. Creig Sharp	Karluk Lake, Kodiak Island	April 28, 1977	brown	Wounded	Fell into fetal position; partner shot bear; it left and was found dead next day.	
139. Kermit Johnson	Behm Canal Ketchikan	May 5, 1977	brown	Wounded	Fired once, hit bear with rifle; it left and charged partner, who killed it.	
140. Robert Muller Kim Dooley	Stoney Creek, Denali National Park	July 27 or August 26, 1977	grizzly	Sow with 2 cubs	No gun; bear chewed man and left.	

					X	
141. Cynthia Dusei-Bacon	Salcha River	August 13, 1977	black	Hunger?		Played dead, screamed, called on walkie-talkie.
142. Norman Creel	Clam Gulch	c. June 6 or 7, 1978	brown?	Surprised		No gun; turned to run, went 5 steps, kicked, yelled; bear left.
143. Marquiss "Mickey" Bryson	Twin Cove, Admiralty Island	October 20, 1978	brown	Surprised		Bear attacked deer hunter from behind; bit head four times, buttocks twice and rib cage once; bear left.
144. Patricia and Quinn Whiting-O'Keefe Chad Hansen	Katiktak, Brooks Range	August 3, 1979	grizzly	Sow with cubs		No weapon; bear struck Patricia once; she feigned death; bear left.
145. Stefan Rydholm	McCarthy, Hidden Lake	c. August 8, 1978	grizzly		X	Biker disappeared; might have been killed by bear. Green nylon rain jacket found shredded and in many pieces with "teeth" punctures.
146. Two injuries/ incidents	Station hotel at Denali National Park	June 1980	grizzlies			
147. Stephen Routh	Cow Lake, 216 miles N.W. of Anchorage	July 29, 1980	black	No warning		Bear attacked as Routh waded ashore from float plane; he fled to water; bear followed; Routh escaped on plane float.
148. Thomas Schulz	Glacier Bay National Monument	August 3, 1980	black?	Lone hiker	X	Possibly killed by bear.
149. Hiroshi Tokura	Denali National Park	August 11 (30?), 1980	2 grizzlies	Too close, surprised		Hiking with 3 companions. Tokura swatted by one of the bears as hikers fled.

Bear Maulings in Alaska (cont.)

Victim	Date	Place	Type of Bear	Apparent Reason for Attack	Details of Attack and Outcome	Fatal
150. Mr. and Mrs. James Wingate, Jr.	c. August 20, 1980	Denali National Park, Mile 8, 1/2 mile N. of road	grizzly		Bear pounced on their tent as wife dove into it for protection. Couple shouted, screamed; bear shredded tent, stood 6 feet away. Husband shouted, and it fled.	
151. Jack Naus	c. September 22, 1981	North end of Admiralty Island	brown	Surprised	Men were deer hunting. They rousted bear out of brush. Jack shot it with a .300 mag. It got up and knocked him down and took a few bites. Partner shot it twice; it ran toward him and then veered off into the woods.	
152. Fred Roberts	October 30, 1981	Spiridon Lake, Kodiak Island	brown	Surprised a sow with cubs	Packing for guide. When bear charged he assumed a fetal position on ground. Bear bit a few times and left, as cubs sought safety.	
153. Dave Pearson	c. 1982	Dry Path, Chichagof Island	brown		While deer hunting, he was mauled; shot bear off himself.	
154. Dennis Figon Tim Gorski	December 1982	Zachar Bay, Kodiak Island	brown	Surprised	Bear charged Figon, bit and slapped him; Gorski shot bear; Figon also shot bear which ran a short distance and died.	
155. Karl Johnson	c. June 5, 1983	Eagle River	black	Surprised	Played dead. Bear sniffed, nibbled lightly, bit into leg. Johnson yelled. Bear left.	

#	Name	Location	Date	Type	Cause	Description
156.	Jim Hunter	Izembek Lagoon, Cold Bay	August 1983	brown	Surprised	Bear galloped from 20 feet away. Hunter shouted; bear hit, knocked him down; bear picked him up with paw under his abdomen and dropped him; picked him up in mouth; Hunter played dead, waited 20 minutes and fled for beach.
157.	Zachary Cook Shane Cardin Luis Manuel Martinez (scouts)	Lost Lake, Delta Junction	July 25, 1984	black		Bear ripped hole in large tent and entered; bit Cook; bear was scared off with firecrackers.
158.	Joel P. and Jane Larson	Troublesome Creek Trail (mile 137.5 Parks Highway)	October 13, 1984		Sow with 2 cubs	No gun; bear bit and clawed both people, then left—seemed concerned for cubs' safety.
159.	Saskia Roggeveem Darrel Tubbs	Denali National Park, Merino Campground	June 12, 1985	grizzly		No gun; woman and friend walking from train depot to youth hostel. Grizzly stood up. Woman ran and fell. Bear attacked and bit her. Approaching train may have scared it off.
160.	Lee Ann Landstrom	Denali National Park, Savage Campground	June 13, 1985	grizzly	Surprised sow with 3 cubs	No gun; Landstrom shouted, waved arms and ran; the bear bit her. Two men chased bear off, and Landstrom climbed a tree.
161.	Nathan Warren and parents	Shotgun Cove, Whittier	June 23, 1985	black	Boar and sow	Boy was asleep in tent next to parents' tent; bear ripped through and dragged him out; parents scared bear away.

Bear Maulings in Alaska (cont.)

Victim	Place	Date	Type of Bear	Apparent Reason for Attack	Details of Attack and Outcome	Fatal
162. Kyle Scholl Diane Nelson, John Pex	Lake Iliamna	July 24 , 1985		Sow with 2 cubs	Sow charged; Scholl ran, was overtaken and knocked to the ground; she bit his head and legs repeatedly, then left to begin mauling Nelson. Pex arrived and fired 2 rounds into sky then shot bear and was charged. Fired 2 more times; fourth shot dropped her.	
163. Ben Moore	Near Healy	September 15, 1985	grizzly	Surprised	Bear charged on all fours. Moore shot it in chest with .357 mag. Bear bit his leg, shook and tossed him six to eight feet. Second shot hit bear in side; bear bit Moore's head. Third shot in bear's mouth killed it.	
164. Chris Kempf	Uganik Island	November 16, 1985	brown	Surprised	Bowhunting for deer. Bear charged. No time to unholster .44. Kemp ran; bear chased him around alders three times. Bear scratched him, then left.	
165. Lee Grimstad	Highway Pass Denali National Park	July 1987	grizzly		Photography mission. Grimstad took pictures of approaching bear. He lay down when bear was within twenty yards; bear bit his legs and left.	
166. Four hunters	Sitka			Wounded	Bear packed off young shooter by the neck; guide rescued victim.	

167. Lawrence W. Jones	Yentna River	September 27, 1988	brown			Moose hunting. Bear surprised hunter, knocked him down; Jones played dead. Bear left, and Jones returned to camp.
168. Duane Christensen Bill Burgess	Uganik Lake, Kodiak Island	November 3, 1988	brown			Bear attacked Christensen while he was gutting deer and knocked him down. He shot bear, but it kept coming. Bear knocked him down, and Burgess shot and killed bear.
169. Harley Sievenpiper	Port Conclusion, Baranof Island	November 4, 1988	brown		X	Deer hunter attracted bear with deer call. Bear attacked, killed hunter.

Dates for the following mauling victim entries were not available.

170. Fisherman	Marka River, Butte Inlet, S.E		brown	Wounded		
171. Alec Flyum	Iliamna Lake		brown			Hollered, waved, played dead.
172. Bill Shively	Young's Bay, Juneau		brown	Surprised	X	Lay still; partner hit bear with hat; bear left.

5

Bears in Man's World

I understand now why many of Alaska's oldtimers hated bears. Besides having to be constantly alert to defend their lives, they could never leave belongings unprotected without worry. Even if we didn't see any bears, the fact remains that they are there. . . .
—Vic Bruss, *ALASKA Magazine*, January 1980

Bears become used to human scent as soon as they enter the areas frequented by humans. They feed in garbage dumps on scraps left or even handed to them by humans. Any natural intolerance of mankind is diminished by the association that the animal has with people. Bears are a dominant animal, particularly the grizzlies. They progressively lose their respect for, or fear of, humankind with any association.—Laszlo Retfalvi in Mike Crammond's *Killer Bears*

Since man's intrusion into wildlife's environment,

man-animal conflicts have escalated. In the case of bruin, it is usually the bear that gets the bad name for pursuing his nature.

Although it is a bit frightening to be confronted by a garbage- or dogfood-eating bear on your deck in the cozy confines of Juneau, Valdez or Petersburg, it is not uncommon for bruin to spend days or weeks in close proximity to some Alaskan towns.

Kodiak Island's Larsen Bay is a typical Alaskan salmon cannery town of approximately two hundred residents. A myriad of dwellings lines the gravel streets of Larsen Bay. The town is split by Humpy Creek, a fifteen- to twenty-foot stream, a couple of feet deep, which harbors a run of humpy salmon during the summer. Although smokehouses and some garbage occasionally attracts bears in the area, the animals are drawn in larger numbers by the arrival of salmon each summer at Humpy Creek. The difference between Larsen Bay villagers and urban dwellers in most of Alaska's larger cities is that they are accustomed to having bears around.

The bears inhabit the streets and lots that the villagers occupy. Dora Aga, a village matriarch, told me about a bear that broke into her brother-in-law's house and dismantled it. She said the locals take the bears in stride, and she gave me several examples.

"There were twelve bears right in the village at one o'clock in the afternoon. A woman was taking her preschoolers to the school. Here's a sow and three cubs comin' down the road. A little farther over is another and three cubs comin' down the road. A little farther, another mother and three cubs—twelve of them right there. And down the creek there are two big boars, so that made fourteen. The woman just turned right around and went home."

Law enforcement officials, as well as the villagers, have grown accustomed to the bears. Stan McCormick, the police officer at Larsen Bay, shared his experience: "One morning about nine o'clock I was walking down to the cannery with another man. There was a bear in the creek fifty feet away from us, busy eatin' salmon. We just stood there and watched it a while. He looked at us and continued to eat. We continued on our way."

These cannery-town dwellers, knowing that their four-pawed visitors will appear and depart every summer, have learned to coexist with bears. And there are several other villages throughout Alaska where this same situation holds true. In light of the fact that bears and men cross paths and share environments peacefully in many areas, a case should be made for coexistence.

While there are many stories of towns such as Larsen Bay, where men peacefully coexist with bears, such a relationship is rare in many towns and more populated areas of Alaska. Jerry Austin, who lives in the rural village of Saint Michael, told me of a frightening encounter with a bear in his town.

"In the early '70s there were several bears around Saint Michael that were a pain to the residents. One evening I was sitting in the YBL shipyard when my cousin ran in and said there was a bear chasing the three neighbor kids down the beach. Dennis went to grab his .30-06, but it wasn't loaded. I always keep one rifle loaded for fast action, so I grabbed my .300 and ran out.

"The kids ran over to where I had my dog team staked out for the summer, and they ran right in with the dogs, but the bear followed. I have never seen my sled dogs quieter, except for one named Jeff. Jeff reached out and grabbed the bear and slowed it down, allowing the kids to reach an old winch-house for safety.

"There were no doors or windows in the house and three kids went in, followed immediately by the bear. Then one kid came flying out the winch window, then the second, then the third kid and then the bear. I shot the bear in the head in the air, and it landed, dead. To this day my neighbor never complains about my sled dogs barking or anything."

Men and bears have interacted since time immemorial, with the beast coming out with the short end of the stick. One need look only at the news accounts over the past decade to verify the presence of bear in man's domain.

The Barn Bear

Some of bears' doings among man are humorous, maybe even human-like. But there is a darker side to bear-man situations which can be and have been extremely tragic. . . . The danger of a fatal confrontation with bruin always exsists.

On a Saturday afternoon in September 1981, Jane Johnston and her two daughters, Shelly and Kathy, were in their barn cleaning horse stalls. As anyone who owns horses knows, riding the horse makes up for the dirty work that goes along with owning one. The women were making the most of their chores with the radio blaring. Their barn was a twenty-by-twenty-four-foot affair with two stalls, a tack room and two paddocks. The rear of the barn bordered a small stream, while the front faced their house.

Their two horses, Ty and Pickles, were free-grazing in the driveway. As the women worked, joking and laughing, Jane looked outside the stall and noticed the horses in the drive. Both stood rigid, staring behind the barn toward the stream—ears erect, nostrils flaring and eyes bulging.

Thinking little of the situation, Jane casually spoke to the animals. "What are you staring at?" Jane looked out the door and back in the direction of their staring. She saw brown, and living in an area frequented by moose, first assumed it was a moose, but then immediately realized it was a bear. Jane shouted, "Moose . . . BEAR!"

As Jane and her daughters stared at the bear, it stood on its hind legs. "He was about fifteen to twenty feet away, and he was huge," said Jane. The alerted bear stood, trying to get their scent, working his nose.

The three ran toward the house. Then Willard, their Pekinese poodle, saw the bear and began barking at it.

As the women ran, Kathy said, "Willie ran past me, toward the bear. The bear ran through the bushes along the creek, paralleling the driveway. Willie ran alongside the bear, six feet away. I turned around and started chasing the dog."

"Shelly and Mom made it to the house and stopped outside the door to wait for me. My sister turned to look for the dog and saw me chasing it. Shelly yelled at the dog, and Mom yelled at me to get in the house."

Kathy reached the dog, six feet from the bear and picked it up, holding it over her shoulder. Simultaneously, the bear reared on his hind legs. "Willie was barking his head off, like a fool," Kathy said. "The bear looked at me and started sniffing his nose, snorting. He towered over me, six feet away and about ten feet tall. He was huge.

"I turned and ran for the house, and the bear

headed for the woods. Mom and Shelly were still standing in the doorway. When I reached the house, Mom said, 'You stupid child,' and began whacking me on the head."

Within five minutes Randy, the man of the house, arrived, grabbed his rifle and went into the brush to investigate. He was concerned that the bear might bother the horses, which had run down the driveway during the melee. Jane said, "Randy saw tracks but not the bear. He returned to the house and called the Alaska State Troopers. We never saw the bear again, but the Fish and Game did. They said it was an extremely large brown bear. Our bear's visit was one of several bear sightings in Anchorage that year."

The spring of 1988 brought a garbage warning to Anchoragites from *The Anchorage Times*, "Bear this in mind: The bears love all your garbage." (Thursday, April 21, 1988)

The man-bear habituation problem is not new; however, the ramifications of protecting bruin and property have some serious implications. Do you shoot a bear that eats your dog's food? Or one that chases your chickens? How big a threat is the bear caught on your property?

Only a few policies are specifically aimed at protecting bears in most Alaskan cities. A general policy adhered to in cities is that firearms cannot be legally discharged within city limits. Another policy that protects bears is the DLP regulation of the Alaska Department of Fish and Game—Defense of Life and Property. A bear may be killed in a non-hunting circumstance only if it is a threat to human life or property.

But what if the human population is to blame for a bear's presence in a neighborhood? Very few towns have instituted a fine for persons attracting bears by allowing garbage to build up around personal property.

A community's improperly disposed garbage is also its greatest attraction for bears. George Petry, a fifteen-year veteran with the Alaska State Troopers, knows that towns could better protect the citizens' property from bears if humans were more careful in cleaning up after themselves. He cites the town of Glennallen as a community with no garbage collection and a big bear problem. "In 1985–86, within a couple of days there were fourteen bears sighted. It was nothing to see one in the Chevron station parking lot."

The Urban Bear

When bears, attracted by a community's waste, become a problem, law enforcement officials are forced to make tough decisions. Chris Thompson, a Soldotna police officer, has had to make such a decision.

It was in the evening about ten or thereabouts. I had received a report that a bear had been spotted over by Soldotna High School. I drove my patrol car over into that area and was unable to locate a bear or anyone who had seen it. A few moments later I was dispatched to Fire Chief Allen Phillips' residence, where someone had seen the bear.

Upon arriving at Chief Phillips' house, I got out of my patrol vehicle, drew my handgun, a .41-magnum Smith and Wesson. I walked around to the north-northeast side of the house and cautiously rounded the corner toward the back. A 175-pound black bear was staring me in the face.

I didn't really want to shoot the animal right beside someone's home, so I backed up, holstered my weapon and radioed my supervisor about the situation. I was told to try to scare the bear off. While I was standing there talking to my supervisor, the bear climbed on the back porch, stood up at the sliding glass doors and proceeded to paw the glass. He then stepped down and moved behind a shed, where I lost sight of him. As I tracked the bear in the nearby woods, I realized he was moving in a parallel line with me, about eight to ten feet away. He showed no signs of fear of humans. Now he moved to another residence and began digging in their garbage.

I hollered and clapped at him, but he only trotted off into the little woods in the subdivision until he found more garbage cans.

I notified my supervisor again that the bear didn't seem to be afraid of people or noise. I had even used my siren on the patrol vehicle, and when another officer had arrived, I shot off some firecrackers with no results.

Knowing the expense of relocating a bear, especially with the population of bears in this area, I couldn't see spending that kind of money and time to move the animal. Sergeant Al Thompson of the ADFG wildlife protection was contacted, and he notified us to go ahead and kill the bear.

Soon my supervisor arrived with an AR-15; I had my 12-gauge shotgun loaded with slugs, and my fellow officer was also armed with a shotgun. Since I was the only one crazy enough, I told them I'd go ahead and move into the brush where I last saw the bear. I went into the thicket area, while probably fifteen or twenty spectators stood at the edge, waiting to see what was going to happen. Within a couple of minutes, I located the bear, which took off running as soon as he saw me, right in the direction of the spectators.

I pulled up on the bear and fired one slug at him, knocking him down. He rolled over, jumped right back on his feet and headed directly toward my supervisor. I could hear the bear crashing through the brush, and then he stopped. My supervisor was calling over the radio, "Where is he? Where is he?"

"The last I saw, he was coming right at ya'," I answered.

So my task was to find the bear. Carefully, I followed a trail of blood and found the bear lying on his back. He was dead.

The slug had put a nice, neat hole the size of a fifty-cent piece through both lungs and right through his rib cage. Since this incident, I've lost all faith in a shotgun slug. It pierced a clean hole, but what normally kills an animal is the shock of a bullet that turns everything inside to jello. This wound looked like I had shot an arrow. It knocked him down and rolled him over, but he came out all right. We sure could have had a mad bear on our hands if I had hit him in his gut.

Some of the spectators were mad that I'd killed the bear. They said there had been no need to kill it, while other people responded with, "What if your kid was playing in the back yard, and the bear strolled up on him and decided to have a meal?"

Once bears lose their fear of man, they can become really dangerous. When this happens, I don't think people and bears can coexist.

It Didn't Have to Happen

Some bears become so people-conscious that they are a real danger. I believe that one of the worst situations involving man and bear is the habituated bear—one that has become so accustomed to people that his fear of man has been replaced with an arrogance or contempt toward man. The following story tells of one such bear, one that roamed about the Indian village of Nabesna in Alaska's Interior. It is a sad reminder of a confrontation with a bear that didn't have to happen.

In Nabesna a man-conditioned grizzly had spent a number of days foraging around the village. Measures usually taken in such a situation include firing shotgun-type cracker shells to scare the animal or transplantation, which unfortunately, is usually rather ineffective. A more effective response in the village might have been to reduce or eliminate the food or garbage to which the bear was attracted.

But the bear remained in the village, and a tragedy resulted.

It wasn't pretty. It never is when a grizzly gets a hold of a person. An animal with three-inch, razor sharp claws, inch-and-a-half canines and boundless muscles with enough strength to break the neck of a barnyard bull with a single swat is an ominous beast. A rogue grizzly used this power on two humans before vanishing into the outlying hills.

As the rescue plane dropped in over the stunted spruce trees and onto the dust-covered bush strip, a handful of men spoke in subdued tones, asking the whereabouts of the bear and the urgency of finding and dispatching it lest it repeat its act. A small Indian girl lay dead beneath a blanket only twenty yards from a village woman's near-lifeless form, which was almost unrecognizable as human.

She lay on a stretcher at the edge of the runway. Her left side was all but mangled—a gaping hole in her left cheek exposed her teeth; her bloody, tattered blouse revealed a missing left breast; gurgling sounds labored from her mouth as she attempted to breathe. The Fish and Game officer and Dan Saunders made an incision into her neck to facilitate her breathing.

Feelings of grief and outrage flooded the two moose hunters who had been summoned to track and destroy the rogue bear. Dan Saunders and Ed had been eating in a roadside lodge when a game enforcement officer asked them to help in this crisis—to find and destroy the renegade bear.

Even though their plans had been to get a bull moose—not a bear—it fell to them to honor the unspoken law of the Alaskan bush . . . to lend a hand in an emergency. The officer showed them on a map the three canyons behind Nabesna that needed to be searched. They chose one of the canyons, and he told them he would try to get men from Chistochina and Slana to search the other two.

No sooner had the plane lifted off than the men hastened to their dreaded duty. Hoping to complete the dismal task ahead of them as quickly as possible and fully realizing the danger that faced them, they threw together light survival packs, expecting to be gone for only a day or two.

An Indian man took them beyond the last signs of human habitation—the rough log cabins and mines of the area—to the last known location of the bear. At the sight of the bear droppings and immense bear tracks, the men gave each other a knowing glance and cold chills swept up their spines. This was no small bear. At that point the Indian returned to the village.

As the hunters left the relatively safe confines of the lower country to head up the canyon, Ed took the lead, instructing Dan to stay at least forty feet to his rear to assure safety and the opportunity for one of them to have a clear shot at the bear should it attack them. They checked their weapons, insuring the maximum load. Both men carried .375 magnums with bullets that packed five thousand foot-pounds of energy.

Splotchy blood on the grass and rocks bore witness of the bear's passing. Ed noted from the blood mixed with intestinal matter that the bear was gut shot—it was in pain and carried a chip on its shoulder. Before the men had gone far, the sun dropped below the canyon rim to the west, and it was time to make camp for the night.

As darkness fell, the men's concern over the surrounding sounds and movements intensified. The men kept a night-long vigil around a hastily constructed and constantly maintained fire and took turns piling wood onto the flames. Their senses were put to the test as every night sound fed their imaginations.

At dawn the men downed instant coffee and beef jerky and commenced their dreaded journey. Their climb up the canyon was compounded by stiffened muscles from the day before. Ed asked Dan to take the point, as he was younger and had better vision. An hour passed. Their muscles limbered; the sore muscles were less painful, and the men's senses became all the more acutely tuned to their environment.

As the sun climbed into the sky, its light touched the mountain tops and the gray of the canyon walls turned an array of pinks and reds. Layers of quartz glittered as the sunlight bathed the escarpments. The men felt the beauty about them contrasted with the stark reality of their mission and the dangerous animal that could appear any moment and without warning.

It was obvious from the blood spoor that the animal was slowing up and taking longer at each stop, stopping every two hundred yards. Ed cautioned Dan to expect the bear in a heartbeat, knowing that if the bear chose to charge them that it would be hell-bent on destroying them as it had the woman and child.

The canyon walls flattened out and the timbered hillsides became high meadows laced with head-high grass and punctuated by alder patches. The hunters followed the wide swath the bear had made through the grass. Tension mounted.

Dan was halfway across a meadow when he stopped abruptly. He had caught sight of movement on the downhill side of a willow clump two hundred yards distant. Both men froze.

Dan found the bear in his scope and saw the big blond diamond on its back. Since the wind was in their favor, the hunters chose to get closer. Ninety yards from the brute they felt the breeze on the backs of their necks. A grizzly lives and dies by his nose, and it didn't betray him now. He instantly stood on hind legs, moaning and bellering—his keg-sized head swinging back and forth, rubbery, dark nostrils sifting the man-scented breeze; he was seeking his enemy.

Dan popped his swivel-mounted scope away, exposing his rifle's iron sights, and released the weapon's safety. He pulled down on the bear's left shoulder. In the fraction of a second Dan needed to prepare for his shot, the bear had mounted his charge—lunging, long claws clasping the earth and pulling it toward himself in rhythmic, sixteen-foot strides.

As Dan touched the trigger, the bullet smacked the bear and dust flew. He fired his second shot into the left shoulder, staggering the bear sideways but failing to stop its forward momentum. His third shot took the beast in the right shoulder, rolling it off its feet. Hind legs tore the grass and scattered the rocks and bushes.

Dan quickly reloaded and fired his final shot into the bear's brain. The dying animal groped toward the hunters, blood gushing from its mouth in its final throes of death. A final groan, and it was over.

Although a welcome wave of relief swept over the men, it was ten minutes before they approached the animal. Dan's knees shook, and he was unable to light a cigarette.

They skinned the carcass and discovered three .30-30 bullets in the left forepaw and one between the shoulders inside the hump. The hide weighed close to a hundred pounds.

On the way out, a day and a half later, they met up with the protection officer. He recognized the hide as that of the man-killer and told the men that the Indian woman had died within minutes after reaching the hospital. He also informed them that the person who had wounded the bear was the dead woman's husband.

The men gave the grieving husband the bear hide and the remainder of their hunting provisions. As they prepared to leave, they were greeted and thanked by all seventeen villagers. The solemnity of their departure served as a reminder once again that this entire tragedy didn't have to happen.

The Bear Cub Capers

Man-bear situations often prove tragic. Sometimes these tragedies are fatal to man, bear or both. The bear that took the life of the Nasbena woman and child paid with its life. Another bear, killed for eating an Anchorage citizen's dog's food, left twin cubs, perpetuating the problem of bears scavenging in the neighborhood.

In June 1988, a Rabbit Creek man shot and killed a brown bear sow that had been visiting his home and

*helping herself (and her twin cubs) to his dog's food. The
surviving cubs, apparently yearlings of about a hundred
pounds, were left to make it on their own. The man's
story was written up anonymously in the paper, and it
instantly became the subject of local debate. The newspaper carried letters to the editor, lauding and disdain-
ing the actions of the man who had shot the bear.*

*No one thought that the cubs would make it through
the winter on their own, but a short time later the cute,
but rambunctious little beasts were captured by Ron
Regnart, a semi-retired commercial fisheries biologist
for the Alaska Department of Fish and Game. I spent an
enjoyable evening with Ron and his wife Claudia, as
they told me their unusual story of capturing twin brown
bear cubs in their dog kennel.*

The bears were coming here and eating the dog
food. We kept a fifty-pound sack of dog food right in the
corner of the porch. One night I was away on a fishing
trip and my wife thought our dog was raiding our
garbage can, but when I came home our dog was tied
up in the middle of the yard and the garbage was
scattered over seventy-five feet. Our neighbor reported
seeing the cubs, so by that time, of course, we knew
who the culprits were.

The cubs had come to our house about three
nights in a row, usually at about ten or eleven o'clock,
before I got the idea of trying to lure them into the
kennel. I had called Fish and Game to ask for a trap, but
all of their traps were being used.

One night the lady next door came home at about
midnight, and as she was unlocking her door, she
looked up and discovered a bear in the tree right over
her doorway. She ran over here to use the telephone
and didn't want to go back. In the meantime, the two

bears moved to the bridge over the creek, and I came within about eight feet of them. I thought maybe I could scare them back into a tree and then call the Department of Fish and Game, but they ran so doggone fast, they left me in the dust.

Our dog kennel is five by twelve by five feet high and constructed of heavy poultry netting. To capture the bears, I held the door open with a stick, tied a piece of monofilament line to it and ran the string up to the porch and underneath the door to our living room. From there, I could look right through our window, spot the cubs in the kennel and trip the door by pulling a wooden handle tied to the string. I also bought a self-closing gate latch and a spring, so the door would shut tightly behind the animals.

Next I cleaned up from under the porch the dog food that the cubs had been raiding and put some canned salmon in strategic spots near the kennel. On the first night the cubs went right to the spot where the dog food had been. When they scraped around and didn't find anything, they got angry and shook the barbeque up and down.

Then the little sow got a whiff of the salmon. I'd put a little piece in a bowl halfway to the kennel. Wow, when she found that salmon, she plunked down on it, put her mouth in there and made a mewing sound—she was in bear heaven.

The male tried to get at it. They didn't fight, but she had her muzzle in there to the point where there wasn't any room for him to operate. He was still standing around, and he wandered over and got a whiff of the salmon in the kennel. But when he couldn't find the door, he stood up, measuring about five feet high, and started shaking the kennel. He nearly shook the thing apart. That's when I realized it wouldn't hold the cubs.

That night I started working on the kennel. I got all the loose boards around our property and tacked them on the outside. Something was still in the brush making noises, and I had to sling a few rocks before I heard whatever it was move away towards the creek.

Now the trap was ready. The next night I rented a video camera. Claudia invited over a neighbor who wanted to see the big capture, but we didn't see the bears for two weeks, I'm sure because it was the Fourth of July and the kids were setting off fireworks like crazy.

Finally, the cubs showed up one night. I was asleep in front of the TV set. All I had to do was wake up and pull the string. My wife was pretty instrumental in the capture of the cubs because she works downstairs late at night and knows what's going on most of the time. Claudia heard the dog barking and woke me saying, "The bears are out there."

I pulled the old rip cord and the door latched. I ran downstairs to set the two wooden clips I'd fashioned, and just after I latched the last one, the male charged the door and slammed into it. He scared me, and I leaped back out of the way as he rammed the gate a couple more times.

As soon as I had the bears, Claudia called Mike McDonald at Fish and Game. We were anxious for him to come out as fast as possible because the bears were so wild. Mike had to drive all the way out from Chugiak. He had called the police and told them he was going to violate some traffic laws. He ran three red lights to get out here and made it in about an hour.

The boar kept on charging, focusing all his attention on me. He got up on a doghouse inside the kennel, and when he turned around, hitting the wire, I could see staples busting out. He didn't know his strength.

These bears were going crazy. I knew they could dig out in a second.

The female soon became completely passive and hid behind the male. When he was on the doghouse making noise and trying to bluff me out, she was behind him with both of her legs over his rump. She would only peek out with one eye. He was the aggressor and her protector, no question about it. I sat down about six feet from them and talked to them in a low monotone, and finally they calmed and lay down.

When the men from ADFG arrived, they darted the boar with a gun first, and he keeled over. They had a hand dart for her. After they darted her twice, she proceeded to forget about us and ate the rest of the dog food. We put her in one of our traveling dog kennels, and when we picked her up, she had the dog pan clasped in her paws. They had to shake it from her grasp.

The game wardens took the bears to the zoo at about one that morning. They went with three orphaned bears from Juneau to a wildlife park near Roseburg, Oregon.

6

Survival by Any Means

O n my Eagle River homestead here near Juneau I've had experiences with bears which have given me a wholesome respect for them as antagonists, and grave doubts about the many stories of tree-climbing escapes.—Paul Satko, *The Alaska Sportsman*, July 1943

A gun actually does something for the psyche of the man who carries it. It allows him to feel more confident and convey confidence in "body language" to the bear. Thus a man standing firm, believing in the infallibility of his gun, has a greater edge for bluffing a bear off. I believe it's the man's confident bearing rather than his gun, that makes the animal flee.—Mike Crammond, *Killer Bears*

Over the years a number of diversions and deterrents have been used in conjunction with bear-man encounters. A common sense diversion is for the fisherman to jettison his salmon when approached by a bear. Hikers have been known to give up their peanut butter and jelly lunches to bruin, giving them a chance to escape. Clothing or a pack sometimes detains a bear long enough for the potential maulee to get away.

When survival is at stake, human beings can be incredibly resourceful. The options aren't many: maybe a specially developed, chemical spray or the nearest climbable tree. But a person confronting a bear must react quickly, as the only real option is survival by any means.

Man's Best Friend?

The subject of dogs in relation to bears has always been controversial. Some dogs have saved their masters, while others have caused the problem, bringing the bear to their master in their effort to escape.

Gust Jensen, an elderly Athapascan Indian from Iliamna Lake country, told me about an experience he had when the dog caused the problem.

"I was on Pile Bay Road; Carl Williams was with me. I seen the black bear. Carl said, 'Well, why don't you go ahead and shoot him.' So I shot him. It was quite a ways. I think I just nicked him. We had Carl's little black dog there that went around chasing the bear.

"This dog ran up and started barkin' at him. The bear was mad already. I had a .270, and I had only a couple shells in the gun. The bear started running, and I shot; but I missed. Before he got up on the road I shot again, and I missed.

"And here that little dog is bringing the bear right to me with no shell in my gun. I didn't know what to do.

I was just standing there, nowhere to run, no place to go; but he was coming so fast.

"Carl, who was down below, had a gun, a .35 Newton. I heard a shot, and that bear dropped almost on my feet. Only thing I was thinkin' was, I had the gun by the barrel and I was gonna try to hit the bear with it. That's the closest I ever come to a bear gettin' me."

Imagine the consternation one would experience if lying in bed in a cabin reading from a good book and a bear suddenly interrupts the peaceful scene.

Gene Kivett was enjoying himself on his bed when his cocker spaniel ran excitedly through the open door of the cabin with a black bear on its heels. Once inside the dwelling, the bear rose on its hind legs, and the scared dog turned protector, sinking its teeth into the nose of the bear.

Kivett yelled and grabbed a stool.

The bear hit the dog, which hit the Yukon stove, turning it over. Now Kivett was confronted by a bear and a fire. As Kivett prepared to jump out a window, the bear backed out the door. Kivett reached his rifle and followed the bear toward the woods where he dispensed with his interruption.

Another veteran old-timer had a run-in with a bear and was mighty glad to have his pooch along.

Bud Branham was checking his trapline during the late winter of 1950, when he came across fresh brown bear tracks. Because his dog Kenai was deaf and Bud didn't think he would be safe, Bud tied him up. He left his dog team and started down into a gully where a moose had been killed earlier by hunters. Bud figured the bear, which should have been in its den, would be feeding on the kill.

Bud dropped into the gully and located the displaced bruin. Just as Bud prepared to fire at the bear, he felt a nudge at his knee and heard Kenai's low whine. He looked down to discover his dog, which had chewed through his lashing. Although Kenai posed a potential problem, Bud fired, little realizing what good fortune the dog represented.

As he pulled the trigger of his .30-30, he was greeted not with the usual shoulder-jerking explosion, but with a *snap*—the rifle had misfired! The bear heard the noise or sensed the presence of Bud and Kenai and came running at a full-scale charge.

Bud fled for the closest, climbable tree and scurried toward its lowest limb, ten feet from the ground. Time slowed. As Bud climbed, Kenai rushed the bear. With Kenai hanging onto the bear's rear end, Bud swung up and over the limb just as the bear swiped at him and hit his boot.

The dog grabbed the bear again, diverting his attention. Time and again the bear returned to reach for Bud only to have the dog clamp onto his anterior portions. Kenai had the upper hand because his light weight allowed him to travel over the crusted snow more easily than his antagonist.

For over an hour Bud waited in his perch. Finally, the dog returned without his playmate, and Bud descended the cottonwood. Even though the dog could not hear Bud's appreciative praise, they shared a mutual understanding.

Another dog rescued its master from a more serious mauling and possible death when it intervened during the summer of 1901. Three prospecting friends—Archie Park, James Leroy and Anton Eide—sought good ground near Mount McKinley, which was relatively unknown to white man at that time.

One day Leroy and Anton, some distance from Archie, took a shot at something in the distance. Archie caught sight of the animal disappearing into the brush and stalked it, believing it was a caribou. Unable to understand his companions' shouts, he continued.

Rounding a clump of brush, he came face to face with a huge bear. Greatly enraged by his wound, the bear attacked and severely mauled Archie.

At the height of the attack, Archie's small black mongrel dog grabbed the bear by the buttocks. After he captured the bear's attention, the dog fled with the bear in hot pursuit, giving Archie a chance to rejoin his companions.

Leroy and Anton were greeted by a gruesome spectre. Miles from the nearest camp, they cleaned Archie's wounds with water, replaced his scalp and sewed it to the adjoining skin with a broad three-cornered sail needle and pieces of sinew unravelled from a showshoe. Archie was able to travel within a few days. A month later his wounds were completely healed, and his scars were hardly noticeable.

Although there are brave dogs who protect their masters, not all valiant canines are fortunate enough to escape the wrath of bears. John Gregg had killed a moose and stored it in a cache about a mile from his Chena Hot Springs home. He later went to the cache and discovered that a large bear had made off with huge portions of his moose.

Gregg salvaged a quarter of the animal and returned it to the cache. Retracing his trail, he discovered the bear only ten feet away and coming hell-bent. Before he had time to shoulder his rifle, the bear had grabbed him by his leg and was dragging him into the woods. With difficulty he finally managed to get his mitts and his rifle's safety off. He put the muzzle six inches from the bear's shoulder and touched off a shot.

Three things happened at that moment: the bear

moaned, Gregg's dog latched onto the bear, and the bruin let go of John. The grizzly hit the dog, breaking its back. Gregg fired again, hitting the bear near the first wound, and the bear fled into the woods. John got to his feet and fired twice more before the bear was out of sight. The bear, weighing seven to eight hundred pounds, was later found dead, but John had to shoot his dog.

Bear Sprays and Other Repellents

Ken Wells of Yakutat told me about an oldtimer who used cans of ether to repel bruin. Whenever the sourdough wanted to rid the neighborhood of bears he wrapped a can of ether with bacon and tossed the bait out on the edge of camp somewhere and waited, listening for bear snores.

"Bear spray" is another deterrent that has come to the attention of the public in the past year or two. This spray differs from bug spray because the spray is not applied to the user, but rather on or toward the threatening bear. The December 1985 *Outdoor Life* carried an article by Stephen Kemp entitled, "Can You Spray A Bear Away?" Kemp's article chronicled Charles Jonkel's efforts to develop a successful deterrent that would save the lives of both humans and bears.

Of all the repellents tested—loud music, a black umbrella, air horns, railroad flares, recorded bear sounds, moth balls, human urine, ammonia and commercial animal repellents—Animal Repel proved most effective.

This spray consists of a liquefied red pepper solution and creates a severe burning sensation. Animal Repel and Halt were the only repellents that caused bears to stop immediately and retreat.

Since the article appeared, modifications have been made, and Animal Repel is being marketed as Counter Assault. It was developed in the mid-1970s through the joint effort of Charles Jonkel, a bear researcher who directs the University of Montana's Border Grizzly Project, and Bill Pounds, a Montana businessman.

On a recent trip to Alaska, Jonkel shared some of his vast bear expertise with Linda Billington, staff writer for the *Anchorage Daily News*. When Linda asked Jonkel how effective Counter Assault was, he replied, "Somebody might come out with something better tomorrow, but out of the six hundred tests I've conducted in the lab, Counter Assault has never failed one single time. There's only been five tests in the wild, with a charging bear. It worked in all five. That's a small sample size, but five to zero is better than, say, five to two." (Sunday, July 24, 1988)

One successful experience with Counter Assault, rated as the first such actual wilderness incident involving the spray, took place during the summer of 1987 in Southeast Alaska. John Hyde, an Alaska Department of Fish and Game visual information specialist, had received a sample of the product the previous year and was skeptical, but carried some in his pack nevertheless.

John was on Admiralty Island later when he noticed a brown bear sow approaching a pair of unarmed kayakers. Joining the kayakers, John tried to scare the sow off by shouting at her, but she was not to be bluffed and came within ten feet of the trio. She aggressively circled the group, chomping her teeth in a threatening manner. She pounded her front paws on the ground and lunged toward one of the kayakers.

John, who had extracted his sample of Counter

Assault from his pack, fired the container into her face. Her reaction was to turn tail and run, stopping, turning and looking back when a hundred yards distant.

John wondered what the effects of the spray would be. How would the spray affect her in the future? Would she be less likely to attack? He was not long in finding out.

Two days later he met the sow again. She was fifty feet away when he sprayed toward the bear. The spray did not reach her, but hung in a mist in the air between the man and the bear. When the bear approached him and encountered the mist, she departed.

On his final encounter with the sow, Hyde merely raised the can toward the bear, and she quickly backed off without needing to be sprayed.

The Fine Art of Tree-Climbing

One escape that has saved some people from a bear mauling is, simply, a tree. More than one person has reason to thank God that a tree grew within a distance reachable from the precarious encounter with bruin.

The *Valdez Miner* described one such run-in. Near Skilak Lake on the Kenai Peninsula, W. M. Nutter had come upon a black bear with a cub at a time when any self-respecting bear would have been in a winter den. The man and bear were a mere forty feet apart when the action began. She got her cub up a tree to escape the man, and he tried to use the same technique to escape her.

"The trouble was that Mr. Nutter did not get far enough up the tree to escape the jaws of the animal, and his differential and other parts were badly damaged.

"The bear was so close to him she made several attempts to claw him out, but he held on to a .22 automatic pistol and in a moment shot the bear where it would do the most good." (Jan. 31, 1936)

Nutter acquired a lacerated leg and a bear skin rug for his troubles.

Another tree climber was a U.S. Forest Service trail foreman. Robert E. McCully was no stranger to the environment around Juneau, traveling trails daily, year-round. He was aware of the bear situation in the neighborhood.

One day in the spring of 1941, he rounded a bend in the trail to discover a sow brownie ten yards distant. How can you react, much less climb a tree with a bear one or two jumps away?

"In that instant I saw the pearly gates fly wide open. Although I was standing under a spruce tree that was just made for easy climbing, I knew that I could not possibly get up out of the bear's reach before she got me. I leaped for a limb just over my head." (*The Alaska Sportsman*, "A Brownie Had Me Up a Tree")

His feet had just cleared the ground when the bear arrived. Reacting from self-preservation he kicked out with a foot, landing a blow to her nose and giving him needed time to climb higher. He kept kicking as she returned until she clasped onto his hip boot and pulled it off. He was able to clamber up into the outstretched arms of the tree to assure his escape. The bear's claw marks were later measured a full eleven feet, six inches above the ground.

I have had more than one person tell me he could escape a bear by climbing a tree. After informing him of the time needed to climb a tree the adherent has usually responded, "Yeah, but you could climb faster if you were scared . . . you'd have your adrenalin pumping." Paul Satko wrote an article called "Don't Count on Climbing a Tree" for *The Alaska Sportsman*, July 1943, in which he questioned the merits of climbing a tree to escape bruin. Paul talked about a bear he encountered in his garden and summarized his thoughts. "The thing which was, to me, most significant about the incident was the speed with which the creature moved. From the time I fired that first shot across his back until I fired the second, which dropped him about twenty-five yards from me in the garden, there certainly wasn't any chance to escape. Finding and climbing a tree was simply out of the question. It was either stop him 'quick' with a high-powered gun, or have a live bear on my neck."

Handguns are Better Than Fists

The general opinion among most Alaskan big-game hunters holds that a handgun is not an adequate defense against a bear attack. For one thing, few pistol shooters practice the many hours needed to be proficient with a handgun. And besides the shooter's accuracy, the handgun does not have sufficient power to repel or stop a bear attack.

The generalization that a handgun is of little consequence in dealing with a charging bear needs to be addressed more specifically. Most agree that a handgun is not an adequate weapon to use against a charging brown/grizzly; however, anyone will admit that a handgun will stop an angry bear faster than a fist.

A pistol versus a grizzly with aggressive, charging tendencies may be far less effective than a handgun versus a black. The handgun may not stop many grizzly bears, but what about the black bear? I hope that the

following examples of bear-man encounters involving handguns will shed some light on the issue and
allow the reader to make a more educated choice
regarding the pros and cons of using a handgun for
defense.

Will a well-placed pistol shot kill a charging brown
bear? Define a "well-placed" pistol shot. Albert Blalock
shot a charging adult brown bear in the nose and didn't
stop it.

In the fall of 1970, Al and his hunting partner Ron
Trumblee had gone waterfowl hunting with their shotguns. Knowing there were bears in the area, they
packed their .44-magnum handguns as defense against
a possible bear attack.

The men heard brush breaking nearby and were
soon face-to-face with an angry mother brownie. As she
charged, Albert leveled his pistol and fired. He said,
"She shook her head and kept coming. When she was
about ten feet away, Ron drew and fired his pistol from
the hip and the bear fell dead four feet in front of me."
(*ALASKA Magazine*, September 1971)

The men then realized that their shotguns would
have been more effective than the handguns. After
skinning the animal, they discovered Al's bullet had
entered the bear's nose while Ron's had broken its
neck. The bear was about ten years old, a seven-and-
one-half foot sow.

In the late 1960s Vic Bruss and his wife had
problems in the bush with bears. Bears shredded their
storage shed one summer while they were at fish camp.
Later Vic said, "It was hard for us to believe the
destruction caused by those bears. It looked as if a
tornado had picked up the contents of the building, put
everything through a grinder, and spewed it back out."
(*ALASKA Magazine*, January 1980)

Later, Vic had a run-in with a sow black bear and tried to facilitate her leaving his homesite. Her cubs had gone up a tree in the middle of his sled dog area, and he moved the dogs so her cubs could retreat with dignity. As a precaution, he strapped on his .44-magnum revolver before he holed up in a shed to take pictures of her and her cubs leaving. When he didn't see her, he opened the shed door, only to see her standing on all fours facing him.

The bear started to enter his shed. He took an aggressive stance and told her to get out. The bear showed no signs of leaving, so he stomped on the floor toward her. Vic said, "Her front paws moved like black lightning . . . the staccato of her claws rebounding off the door and frame. . . . The speed at which she could move was frightening. She was too fast for me to see the movement."

She ground her teeth, and in a blur she came for him. He popped a cap and dropped the bear. What would have happened had Vic not had a pistol?

Maurice Goff had never heard of a bear attacking at night when he and a friend were trout fishing near Skilak Lake on the Kenai Peninsula. The night before their scheduled return flight to Anchorage, Maurice walked to a stream to clean the dishes and stumbled onto a bear cache not far from their campsite. He fell face first into a large depression full of rotting salmon; evidently a bear had dug several holes and filled them with the silvery menu with plans to return.

After cleaning up, the men bedded down for the night, heads toward the campfire. Maurice placed the flashlight near his head; a .45-caliber pistol lay nearby. Their shotgun was leaning against a tree, handy in case they saw ducks before their morning departure.

During the night they had a visitor. Maurice woke

up, a foul odor filling his nostrils. The head of a huge brown bear was inches from his face. Maurice reacted on instinct, yelling, throwing out his hands and pushing at the head of the bear.

The bear jumped on Maurice. It swatted at him in his sleeping bag as he screamed, prayed, cussed simultaneously, futilely attempting to push the beast away. Suddenly, the bear vanished into the nearby stream.

Before the startled Jack could discover what had happened, the bear returned and knocked him down. In a flurry, the bear thrust and parried and ghosted into the darkness only to return time after time.

Between bear raids, both men yelled and frantically sought the pistol (having forgotten the shotgun). Finally, Maurice found the pistol, pulled it from its holster and emptied the gun into the charging hulk.

The bear altered its course, and Maurice scrambled for a tree. He begged Jack to do likewise, but Jack refused to do so until he got his hands on the scatter gun. Moments later Maurice felt the barrel of the shotgun and discovered Jack was on his way up the foot-thick cottonwood. Hearing nothing below except the roaring of the stream, they considered huddling in their perch, twenty feet from the ground, until daylight.

The problem was that although Jack was fully clothed except for shoes, Maurice was wearing only long underwear. In the blackness they discovered by matchlight that it was half past midnight. It would be nearly impossible to withstand the cold until daylight, so they climbed down.

They retrieved the .45 and loaded it. Jack got his .38 revolver from his tackle box. They got a fire going and examined their injuries. Jack had a bruise below his elbow and some bruises on his body. Maurice had a scratch on his head and face and was missing the skin on his left shin from his ankle to his knee.

Finally, daylight arrived, and they examined the area where they had last heard the bear, finding matted blood and signs of the bear's struggle. They found six-inch-wide tracks and estimated the bear's weight at six to eight hundred pounds. They didn't like the idea of leaving a wounded bear in the woods and chose to go airborne to spot for the animal before their return to Anchorage. About a half mile upstream from their camp, they observed a very dead brown bear on a gravel bar.

There have been several well-documented incidents in which handguns have played a life-saving role. Louie Kis' experience received national attention in the fall of 1987 when his story was printed in Outdoor Life *and other national magazines. When I first heard that Louie was unceremoniously dumped onto the ground and chomped on by a grizzly with only a .357 handgun for a weapon, I called him for his account. Louie was more than cooperative and sent me his comments on his experience, mentioning three other men who had confronted bears with handguns.*

Louie has successfully relocated many grizzlies during his tenure as a Regional Warden Supervisor for the Montana Department of Fish, Wildlife and Parks. His story follows:

Contrary to popular belief, grizzly bears can be killed with small-caliber pistols provided the bullet placement is exact. However, poor placement of heavy, high-velocity slugs will not provide for an instant kill, even on less powerful animals such as whitetailed deer.

Most animals that have been severely injured

develop a tremendous will to live and require well-placed bullets to kill them; for instance, try destroying a deer that has been badly hit by a car on the highway. After thirty-five years of destroying maimed wildlife of various species, I have found they are slow to die unless bullet placement is exact.

I think grizzly bears are no harder or easier to kill than other species with the same size bone and muscle structure. We need only to carefully check a grizzly skull in order to determine the vulnerable spots where the brain is less protected by bone structure.

Thin bone areas include the upper rear of the mouth, through the eyes or nose or under the chin. However, hitting a charging bear in the eye is somewhat difficult to do. Having dealt with many bears as a wildlife officer, I found it expedient to consider the vulnerable spots in case, for human protection, an animal had to be destroyed with a sidearm.

I do not recommend shooting grizzly bears with a pistol except under dire circumstances when no other alternative seems available. As stated earlier, most calibers will handle a grizzly; however, I highly recommend one use a large, high-velocity caliber with plenty of fire power, such as a .44 magnum with a "banana clip," in case bullet placement is not exact. Bullet type is very important; one should use heavy solids, not hollow points.

I had the opportunity to test .357, 158-grain, hollow-point, jacketed bullets on a rather large male grizzly at point-blank range as the bear was gnawing on my right leg. Two hits just above his right eye failed to penetrate the skull bone and only flattened out and coursed down through the zygomatic arch, ending up in the neck area under the skin. Two others turned and traveled toward the bear's shoulder. Needless to say, these were not instant killing shots, but no doubt "smarted a bit." After I got the bear's attention, he released my right leg and raised his head, pushing my Smith and Wesson .357 upwards, and one round discharged into the sky.

Somehow, I was able to snap the last cartridge under his chin into the base of the skull, killing the mean son of a bitch instantly.

The entire firing of the six rounds took place in approximately five seconds or less, giving the bear very little time to maul me. The bear did manage to puncture my right tibia just below the knee, shatter the fibula and mangle the main nerve leading to my right foot. Had the sixth round failed, who knows what the outcome would have been. I did have back-up, but I'm sure I would have been severely mauled, if not killed, by the enraged bear in a matter of seconds.

By the grace of God and Smith and Wesson, I have few lasting effects from the incident other than scars on my leg, but my wife says I had deformed legs anyway.

In addition to the vulnerable spots mentioned earlier, the base of the ear is also a good immobilizing shot but seldom presents itself when you are being attacked. In fact, the problem is being able to place your shot expertly, if at all, while being tossed about by four- to six-hundred-plus pounds of enraged bear. Being able to keep one's "cool" is an asset when at the mercy of a large carnivore.

I prefer a shotgun for close-range work on bear (meaning ten to thirty feet). Over that range, I suspect a heavy-caliber rifle is best. The shotgun should have an extended magazine and a short barrel. Some prefer an auto loader such as the Remington 1100, saying that it can be operated with only one hand if the bear is biting the other hand. This is a good point; however,

I prefer a repeating-action type such as the Remington 870 or Winchester Model 12 with slug barrel.

In my case, the shotgun would probably not have worked since I walked directly into the bear and probably would have had problems firing at such close range. If you anticipate an extremely tight situation with a bear, I suggest the heavy-caliber revolver of double action, certainly not a single-action type as it takes too long to draw the hammer back.

Naturally, I prefer to shoot a bear with a rifle at a distance or with a slug shotgun at close range, but if the chips are down, don't discount a large-caliber, double-action revolver.

Three other incidents come to my mind when considering cases in which a pistol may have prevented a mauling; however, in two cases the bears apparently didn't want to take on the shooter.

In 1979 or 1980, I was called to the North Fork of the Flathead to pursue a grizzly female wounded by a neophyte from California who had walked up to the sleeping bear thinking it was caught in a snare. The bear jumped up and the shooter, who carried a .357 revolver, opened fire with one shot, hitting the bear near the jaw. The bullet coursed back at an angle into the neck of the bear. I trailed the animal in heavy brush for a mile before finding it dead along the river.

Another incident involved a camp worker from Kalispell, Montana, who was hiking in the Bob Marshall wilderness and came upon a large, male grizzly digging for food in light snow. The bear apparently didn't notice the shooter and came toward him. At twenty feet, the worker panicked and shot the bear with a .41-mag, single-action revolver. The bear went down and rolled around until the worker finished the bear off by shooting it in the head area.

The third incident happened in the North Fork. In the early 1960s a wildlife worker surveying a study area approached a grizzly bear in a black bear snare. The grizzly charged, pulling snare and drag, and was almost upon the worker when he became caught in a windfall tree. The worker, using an H&R .22-caliber "nine shooter," was able to destroy the bear, although the animal died slowly. No doubt the bear would have seriously mauled the biologist or killed him if he had not been armed—even poorly armed with a .22-caliber pistol.

Since my own accident, many people have asked me if I feel any animosity toward bears. In general, no. Toward the one that attacked me, yes. He had his chance to go free but let his ego get the best of him. He was big, mean and angry and was responsible for his own downfall—the same thing happens to humans quite often.

Don't get me wrong, I expect bears to know their place and tend to their own business, and I'll tend to mine and not intentionally provoke them. My motto is "be especially alert in bear country, carry a big gun and shoot to kill only when necessary."

Obviously, when confronted with an enraged, charging bear, one should first immobilize the beast or at least slow him down a bit, allowing for careful placement of bullets in instant killing areas such as the spine or neck vertebrae. Then the bear can be finished off with a brain shot if necessary. For many years I have carried a .300 Weatherby mag when following wounded grizzly or black bear. I use 180-grain bullets; however, 200-grain may be just as good or better.

If I was to start out after a grizzly bear tomorrow, that gun would be my weapon. I recall a large male, cattle-killing grizzly in a trap whirling around to charge me and three others, only to get tangled in some timber. I had a .243. One shot from the .30-30 killed the bear; however, I prefer the large caliber, as I'm prone to wobble a bit in times of stress.

Remember, the only "safe" bear is a distant bear.

Jerry Austin of Saint Michael also found his pistol comforting in a tight spot with a bear.

In the late 60s I was asked by some Eskimos on Stewart Island to help them shoot a grizzly that kept chasing villagers from Stebbins. I had the biggest gun around in those days, a .300 Win Mag Browning bolt-action.

One of the elders and his son, who was in the National Guard, took me over to where the bear had just chased some women. The father had a rifle and the son had an M-14 from the armory, a .45 auto, and a .38 snub-nose. And I decided to carry my .44, as well.

We briefly saw the animal, and it went into heavy willows about three hundred yards from us. The father instructed us to cover him, and he walked up to the spot where the bear had disappeared into the brush. I was standing about ten feet from the willows when I heard the son mutter, "BBB ... BBB ... BBB ... BEAR!"

He dropped his M-14 and started running away across the tundra. I turned around as the bear lunged for me. I put the barrel of my .44 in his mouth and fired, and we both went down with the momentum. I rolled out of the mess with my .44, ready to shoot again as my rifle was knocked out of my hands, but the one shot from my .44 had done the trick. The bullet, a 180-grain Nosler, had glanced off the skull and broke the bear's neck. The bear squared nine foot, ten inches and to date is still the largest grizzly I've ever killed.

The father and I started skinning the bear, and the son came walking back over, pretty shook up. While we were skinning, all of a sudden there was a gunshot and here was the son, five feet away with a smoking .45. We asked him what in the heck he was doing, and he just shrugged.

The next day in the village a little kid came up to me and asked if I'd heard about the huge bear that the son had bagged that evening, and then I understood why he had taken that shot!

I think of all these fishermen out there with .22s and .38s thinking they'll scare off a bear, when in reality even a .44 mag is a last-action type of resource. The one thing I've found, though, is that a properly holstered, large handgun is very handy to have if you get rolled around on the ground like I did that once. At least you've got something. Almost every bear mauling I've heard of could have been prevented or at least been less serious if the person had a properly holstered .44. I can tell you it's pretty hard to hang on to a rifle when you're going head over heels.

The Decision to Shoot

In pondering diversions and deterrents it is wise to consider Max Schwab's comments. Max is a registered guide from Talkeetna who sent me some suggestions about coupling precautionary action and common sense to avoid problems with bears.

I strongly believe that firearms should not be relied upon for defense from bears, because it results in many bears being killed unnecessarily and because there are too many situations where a bear can be upon you much faster than you can do anything about it with a gun. Not to mention that a bear is much too beautiful and valuable a creature to waste by shooting in self-defense. It's much better to not get yourself in a situation where you have to shoot, because by then, it is too late for either you or the bear. Also, bears tend to change their minds about grabbing people at the last second and run away instead. I will relate a couple instances where I shot bears in self-defense, but I was hesitant to do so, because first, I'll never know if the bear would have changed his mind before he did any actual damage to me, and second, I know that if I had been a better woodsman I could have avoided the confrontation.

People tend to brag about their close encounters with bears, but I have more respect for those who have spent their lives in bear country and have avoided dangerous contact with them. I relate the following instances with the hope that it may prevent some bear from dying for no purpose.

One time in mid-October, I was picking the last of the blueberries before the frosts and snow got them. I had been picking for perhaps a half hour when I heard some noise in the bushes about two hundred feet away. At first, I thought it was a moose, but it didn't take long to realize that it was a grizzly bear and that he appeared to be beaming in on my scent and heading straight for me. A couple of tense seconds passed before I located my rifle leaning against a stump and grabbed it. By then, the bear was coming at full speed, and I can't emphasize enough how fast a bear can move even in dense brush. I fired the first shot when the bear was about a hundred feet distant. He kept coming full speed, and I kept firing until he was about fifteen feet away. I was feverishly working the bolt of my rifle to load and fire the fourth and last shot.

Bears have expressions on their faces the same as people, and this one had an expression of eagerness. My last shot turned the bear, and he brushed by me instead of bowling me over. He ran another fifty feet and fell dead. He had two bullet holes—one superficial and one through the chest. I've wondered many times if he would have turned had I not fired that last shot.

Another time, I was fishing a salmon stream that was bordered by dense brush. I had walked along about a half mile of stream looking for a good salmon. I had seen many fresh signs of bears and had even caught glimpses of a few bears that moved back into the bushes when they saw me. I circled away from the stream to avoid a particularly dense section of alders.

When I got back to the stream bank and looked down, I saw two cubs and then a mama grizzly not ten feet away. They hadn't seen me because I was on the bank above them and they were in the fast-flowing, noisy stream looking for fish.

I immediately backed away on tiptoes—with my heart and stomach in my throat. I got about a hundred feet away and was starting to think I was safe when I heard a commotion from the stream. I could hear some angry-sounding grunts, and I could see branches waving and small trees being knocked down. I thought surely the sow was confused as to my exact location, so I yelled to let her know where I was. My double-barreled 12-gauge was ready with buckshot, but I didn't think I'd need it.

My feet were starting to leave without me, and by the time my brain told my finger to pull the trigger that bear was not more that three feet from the end of the barrel. I thought I was done for. The expression she had on her face was one of rage and intent to do me harm. The charge of buckshot all went into one hole the size of a quarter, about an inch from her eye and it stopped her as if she had run into a brick wall.

I've always asked myself if I could have prevented her death by making more noise than I did or by foregoing my salmon dinner when I saw all that fresh bear sign.

A number of diversions may give a person a better chance to escape a bear confrontation. Some deterrents work, some better than others. If you're planning to avoid a serious encounter by climbing a tree, put yourself to the test. Look at other deterrents like Counter Assault. Consider the advantages of carrying a handgun; they have saved lives and killed bears. If a bear were chewing on me and I had the choice of using a handgun or my fists, I'd take the handgun any day.

Index